1. The fine 'Art Nouveau' case and stand of a 17 ¼-inch Stella by Mermod Frères, Ste-Croix, c. 1900 (Grace Thompson collection)

The Musical Box Handbook

2nd Edition • Volume 2 • Disc Boxes

Illustrated by Philip Weston
Additional drawings by
Adrian Little

Graham Webb

The Vestal Press Ltd.
Vestal, New York 13850

Library of Congress Cataloging-in-Publication Data
(Revised for vol. 2)

Webb, Graham.
 The musical box handbook.

 Rev. ed. of: The cylinder musical box handbook.
1968, and The disc musical box handbook. 1971.
 Includes index.
 Contents: v. 1. Cylinder boxes—v. 2. Disc boxes.
 1. Music box. I. Webb, Graham. Cylinder musical
box handbook. II. Webb, Graham. Disc musical box
handbook. III. Title.
ML1066.W4 1984 789'.8 84-5202
 ISBN 0-911572-36-8 (pbk. : v.1)
 ISBN 0-911572-51-1 (pbk. : v.2)

for Jo

CONTENTS

Introduction	xi
1. The Disc Musical Box	1
2. Development	4
3. The Principal Manufacturers	20
4. Rare Types of Disc Musical Box	37
5. How to Choose a Disc Musical Box	62
6. Cleaning a Disc Musical Movement	84
7. Restoring a Disc Musical Box Case	109
8. Care and Repair of Discs	117
9. Minor Adjustments and Repairs	137
10. Replacing Broken Teeth	163
11. Replacing Lead Tuning Weights	174
12. Rust Affected Bed-Plate Assembly	184
13. Disc Musical Box Dampers	200
14. A List of Disc Musical Boxes	216
15. Tuning Scales for Combs	245
16. List of Manufacturers and Agents	301
17. An Essential Bibliography	315

ACKNOWLEDGEMENTS

It must always be said that a book such as this is dependent on the co-operation of many people. Sincere thanks go to: Bob Minney; Ronald Pearsall; the late Frank Greenacre; Colyn Gates; the late Hughes Ryder, sometime Hon. Treasurer, Musical Box Society International; Patch Pearce; Keith Harding, Archivist, Musical Box Society of G.B.; Clifford Burnett; Ronald Lee; Gerry Planus, sometime Hon. Vice President MBSGB; David Tallis, sometime Hon. Treasurer of that Society; William Nevard; Michael Gilbert; Alfred and Grace Thompson; George and Gloria Helston; Richard Baines, and John Cowderoy.

Special thanks for their researches: Drs. Luuk Goldhoorn of Utrecht; Arthur W.J.G. Ord-Hume, sometime Editor, Journal of MBSGB; Hendrik H. Strengers, Grabijnhof 28, Delft, and to Q. David Bowers, for allowing me the freedom of the pages of his *Encyclopedia of Automatic Musical Instruments* (Vestal Press, 1972).

For tuning scales I am especially grateful to Arthur Coombs, who supplied the Polyphon scales and others for the original edition, and subsequent corrections for this one; Ralph M. Heintz, sometime President MBSI, and my good friend, for very many of the new scales; Jim Wier; H.H. Strengers; Robin Timms, for scales and use of his musical knowledge; Patrick MacCrossan; James O. Spriggs; Michael Hallett; and Jim Hall, for the Chordephon scale.

Grateful thanks too, to Adrian Little, for his technical advice and the extra drawings, and Ruth Kelly-Webb for her help.

Finally I acknowledge my debt to both societies mentioned.

NOTES ON THE SECOND EDITION

Some fifteen years have elapsed since the first edition of this work was published which means the manuscript left the author's hands in 1970. Since then, as with Volume 1 (Cylinder Boxes), much has been learned about the disc musical box, its makers, its history, and its repair.

In this edition will be found much about the development of disc musical boxes that has never before been published. Information on such well-known firms as Leipziger Musikwerke, Symphonion, and Polyphon, that is sure to surprise even those who have lately researched the subject. For much of this information I have to thank my friend Drs. Luuk Goldhoorn of Utrecht, while some has been the result of my own researches for this and other books.

Some chapters have been entirely rewritten to take account of improved knowledge, methods of repair, and availability of spares. Others have been left almost untouched except to extend them where necessary, and one extra chapter has been added. Apart from this, the 'List of Disc Musical Boxes', and 'List of Manufacturers and Agents', have been considerably enlarged, so that the whole now represents the most up-to-date and comprehensive work available on the subject.

Thanks to a number of friends and others, the chapter 'Tuning Scales for Combs', though by no means complete, is massively enlarged, while those scales originally provided have been corrected where necessary. When using these scales, please read the introduction to that chapter!

In particular with disc musical boxes, because original mass production methods made it possible, a large number of spare parts are now available, particularly for Polyphon and Regina machines. This factor, coupled with advanced techniques, makes it possible for far more work to be done by the knowledgeable amateur, to such a degree, in fact, that almost any disc box, whatever its condition, can be brought back to sound and look as good as ever. It has to be said, however, that knowledge and care are the essentials, and knowledge includes the ability to know when professional assistance is required!

The first edition of this work was well received. Through the years I have had the pleasure of seeing good work that has directly stemmed from the use of it. I hope this edition will prove as popular and helpful.

Ship Street,
The Lanes,
Brighton, England.

INTRODUCTION

This book is designed as a companion volume to *The Musical Box Handbook (Cylinder Boxes)*. It is hoped that these two books together will not only provide some of the basic knowledge desirable when forming a collection, but will also continue to serve as a guide to the maintenance of the musical boxes obtained.

The disc musical box, like all mechanisms, requires a certain amount of care. Once put in good order, however, it will be found to be extremely robust, and will continue to give good service for many years. Many disc machines were, of course, expressly designed for the rough and tumble of commercial use, and few of these escaped the odd nasty jolt administered for not producing music in exchange for a penny.

For almost the whole of the nineteenth century, and in particular during the second half, there had been available a vast range of mechanical musical instruments, both for domestic and commercial use. By far the most popular of these was the cylinder musical box. This machine reigned supreme as the home entertainer. During the period preceding the invention of the disc musical box there had been many improvements in the design of cylinder boxes. Possibly the most significant of these improvements was the introduction of the interchangeable cylinder movement, which enabled a library of cylinders to be built up, and so overcame the lack of variety of music played by any one musical box—a basic fault up to this time. The interchangeable box also had its problems, chief among them being the cost, first of the machine, and then of the separate cylinders. In this respect the introduction of the disc musical box was more of an improvement than an entirely new invention, since not only was it much cheaper to add to the stock of tunes, but the original machine was also far less expensive.

A natural progression from the sturdy smaller disc machines was the upright coin-operated instrument to be found almost everywhere within a few years of the beginning of manufacture of the disc musical box.

The penny slot-machine automatically springs to mind when disc boxes are mentioned, and these are the machines for which the hunt is on today. What is more evocative than *The Honeysuckle and the Bee* rendered in perfect melody after the rattle of an inserted penny? Seven feet high and bedecked with carved lumps and turned knobs, who could fail to be impressed by its endearing ugliness?

Who would have thought that the downfall of these tuneful giants would be brought about by an insignificant little machine which looked like nothing more than a sewing-machine with an ear trumpet? First, the Edison Phonograph and later the Victor Talking Machine began the move away from musical boxes and mechanical music, and led the way for the reproduced music still very much with us today. It is interesting to speculate as to what would have become of the disc musical box idea at all had Thomas Edison been as quick to develop his invention as the disc box manufacturers were with theirs! In fact, the first words were spoken into a recording machine by Edison in 1877, some five years *before* the first patent of a disc movement was registered! Had the new 'talking machine' been in the hands of some enterprising business man, perhaps the phonograph would have developed so quickly as to swamp the musical box market completely, as of course it eventually did, before the disc machine could get started.

Whatever could have been the case, we have now a great revival in popularity for disc musical boxes. Let us then cherish those machines which are left to us.

TRANSLATIONS

British-American translations of terms which appear in books by Graham Webb:

Araldite	epoxy
Bakers Fluid	an acid flux—hydrochloric acid with zinc dissolved in it. Also called Killed Spirits of Salts.
blinding	covering the carcase wood with thick solid solored polish—used instead of veneer.
"Brummer" stopping	trade name for a wood filler
carcase	the basic body of a piece of furniture. carcase wood—the basic wood from which the piece is made.
cotton wool	a type of cotton wadding
cramp	C clamp
"Croid"	trade name for cold animal (hide) glue
flour paper	Baker's paper, used to line pans in a commercial baking establishment.
"Harracks" solvent stripper and "Perfecta" remover	solvent strippers that dissolve finish base, but which are not typical chemical strippers

Horolene	trade name for a water-based ammonia cleaning fluid used for clocks, etc.
methylated spirits	methyl alcohol
paraffin	kerosene
Piqué	the setting of pieces of metal into veneer wood, tortoiseshell etc. to make a pattern or design. *Not* metal stringing.
polisher	one who does refinishing
polythene	polyethylene
powder colours	the various natural colors used by refinishers to color the polish
proud	a term used when one surface projects above another
Radflush	a commercial automobile radiator flush
silver steel	a high alloy steel; tool steel
Timberfill	an epoxy-based wood filler

THE DISC MUSICAL BOX

A disc musical box is best described as a wooden case enclosing a musical movement employing projections or holes on an interchangeable revolving metal disc to dictate the melody. The projections or holes of the disc cause star wheels to turn, plucking the tuned teeth of a metal comb or combs in sequence so as to cause a tune to be played. The discs are interchangeable so as to allow any amount of tunes, limited only by the number of discs available. The discs from any one machine will play on any machine of the same make, size and type of comb.

The disc machine consists of two main assemblies: the bed-plate assembly containing those parts which make the music from the disc, and the motor assembly, which drives the disc.

Bed-plate assembly

The bed-plate assembly consists basically of the comb or combs, the star wheel assembly which plucks them, the dampers and brakes which control the actions of both, and a pressure bar to hold the disc in position.

Motor assembly

The motor assembly contains a spring as a driving force, held in check by a series of wheels terminating in an endless screw which is fitted with an air brake, usually in the form of a pair of fans, and a drive wheel to rotate the disc.

There are two main types of disc musical box: upright machines, which are usually activated by a coin and play with the disc in a vertical position, and table machines which generally have a manual on/off control, and play with the disc in a horizontal position. There are exceptions to both types.

THE DISC MUSICAL BOX

Upright disc machines

With rare exceptions, the two assemblies of the upright coin-operated machine are entirely separate. The bed-plate assembly is bolted or screwed to the back of the case, and the motor assembly is fixed to the base of the case, the two assemblies meeting only at the drive wheel for the disc, though some instruments have the assemblies bolted together. The drive wheel engages with holes in the periphery of the disc to drive it. The coin mechanism consists of a chute down which the coin travels to a pan at one end of a counterbalanced arm. The extra weight of the coin causes the arm to move, allowing the governor to run by removing a trip, and play commences. At some point during play, the coin pan is tilted, allowing the coin to fall into a drawer. At this stage the arm is kept off-balance until the end of the tune is reached. A sprag riding on a wheel is then allowed to enter a hole, the counter-balance operates, and the trip engages the endless screw once more.

Table models

Table-model disc machines were generally made for home use, and with a few exceptions are smaller—at least in the case—than upright machines. The motor assembly is normally attached to the underside of the bed-plate assembly which is fixed horizontally, on shelves, across the centre of the case. There are two main types of drive for table-model discs. Usually smaller sizes of disc are driven from the centre spindle, which revolves; larger discs are normally driven by a drive wheel which engages with holes in the periphery of the disc, as with upright instruments. Most table models are controlled by a push/pull button at the side or front of the case. When the button is pulled out the tune commences and generally continues to play, after the control is pushed in, until the tune ends.

Disc musical box cases

The cases of table-model machines vary considerably in design. Although the period of the disc musical box was short, the cases show infinite variety. It must be admitted, however, being turn-of-the-century, German examples tend towards a rather heavy look. Some better-class machines are of fine quality, with beautiful inlay and marquetry on the lids. Some, in particular the American Regina, are of quality woods, quite plain and with a simplicity of style which lives quite well with the furniture of today. Later and cheaper boxes are the exact opposite, and display garish transfer finishes of the very worst design.

Upright disc machine cases vary little in design, except that as they get later they tend to get plainer and simpler. It must be remembered that these were commercial machines and were designed for the gin palaces and hotels of the turn-of-the-century, with their tassels, dark woods, and cut-glass mirrors.

DEVELOPMENT

In November 1882, Miguel Boom of Haiti patented in the United States of America an idea which appears to have been the forerunner of the disc musical box we know. The patented invention consisted of a mechanism apparently driven by a hand crank, having a revolving disc in which were set moveable chisel-edged pegs which could be arranged to play a tune of choice upon a musical comb set in the case at right angles to the surface of the disc. That the idea was in no way commercial is evident. The very fact that it was necessary to move the pegs to change the tune — a complicated maneuver even with a knowledge of music —

2. Detail of the earlier, miniature, disc movement. Swiss, c. 1815. (David Tallis collection)

DEVELOPMENT

would have been sufficient to deter most of the possible customers from what would have seemed at most a gimmick, though later a similar idea was sold commercially, but appears not to have been successful.

It could be argued that the disc musical box had been in existence in another form some three-quarters of a century before Boom's patent. Found in small flat objects such as watches, patch boxes, and the like, the earlier type of disc musical movement began to be used shortly after the tuned steel tooth became a means of producing a tune. This disc or platform movement was used as an alternative to the cylinder movement for many years, in articles where it was not possible for the cylinder movement to be fitted, though, apart from its usefulness in this respect, it did not constitute a challenge, in view of the far greater versatility of the cylinder movement.

In effect, the major basic difference between the early disc movement and the later one (size apart) was that later discs were interchangeable. It was this interchangeability which made the disc movement the dominant type of musical box in the closing stages of the nineteenth century.

Apart from the early, miniature, disc movement, the advent of the disc musical box was presaged in another form, one that, since it originated in Leipzig, must have been highly influential, in that it showed how effectively a large disc could be used as a tune-carrier.

(F.E.) Paul Ehrlich began manufacture of his card disc-playing organette, eventually to be known as the 'Ariston', between 1876 and 1877, the year that Edison invented the cylinder phonograph. Ehrlich's organette became immensely popular. By 1888 some 30,000 were being made each year, and by 1890 over 200,000 had been sold (*Zeitschrift fur Instrumentenbau*', 21st. April, 1890).

The popularity of the Ariston was not entirely due, as the German press would have it, to the 'excellent and perfect arrangement of parts', nor, entirely, to the organette's inexpensive character. Much of it must have been because of the easy and cheap availability of new tunes, a catalogue of some 4000 of which was available by 1890.

It was in the success of the Ariston, with its easily changeable discs and the constant supply of new tunes, that the seed of the disc musical box was sown in the early part of the 1880s.

Ehrlich's only serious rival in the German organette field was the firm of Ch. F. Pietschmann & Sohn of Berlin, whose main instrument was the Herophon, using a stationary square 'disc' as note carrier. In

DEVELOPMENT

1888 this firm was producing some 13,000 instruments per year. In the Herophon, the mechanism turns under the 'disc', rather than the disc turning over the mechanism as in the Ariston.

In all known early attempts at making a viable disc musical box, from Miguel Boom on, one or other of these already successful designs of note carrier was used, either the revolving disc of Ehrlich, or the stationary 'disc' of the Herophon, though of course both of the original types of disc were of card, and without projections.

Boom's machine had used a revolving disc, the movable projections of which plucked the teeth of a stationary comb with its teeth pointing downward to the surface of the disc below. The idea patented by Ellis Parr in his home country of England in September in 1885, and also in several countries over a period of two years, again used a revolving disc to pluck a set of perpendicular teeth, still with direct action between teeth and projections. Meanwhile in Germany both (F.E.) Paul Ehrlich, already well entrenched in making mechanical musical instruments, and (Oskar) Paul Lochmann, an engineer of some experience, were working on similar lines, presumably, but by no means certainly, separately. Lochmann was on the same track as Ellis Parr and in 1885 we see the result of his work in a patent for a musical box having two combs, one either side of the centre drive, with direct contact with notes or pins on a square note-sheet. This time the combs revolved under a stationary 'disc' very much as in the 'Herophon' organette. The note carrier was set in a square frame over the combs beneath a hinged 'lid' that formed a firm backing to the thin sheet. Though it may be that some of these machines were marketed there are certainly none known to exist today and the model was short lived. The material used for the note carrier, and how the projections were set, is still something of a mystery. In other texts, there is reference to 'cardboard discs', but none to projections, though these of course would have had to be metal.

During this period, Ehrlich, with the backing of the experience of his highly successful mechanical musical instrument organization, was working with the same aim, a viable disc musical box, in two directions. One was the use of a version of his card disc, as used for the Ariston organette, with a lever-plucking device to pluck the teeth of the comb, patented in Britain on 12th. May 1886, eventually to come to fruition as a commercial instrument in the 'Baskánion' (Bascanion). The other direction of inquiry resulted in a machine with vertically mounted combs, the teeth of which were plucked by the projections of a

DEVELOPMENT

3. Earliest known surviving version of the Symphonion disc musical box, c. 1887. (Graham Webb)

4. The lid of the early Symphonion in Plate 3, showing colourful transfers on a black-polish background.

revolving disc, patented in Britain as co-patentee with G.A.F. Muller, in July of the same year.

With the above in mind, it is clear that Ehrlich was well in the running in the early search for a commercial disc musical box. Though at this time it is still not clear what relationship existed between Ehrlich and Lochmann, there is no doubt there must have been a fairly strong link, if only because of the great similarity between some models of Symphonion, Lochmann's instrument, and some of Monopol, that of Ehrlich. This similarity is found in some smaller movements, used in table models and wall clocks, the designs of which were set during the period up to, say, 1895.

Paul Ehrlich, in fact, had far more to do with the early disc musical box than has so far been disclosed in modern literature on the subject. On 2nd April, 1883, a German patent was granted to 'Fabrik Leipziger Musikwerke', formerly Paul Ehrlich & Co. The patent, number 21715, relates to a method of opening and closing pipes with the use of levers, acted upon by a disc. This patent obviously relates to organettes, but does include a disc. Another patent, granted on 25th. September, 1883,

DEVELOPMENT

relates to a similar device, using discs of various diameters, and with projections. This was numbered 24106.

The reason these patents are mentioned here is that both of the numbers appear on the discs of the earliest known Symphonion, made by (Oskar) Paul Lochmann. In the *Zeitschrift fur Instrumentenbau* of 21st. February, 1891, the Editor writes (in rough translation): 'From an authoritative source we have learned that the musical instrument Symphonion, manufactured by the Fabrik Lochmannscher Musikwerke, is under cover of Ehrlich's Ariston patent (number 21715 and addenda). The Lochmannscher Musikwerke has obtained a license from the Fabrik Leipziger Musikwerke, formerly Paul Lochmann & Co., to build this type of instrument.' It is interesting that in the following issues of the journal, no protest from Lochmann is heard!

Also of much interest with regard to disc musical boxes are the German patents number 33782, dated 19th. June, 1885, and an improvement, 40943, dated 7th. November, 1886. These patents relate to the 'Ariston', but this time a star wheel—albeit with only four teeth—is used 'for lifting a bar which in its turn strikes a key of a piano.' Alfred Dolge* tells us "In Germany about the year 1887, Paul Ehrlich, patented the 'Ariston' mechanism, which played 36 notes'. Here he is referring to the disc piano-playing device, but, in fact, we have the first known mention of a star wheel.

Ellis Parr and Paul Lochmann came together. We find Ellis Parr in an interview saying—'Mr Lochmann, my German co-patentee made precisely the same invention only a week after I made mine . . . At first I took action against him to prevent his interfering with the sale in England, but eventually we became partners . . .' The interview was with *The Pall Mall Budget* for 16th. February 1888, and by this time the Symphonion as the machine was called was selling well. The Symphonion in question was by now a recognizable disc musical box, having a motor beneath a bed-plate on which were two stationary combs, the motor centre-driving a round disc, and star wheels being intermediary between disc projections and comb teeth. The disc projections were a single finger of metal stamped from the metal disc and bent at right angles. Dampering was effected in a most interesting way, the (musically) lower of the two combs used a much more robust version of individual

*Alfred Dolge *Pianos And Their Makers*, Dover Publications Ltd., 1972.

DEVELOPMENT

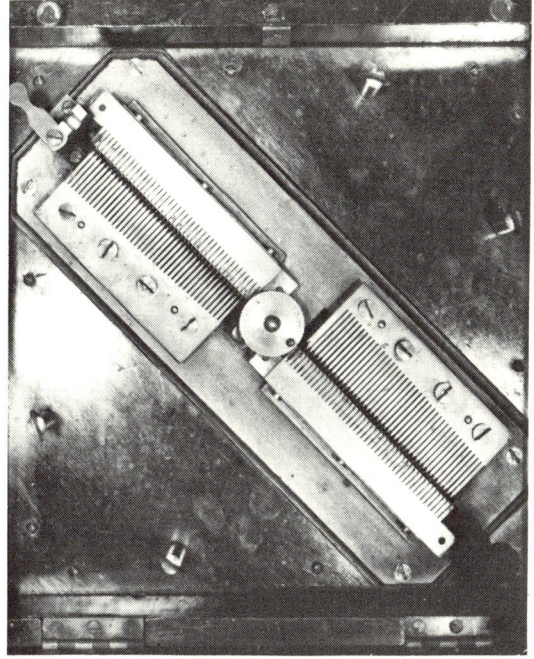

5. The bed-plate assembly of the Symphonion in Plate 3. The centre drive wheel bears the legend: 'PAUL LOCHMANNS AND ELLIS PARRS PATENT'.

cylinder musical box dampers, while the higher comb used a simple strip of felt that was pushed on to the tooth to be played by the star wheel to stop it vibrating before being plucked again. Braking of star wheels was obtained by a series of strips of spring metal arranged beneath the movement. Each of the strips 'cupped' the lower tooth of a star wheel, holding it lightly in position and allowing it to move out when necessary, cupping in turn the next tooth. On the centre drive wheel was found the legend "PAUL LOCHMANNS AND ELLIS PARRS PATENT". This machine was the subject of an article in the magazine *Invention* for 10th. December 1887, so it must have been in production for some while before that. Exactly what part Ellis Parr played in this later design is not known, but by 1888 he does appear as sole English agent for the machine. Also in this year a review of total German activity in

DEVELOPMENT

the making of mechanical musical instruments* shows the firm of Kuhne, Lochmann and Co. to be producing 15,000 Symphonions per year. At the same time Paul Ehrlich and Co. were producing 30,000 instruments a year, mainly Ariston organettes. Symphonion was alone in the production of disc musical boxes.

At the beginning combs for the new style of musical box were obtained from Switzerland, mainly Ste-Croix, since the Germans had no knowledge of their technology, though the Swiss, naturally enough, frowned on any comb maker who supplied what could clearly be seen as a serious rival industry. Chapuis† tells us that one comb maker at least, Jules Besse of Ste-Croix, established himself in Leipzig to supply the new industry, and many workers were obtained by advertising. The wheels and general design of the motor assembly owed much to cylinder musical box design.

Paul Lochmann's firm started in January 1886. The first advertisement for Symphonion to be found so far is that of Wilhelm Dietrich, Leipzig, dated 11th. July, 1886. On 11th. August of the same year Messrs. Breitkopf & Hartel, also of Leipzig, were advertising '. . . Symphonions, manivelle and with motor-drive, with 60, 72 and 84 steel teeth.' An important German patent—number 38822—was granted to Lochmann on 19th. February 1886, which related to a 'dampering system for musical machine'. 'By the use of star wheels for the transfer of the movement of the projections to the teeth is a dampering device in use'. The importance of this patent is not in the dampering device, which, it seems, was not practical, but in the proof it gives us that star wheels were already invented, and used in at least a prototype instrument. On 1st. March, only just over a week later, Lochmann applied for a German patent under the sub-title: 'Use of a star wheel for plucking musical box teeth'. The application was refused, and because of this there are no details available.

From the above, from Ehrlich's 1885 patent, and from knowledge of the early Symphonions extant, considered to date from about 1887, we have enough information to say, without doubt, that the star wheel was not the invention of Paul Wendland, at least, as modern histories have

*Kuhlow's Review. This shows a total of 82,500 mechanical musical instruments made yearly in Germany, with 44,000 exported.
† Alfred Chapuis, *Histoire de la Boîte à Musique et de la Musique Mećanique*, Scriptar S A., 1955. Now available in translation, MBSI.

it, in 1889. In 1896, Paul Ehrlich was to claim a monopoly of the use of star wheels, presumably because of his early patent. He lost his case, and also lost the appeal that followed!

Reports of the Leipzig Chamber of Commerce (*Leipziger Handelskammer*) said in 1887 that the Symphonion, now manufactured in different sizes and qualities, was doing well, although its construction was a painstaking operation. The demand, it said, especially for the 'small' items, required the enlarging of the factory. In 1888 the demand for Symphonions was growing so great that the company must become a Limited Company. Nevertheless, in September of that year the editor of *Zeitschrift* wrote (rough translation): 'Perhaps for reasons of economy, the material used for the (Symphonion) combs is too brittle. The tips of the teeth break very easily. The makers have recently bought better steel to avoid the problem'. It was also about this time that the company improved the disc projections by adding a second finger of metal behind the projection to reinforce it, forming a kind of backward 'h'.

By at least May, 1889, Symphonion was no longer alone. Leipziger Musikwerke had begun production of the Baskánion (Bascanion), as already described, a card disc-playing lever-plucking machine. This is mentioned in an advertisement of 11th. May, 1889. The instrument was still in production at Easter 1891. In a review of the Easter Fair the editor of a trade paper said: 'There is not much that is new. . . . In the

6. The black-polish case of the Baskánion by Leipzig Musikwerke (formerly Paul Ehrlich). (Grace Thompson collection).

DEVELOPMENT

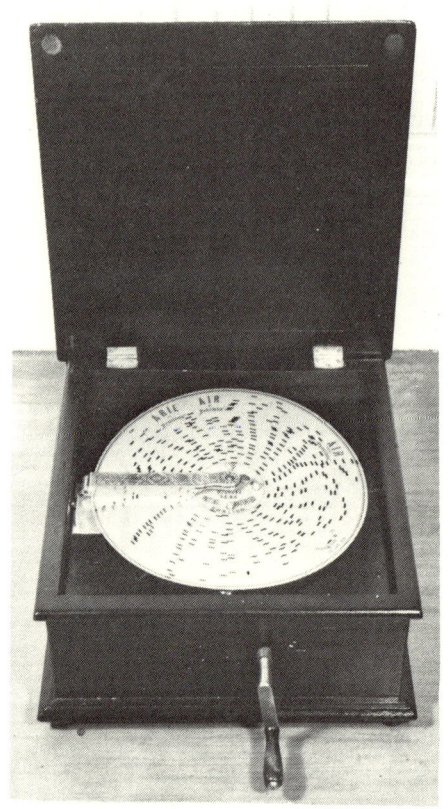

7. The Baskánion shown open, with its card disc, similar to that of the Ariston.

Fabrik Leipziger Musikwerke stand . . . the known products such as: Ariston; Aristonette; Daimonion; Bascanion (sic) (the kind of musical boxes of Switzerland with changeable Ariston discs) . . .'.

Interestingly, in the review of the previous Easter Fair, the same editor says that among the instruments with steel combs, the Symphonion is the best up to that date. There had to be at least one other machine

DEVELOPMENT

8. Bed-plate assembly of the Baskánion, showing the levers that pluck the comb.

9. A catalogue cut of a hand-crank version of the Baskánion.

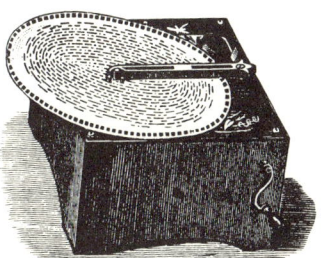

10. A cut from an early catalogue showing a hand-crank version of the early Polyphon.

with which to compare, this being the Baskánion. The Polyphon was yet to arrive.

Proving yet another connection between Ehrlich and Lochmann, the Michaelmas Fair of 1891 saw a new Symphonion instrument, the Sublime Harmonie Piccolo 'Meteor'. With this machine, it was possible to play discs of various diameters, for tunes of different lengths. The variation in disc sizes was based on German Patent 37234, the third addition to the Ariston, Ehrlich, patent, 21715. The instrument does not appear to have been a success; in subsequent Fair reviews it is not mentioned.

In an advertisement for 21st. November, 1890, and repeated until 1st.

13

DEVELOPMENT

June, 1891, came the following, from the house of Hugo Hennig, Berlin (rough translation): 'Surprising novelty/"Polyphon"/Musical Box/40 keys/Acting by hand or mechanical,/with changeable *card* discs (*Papp-Noten!*).'

The firm of Brachhausen & Riessner, comprised of Gustave Brachhausen and Paul Riessner, the former a foreman at the Symphonion factory, the latter an engineer with the firm, had actually shown their 'Polyphon' in October, 1890 at the Michaelmas Fair in Leipzig. The new machine was on display for only a short time. It was withdrawn by the manufacturer. The instrument was pursued from the start by its competitors. From this we can assume that Symphonion (or possibly Ehrlich?) had warned the company off because of existing patents. The instrument was comparable with the Symphonion, but it played with card discs.

Whatever the earlier objections, they must have been overcome quickly, from the fact that Hugo Hennig, though a relative newcomer as an agent, was advertising the Polyphon, and that it was exhibited at the Easter Fair, in March 1891. The card disc was obviously a major drawback, and at some period during the same year a metal disc appeared, and the machine became an early example of that so well known today. On 21st. November, 1891, a year to the day from the first known advertisement, another appeared, showing what appears to be a 15½-inch table Polyphon, with 156 notes (2 × 78 with opposed combs), and a metal (zinc) disc. The advertisement bears the legend 'Patented in all Countries'. The machine was available in several sizes.

Once their Polyphon had reached its basic state, Brachhausen and Riessner continued to improve it. Among other things, they attempted many different types of damper, not only to avoid infringements but also to improve on Lochmann's methods. They also used a new type of projection, this in fact a singular improvement on the double finger of Symphonion. The method they used involved a single cutter, the shape of which caused the metal finger to curl as it was cut to bring the top of the finger in contact with the surface of the disc, forming a bridge of considerable strength in one simple operation. Despite all their efforts the owners of Polyphon were sued by Lochmann for infringement of his patents in regard to, among other things, disc projections. The case dragged on for many months, the eventual outcome being that the defendants, Polyphon, won the litigation. Ironically Symphonion eventually used these same projections, as did most of the disc box makers to follow.

Though, it seems, opposed, double combs (duplex) arrived early on the scene, and these were necessary for volume if a commercial, coin operated, machine of any size was to be attempted. In addition, there were many other problems to overcome, not least being the metal for the discs, their larger size, and a dependable method of dampering for excessive use. Musical Box Society member Mr. Cramp of Horsham, England, has hazarded that the numbers to be found on the bronze rivet on the outside of the spring of upright Polyphons is, in fact, a date of manufacture of at least the spring. It is interesting to note that no one appears to have found a set of these numbers which would make the date earlier than the last years of the 1890s. It could be said that possibly the dating of the springs was not begun until this time, but it would seem that all but a very few do have these numbers and these few could well be replacement springs. A further clue is the catalogue of disc musical boxes originally published in the United States and dated 1894–95. This catalogue is in the collection of another member of the Musical Box Society, Mrs. Ruth Bornand of Pelham, New York. The catalogue lists eleven Symphonions including a large 'Hall Clock', four Reginas, and two Polyphons. In no case is there a disc-size of over 15½-inches, although double combs are in evidence and the discs are made of steel.

By 1895, just ten years after the first serious patent had been taken out, Swiss makers of cylinder musical boxes began to fight back against the German instrument that had made such heavy inroads into the market once almost exclusively theirs.

In that year Mermod Frères of Ste-Croix, established in 1815 and recognised as makers of excellent cylinder musical boxes, and innovators of many practical improvements, began manufacture of the Stella. They exhibited it at the Geneva Exposition of 1896.

According to Chapuis*, the idea used in the Stella—a projectionless disc allowing star wheel teeth to rise through its perforations to be drawn forward, turning the star wheels to pluck the teeth of the comb—was first brought to Switzerland by its originator, André Junod, returning after being in the United States. The firm of Harmonia of L'Auberson was first to make such a machine. Though some Harmonia instruments ex-

*Leipzig Trade Journal.

DEVELOPMENT

ist, and the company must have continued to make its version, the Stella is far better known.

Of the two main centres of musical box manufacture, Ste-Croix was by far the more active in making disc machines. By 1895(?), five firms were involved in the work*. Gueissaz fils et Cie. (of whose output nothing is known), and Barnett H. Abrahams (makers of 'the Britannia' and Imperial); Mermod Frères (Stella and Mira); E. Paillard et Cie.; and Hermann Thorens, these last three of Ste-Croix itself. All of these five exhibited at the 1900 International Exhibition in Paris.

Mermod Frères showed that they could now supply six different sizes of disc movement, with combs having teeth of from 80 to 254 teeth, played by discs of from 9.6 inches to a massive 32 inches—this last size now unknown.

Hermann Thorens offered three interesting machines, all coin-operated: a movement with bell accompaniment—described by L. Ph. Mermod, a member of the international jury, as 'a new application'; a box with a reed organ section as well as its two combs (this was the year of the introduction of Adler's reed organ accompanied 'Fortuna Marvel'), and an auto-change disc box (under a patent the British version of which was number 9688, granted 8th. May, 1899). Thorens is known for the Edelweiss and Helvetia boxes made in both 'lever-plucker' and more normal format.

At the International Exposition of 1906 in Milan, E. Paillard et Cie. among their exhibits also showed three unusual disc boxes: one with four combs 'Sublime Harmonie Tremolo Zither' (Paillard et Cie. were responsible in 1874/5 for 'Sublime Harmonie' cylinder boxes); a 'shifting disc' box, playing either two tunes or one long tune (a mechanism now associated with Mermod Frères) and an auto-change box.

In Geneva, from 1896, a company formed by three cylinder musical box houses, Rivenc, Langdorff and Billon, was making, first the Gloria, and later Polymnia disc boxes. The only other known (?) maker of disc boxes in this area was the partnership of Schramli & Tschudin, who, among other things, made an example named the Sun. Very little is known of this machine and no examples appear to exist.

With these Swiss makers, and those German firms who entered the market late, even though there were many excellent instruments made, particularly by Mermod Frères, there was never a serious threat to the

*Chapuis, *Histoire de la Boîte à Musique*

DEVELOPMENT

three big manufacturers, Symphonion, Polyphon, and Regina, this last company having been established in New Jersey in 1892 by Gustave Brachhausen. Regina continued for some time to buy parts from Polyphon to make up and sell under their own name, and for this reason some of the discs of the two companies are interchangeable. Here again like sizes of discs stop at the 15½-inch. Around 1895 Symphonion decided to follow Polyphon in evading the particularly high U.S. tariffs by opening the Symphonion Music Box Co. with offices in New York and a factory in New Jersey, where the Imperial Symphonion was made, though it is thought that relatively little manufacturing was done. Discs were made but these too were augmented by those imported from the parent company. About 1900 the Imperial Company ceased to function, this at about the same time that the parent company came under the aegis of Hupfeld.

The last years of the nineteenth century saw many new companies in the disc musical box field. Though these were, and are, overshadowed by 'the big three', who between them took some ninety per cent of the total market, this does not mean they are inferior, or that they did not have a relatively good, albeit short, business life. There were, of course, because of the constant need to beware of already existing patents, some instruments that were rather over complicated in their mechanism, but in the main these secondary firms made good machines, many of which would have sold considerably better had they been earlier in the field, or more competently marketed.

The main markets for disc boxes were Russia and Britain, though of course the whole of Europe was open to the new machine, and the United States. Symphonion at least appears to have found a good market in Australia and New Zealand. The last years of the nineteenth, and the beginning of the twentieth century formed a period of particular opulence and wealth. Main agencies were formed to sell the machines and they could be seen everywhere. Particularly popular were the coin-operated upright machines which appeared in any public place thought a possible source of coins. In 1896, the auto-change disc musical box made an appearance as what can truly be called the first juke-box. A set of discs was available in the machine. By means of a lever a tune could be selected, and the insertion of a coin put the machinery into motion. The disc was lifted into place, played the tune, and returned to the rack, truly a sight to watch. Polyphon were responsible for this step forward, which did away with the necessity of changing the disc by hand. Before

DEVELOPMENT

the arrival of the auto-change machine, the changing of discs must have really been a nuisance in a cafe or public-house.

Several companies followed Polyphon with auto-change machines, Regina becoming by far the most prolific in the field with Polyphon second a long way behind. Symphonion, who introduced changers rather late in the day, and who made more different designs including table models, sold very few.

There were many attempts to make a different sound. Bells had been used to accompany disc boxes almost from their inception. They took three forms: the classic style already used in cylinder musical boxes; tuned metal bars, and tuned tubular bells. There were various attempts in other directions. Symphonion together with Monopol used a scheme of comb tuning with some of their boxes to give a so-called harmonic effect. More normal double comb mechanisms of the 'opposed-combs' type were used to increase volume.

Occasionally a more brilliant effect was achieved accidentally, making for an especially fine sound in a particular example of an otherwise ordinary range. The apogee of harmony in a disc box was obtained by Symphonion in their Eroica triple-disc machine. The three discs, each with their own musical arrangement of a particular tune, played on three sets of 'sublime harmonie' combs making an excellent sound. Symphonion, as did several other companies, made a double-disc machine, but the only other triple-disc instruments were a larger size sold by both German and American Symphonion (Bowers, *Encyclopedia*).

At about the same time as the auto-change was conceived, a different idea was patented (1896) by Keller and Bortmann of Leipzig. The patent was for a disc shifting device allowing two tunes to be played by one disc. After playing a tune for one revolution, the disc was moved to present another set of projections to the star wheels and enable another tune to be played. Mermod Frères, the assignees of the patent, are believed to have made mechanisms using this idea that were placed in 'Sirion' and 'New Century' disc boxes. T. Alwin Plessing patented another shifting-disc mechanism in 1897 that was subsequently used in 'Tannhauser' boxes. A shifting-disc box was shown at the International Exposition of 1906 in Milan by E. Paillard & Cie. of Ste-Croix. None of these last are known, and all types are extremely rare. (see A List of Disc Musical Boxes)

A major move to obtain a different sound was made by Adler, who presented their 'Fortuna Marvel' box, an upright machine using reed or-

DEVELOPMENT

gan, drum and triangle to accompany the combs. Shown in 1900 the Fortuna Marvel attracted a great deal of attention. In the same year the company passed to the ownership of J.H. Zimmermann who changed the name of the whole range to cash-in on the popularity of this model.

The next major step in the development of the disc box was the 'disc piano orchestrion', which was in fact a set of strings and various other instruments played by a disc in a cabinet similar to that of the larger ordinary disc machines. Adler had added a reed organ sound with drum and cymbal to the comb mechanism of the Fortuna, but the disc orchestrion was a new departure. Using a projectionless disc and going back to the lever system, the machine does not seem to have caught on in England since few if any were imported, although Polyphon exported some to the United States for Regina, who later manufactured some for themselves.

Symphonion made disc orchestrions too and each company moved on to using a paper roll to dictate the melody, so taking the instrument out of the realm of disc musical boxes. The shadow of the phonograph had hung over the disc musical box from the beginning of its life, long before the patenting of Miguel Boom's idea. Little had been done, however, to market the idea seriously until the disc musical box was well entrenched. Then in 1901, a massive advertising campaign was launched in the United States by the Victor Talking Machine Company, the first to attempt seriously to promote the sale of the disc-playing gramophone. From this beginning, the writing was on the wall. What was certainly an innovation was the disc musical box with attachment to play gramophone records. It was made by several companies.

One by one giant and pigmy alike began to falter. First of the major companies to go to the wall was Polyphon. For all intents and purposes business ceased in 1914, though the firm staggered on until 1917, when it was merged with *Deutsche Grammophon*, a gramophone company. Symphonion had changed hands in about 1900, Ludwig Hupfeld A.G. acquiring a major shareholding, but the firm continued in business into the 1920s. Symphonion Manufacturing Company, New York, makers of the Imperial Symphonion range, had lasted little more than five years, closing in 1900. Regina sold its last musical box in 1921.

THE PRINCIPAL MANUFACTURERS

There were, of course, many makers of disc musical boxes over their relatively short period of manufacture. By far the most prolific, however, and so most important, were the 'big three': Symphonion, Polyphon and Regina. This is particularly so in coin-operated machines, where a commercial interest made it necessary to have a good service organization behind an instrument relied upon to earn money.

Information about other makers may be found in the chapters 'A List of Disc Musical Boxes' and 'A List of Manufacturers and Agents'. Some early history of the disc musical box, which of course includes that of the firms mentioned here, particularly Symphonion, is to be found in the chapter 'Development'.

SYMPHONION

To the Symphonion belongs the distinction of being the first commercial disc musical box. (Oskar) Paul Lochmann, founder of the company, had been a manufacturer of several types of machinery including the table fountains that were popular during the third quarter of the 19th century before he began to produce the Symphonion at Gohlis, a suburb of Leipzig. The early history of the Symphonion is also that of the early development of the disc musical box.

The Lochmann factory was founded in January 1886, and by July of that year the Symphonion was being advertised by Wilhelm Dietrich of Leipzig, already an agent for Ariston, Herophon, Clariaphon, Orpheus, and Melophon, all of them using discs. By this time, or within a month, the Symphonion was being produced in three sizes, 60, 72, and 84 teeth, each available in a manivelle (hand-turned) or mechanical model.

11. An upright, coin operated, 25-inch disc Symphonion with disc bin. (Graham Webb).

Also by this time the instrument, though showing its basically Swiss origin in the design of the movement and the combs, was complete with star wheels, and quite similar to the design generally known today. Two things, however, tie the Symphonion to the then extremely popular Ariston, a card-disc organette manufactured by (F.E.) Paul Ehrlich. First is the making of each model in hand-crank form, as with organ-

THE PRINCIPAL MANUFACTURERS

ettes, but the second is far more important: the numbers of two patents granted to Ehrlich were printed on Symphonion discs. Both of these German patents, 21715 (5th. May, 1882) and 24106 (25th. September, 1883) relate to discs, the second, an addendum to the first, including those with projections. Apart from the discs, Ehrlich also had patented the star wheel itself. He was granted German patent 33782 (19th. June, 1885) and another, 40943 (7th. November, 1886), an improvement on the first. Though the star wheel was for use with his piano-player, using Ariston type card-discs, and with only four teeth, it seems the first patent was sufficient to cause the failure of a patent application on 1st. March, 1886, by Lochmann for 'Use of a star wheel for plucking musical box teeth'. Interestingly, Lochmann had been granted German patent 38822 on 19th. February, 1886 for a 'Dampering system for a musical machine', in which a dampering device was caused to act by the use of star wheels for the transfer of the movement of projections to the teeth. The dampering device was not practical, but the interest lies in the fact that star wheels were already in use at this time—presumably under license from Ehrlich.

With the now obvious cooperation of Ehrlich's company—even if only under the license—Lochmann's success with the Symphonion was rapid and large. A survey for 1887 of Leipzig trade, published by the *Leipziger Handelskammer* (Chamber of Commerce) stated (rough translation): 'Symphonion, now manufactured in different sizes and qualities, are doing well, although their construction is painstaking. The demand, especially for the smaller items, requires enlargement of the factory'. For 1888, from the same source we get: 'Demand is growing so fast that the company will have to become Limited'. We learn from another source, *Kuhlow's Review*, that in this year production reached 15,000 machines per year, worth 400,000 marks, and the firm employed 180 men. Again in the same year, two problems in manufacture were overcome. It was found that the comb steel was too brittle, and that the tooth tips broke too easily. The company was forced to buy better steel. Similarly, the single-tongue projection had been found to be too weak for constant use, and a second projection was designed, to curve behind the first, reinforcing it.

It was not, in fact, until June, 1889, that the change was made to a Limited Company, and in the same year the factory was considerably enlarged, with business still booming.

The year 1889 saw Symphonion's monopoly broken as the only com-

THE PRINCIPAL MANUFACTURERS

12. A good example of a rare 17¼-inch disc Symphonion table model. (Grace Thompson collection).

THE PRINCIPAL MANUFACTURERS

mercial disc musical box. The Baskánion, a steel comb lever-plucking card-disc musical box, made by Fabrik Leipziger Musikwerke (formerly Paul Ehrlich), made its appearance at least as early as 11th. May, 1889, when it was advertised. A review of the Easter Fair for 1890, states: 'The Symphonion is, up to now, the best of the instruments with steel combs'. Thus proving at least one rival—the Baskánion—if not more! The new machine used Ariston style card-discs. It does not seem to have been very successful, from the fact that only one is known to exist today, though its manufacture continued until at least the Easter Fair of 1891. The Ehrlich factory had far more success with their 'Monopol', introduced in April, 1893, a classic metal-disc box.

Symphonion continued to prosper, though the advent of the Polyphon, first in 1890 as a card-disc instrument, and then in late 1891 much more seriously as a metal disc machine, was to cause them problems and eventually move them into second place.

That the firm was still somehow involved with Paul Ehrlich's Fabrik Leipziger Musikwerke, was shown yet again at the Leipzig Michaelmas Fair for 1891. A new machine, the Sublime Harmonie Piccolo 'Meteor' was introduced. It was claimed that the instrument could play discs of different diameters, and so play for different lengths of time. This idea stems directly from yet another addition to Paul Ehrlich's Ariston German patent 21715, numbered 37234. The Meteor does not appear to have been a success. None are known today.

The *Polyphonmusikwerke* must have been a thorn in the side of Lochmann, particularly since the factories were in the same area. It was not long before Lochmann brought a law suit against Brachhausen for infringement of the patent rights of Symphonion on disc projections, although in fact projections used for discs were not only different in shape, but much more robust. The suit continued for some time before judgement was made for Polyphon. Although Symphonion grew quickly, Polyphon set a tremendous pace, putting Symphonion in second place in production and sales in a couple of years, mainly due, one feels, to more extensive advertising and better sales technique. At the height of production, Symphonion employed 400 workers, some of these women, but Polyphon had considerably more employees.

The 1890's proved to be the heyday of the disc musical industry, and Symphonion continued to do excellent business. Among the many innovations were several types of disc-playing clocks. Excellent selling

THE PRINCIPAL MANUFACTURERS

items were the multiple-disc machine of which the Company appears to have been the only successful manufacturer. In particular the 'Eroica' three-disc machines must have had a good reception with their distinctive and beautiful sound. This machine is discussed in the chapter 'Rare Types of Disc Musical Box'. Also manufactured was the 'Rococo', a model which used a normal 11⅞-inch disc movement in a most attractive case with the appearance of elaborately-carved wood. Perhaps the most striking of Symphonion cases however, was the 'Gambrinus' which, again housing an 11⅞-inch movement, was a coin-operated machine in the shape of a beer barrel with the 'Beer King' perched on top holding in one hand a large beer jug and in the other a beer stein. This machine was made to stand on the counter of a bar or beer cellar. Although found very occasionally in Europe, it does not seem to have been sold in Britain, probably because of the Germanic design of the figure.

In 1895 or thereabouts, Symphonion opened a factory in Asbury Park, New Jersey; the registered offices and showrooms for the new 'Symphonion Manufacturing Company' were in New York City. Machines made at this factory and distributed through the New York showrooms were of similar appearance in case design to the Regina. The Imperial Symphonion range included a three-disc machine which was entirely different in case design and size of disc to the European equivalent (see the chapter 'Rare Types of Disc Musical Box').

In 1896 an association was formed of 18 companies *Verein Deutscher Musikwerke-Grossisten* (Association of German Wholesale Dealers in Musical Products) and Symphonion was one of the sole agencies this group obtained together with those of Orphenion and Kalliope. A member of the Association was the firm of Ludwig Hupfeld of Leipzig, already large manufacturers of mechanical musical instruments in its own right. About 1900 Ludwig Hupfeld acquired a controlling interest in Symphonion, and Paul Lochmann left the company he had founded, to form Lochmann Original Musikwerke, makers of the fine machines of that name. In the same year Symphonion opened showrooms and repair shops in London at Ely Place. Also in the same year the American branch of the firm was closed. The parent company continued to do good business for many years. Though not more than a handful still exist the company made several different models of autochange disc machines, including two table model versions. It also went

THE PRINCIPAL MANUFACTURERS

13. View of the interior of a 19⅛-inch disc upright coin-operated Symphonion. (Graham Webb).

into the disc orchestrion business and quite naturally sold electric pianos and orchestrions proper. The company continued well into the 1920s after taking over Polyphon's disc musical box business selling the once rival Symphonion and Polyphon machines together, though most of the business was in gramophones.

THE PRINCIPAL MANUFACTURERS
POLYPHON

By the time Gustave Brachhausen and Paul Riessner left the Symphonion works and set up *Polyphonmusikwerke*, A.G. in Gohlis, Leipzig, (the same area and town as their former employers), the greater part of the early development of disc machines for the music box market had been accomplished. The early problems with the material from which the disc was made had been solved and the zinc now being used was proving a fairly good, if not perfect, choice. The projections had been made stronger by using two pieces of metal cut from the disc, one bent over behind the other to form a support.

14. A most rare table model 17½-inch disc Polyphon with bells. (Vickie Glasgow collection).

THE PRINCIPAL MANUFACTURERS

For Polyphon there remained some improvements to make. The first was immediate, in that the projections used by Polyphon from the beginning were different from those of Symphonion. The strength of the projections was obtained by cutting a single tongue from the metal and curling it over to touch the surface of the disc to form a bridge. In spite of the difference in form of these projections, Symphonion sought a decision from the courts against Polyphon for infringement of projection patents among other things. The case carried on for some time before a decision was made for Polyphon.

From the beginning one of the main problems to beset disc musical box manufacturers was that of a suitable means of damping the notes before they were struck again. It was not only necessary to make a set of dampers which worked, a comparatively easy job, but to make them strong enough and simple enough to last a long time. Many types of damper were tried, and used with varying degrees of success. To give an example, there are at least six different types of damper to be found in the 15½-inch size Polyphon alone. It is not known which firm was responsible for the D-shaped dampers which were eventually used not only by Polyphon but, with slight variations, by quite a few others including Symphonion. The dampers, running vertically between the teeth from a brass bar, were easy to fit and long lasting, proof of this being the large numbers of disc machines having good dampers when found even now.

Polyphon was soon taking the lead in the disc box market, and the company also produced many clocks of various sizes fitted with a disc movement, some of these being provided with coin slots so that as well as sounding a tune on the hour they could also be used to earn money for the owner. Disc clocks are discussed more fully under the heading 'Rare Types of Disc Musical Box'. The boom in disc machines continued and Polyphon quickly became the most popular make. The company, having started life in a large house, adding bits to the premises as the need for more room arose, eventually moved to a large factory at Wahren, still in Leipzig, where all the various processes of manufacture could be undertaken in better surroundings.

In 1892, while sales were still on the increase, Gustave Brachhausen left the Company to go to America. It is enough to say at the moment that for some time Polyphon supplied parts and discs to be assembled in America by Regina.

Without its prime founder, Polyphon continued to thrive and after

THE PRINCIPAL MANUFACTURERS

some years the already large factory was altered considerably to enable the company to employ more workers and continue expansion. Unfortunately, shortly after the alterations were completed on 6th. July 1899, a fire broke out in the joinery department of the factory. It seems to have started in a pile of shavings and spread very rapidly among the piles of timbers, taking in the mounting shop. Many firemen from the surrounding countryside were involved in fighting the fire and even the military

15. An exceptionally rare 22-inch disc autochange Polyphon with integral disc bin. (Michael Gilbert collection).

was called in. The fire was fanned by a stiff breeze, and the fire fighters were hampered by lack of water. Eventually the fire was brought under control, luckily before the main machinery halls had sustained much damage. It was found that the workshops for the finer work, which were in the basement, were undamaged also, so that by setting up temporary buildings on the grounds of the factory full production could be resumed almost at once. At that time there were 780 people—many of them women—employed at the factory, who must have breathed a sign of relief that none were to be laid off.

During the period preceding the fire, Polyphon had continued to build

16. An interior view of the 22-inch disc autochange Polyphon. Note the discs commence play upside down.

THE PRINCIPAL MANUFACTURERS

up the number of models produced. The whole range now included 19⅝-inch, 22-inch, and 24½-inch sizes in various styles such as the 'folding-top' table boxes, (which are very rarely found), upright models, with and without disc bins, and the auto-change models (see 'Rare Types of Disc Musical Box'). At just about the turn-of-the-century came an exciting new machine, the 'Polyphon-Concerto', this being a disc orchestrion playing on piano, bass drum, snare drum, and glockenspiel. Many of the Concertos were imported into the United States by Regina, who subsequently assembled them in America from Polyphon parts. Later the Concerto was also made to play with a paper roll, disc or roll models being offered as a choice.

A sign of the increasing interest in recordings and the corresponding decrease in the sale of musical boxes was the 'Gramopolyphon', also named 'Polygraphon'. This was an ordinary table or upright Polyphon with an attachment to play the new type of disc, a gramophone record, as well as the musical box disc. The machine was made in many more models and to a more sophisticated pattern by Regina in the United States, and others (see 'Rare Types of Disc Musical Box').

During the next decade Polyphon was to turn more and more to the selling of gramophones as well as pneumatic pianos and orchestrions. In 1917 the firm merged with *Deutsche Grammophon* and turned away from disc musical boxes, though the name continued with Symphonion, and survived through the twenties and thirties selling gramophones and non-musical items. Among their many products had been motor cars and typewriters.

THE REGINA MUSIC BOX COMPANY

There is no doubt that collectors of musical boxes generally, and not just those in the United States, consider that the Regina disc music box has by far the finest sound. Couple this sound with a case design which is more readily assimilated into the modern home due to the simplicity of line which it displays, and you have a machine which any collector might be justifiably proud to own. The excellent sound is the result of using the case fully as a sounding board, a technique which was perfected by Regina. The simplicity usually found in the casework may well have been due to a lack of carvers in the German style, which had been such a feature of the European machines. Another reason might be

17. A good example of the rare 20¾-inch disc Regina autochange. (Graham Webb).

that the home market simply called for elegance of line, popularized by the "Arts & Crafts" movement. Whatever the reason, we can be grateful for it now.

The story of Regina begins in September 1892, when Gustave Brachhausen, co-founder of Polyphon, arrived in the United States of America with five workmen. He settled in Jersey City, New Jersey, and started the Regina Music Box Company. Brachhausen, then, has played a large part in the three major disc musical box companies: Symphonion, where he was foreman for Paul Lochmann; Polyphon, of which he was co-founder; and now Regina, the first company ever to make disc musical boxes in America. During the first year or so of his American life Brachhausen spent much of his time applying for U.S. patent rights, for some of which his co-patentee was Paul Riessner, the 'other half' of Polyphon. By the spring of 1894 the Regina Company had been incorporated and had three main shareholders, Brachhausen, Riessner and Johannas J. Korner of Leipzig, a backer. The company began its swift climb to fame.

18. Detail of the rare 'folding top' or 'accordion' 27-inch disc Regina, showing the combs and various parts of the bed-plate assembly. (Dr. Peter Whitehead collection).

THE PRINCIPAL MANUFACTURERS

In the beginning, Regina imported both parts and discs for the machines from Polyphon in Leipzig and assembled them in the factory in Jersey City. As time went on, however, more and more of the mechanism and the discs were made in America. The early practice of obtaining parts and discs from Polyphon has had the effect of making most discs up to and including the 15½-inch size interchangeable between the two machines. The fact that the interchangeability ends at this size adds weight to the theory that the larger coin-operated machines were not manufactured until about 1895. There are exceptions to the sizes of discs below 15½-inches which would fit either make of machine, but this is simply because there is not an equivalent machine made by the other company; such a case is the 11¼-inch Polyphon, with bells added. The disc for this machine will not even play on an ordinary 11¼-inch Polyphon. Regina used the sizes 20¾ inches and 27 inches for their large upright machines and also made the two sizes in table models of the double-lid type. Although in the main the cases were plain, many different styles of cases were made both for general sale and by order.

By 1895, Regina was in full swing and rapidly increasing sales. Not a little of this success was due to the enthusiasm of Gustave Brachhausen, who would make a tour of the country from time to time drumming up new business and keeping regular distributors happy. The original building in West Cherry Street, Rahway, New Jersey, to which Regina had moved when in need of larger premises, was enlarged, and later another building was acquired to house the cabinet-making side of the business. When, in 1896, the automatic disc-changing machine came into being, Regina went into the business of supplying, servicing, and collecting the money from these new-style machines. Just as with modern juke-boxes, 'records' were changed periodically by the Company. The machines were made in 15½-inch, 20¾-inch and 27-inch disc sizes.

Regina went from strength to strength and at the height of production was grossing two million dollars a year. This, however, was not to last. After weathering a country-wide recession in the first year of the new century, the company was hit badly in 1903 by the massive campaigns to sell disc grammophones which had been mounted by the Victor Talking Machine Company and others. Although the company continued to make musical boxes until 1919, there was never really a recovery from this setback. Many diversifications of production were tried, the first as

THE PRINCIPAL MANUFACTURERS

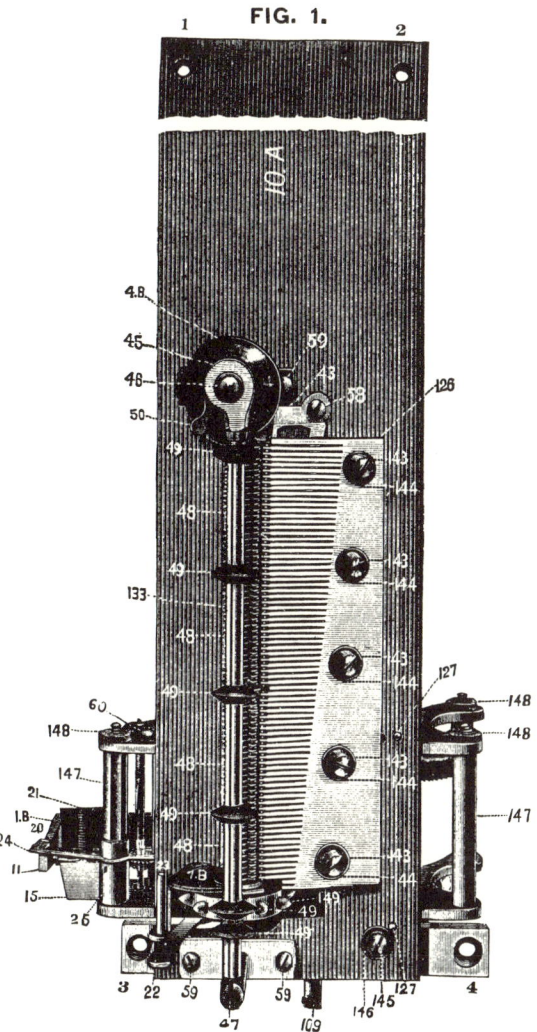

19. A cut showing a 15½-inch disc, single comb Regina bed-plate assembly looking remarkably like that of a Polyphon of the same size. (Drs. L. Goldhoorn Archives).

THE PRINCIPAL MANUFACTURERS

early as 1902 when a hand-operated vacuum cleaner was introduced. In 1903 Regina imported disc Orchestrions from Polyphon which used a disc larger than any used before by either company, the size being 32 inches. The Orchestrion played piano, tuned tubular bells, drum, and triangle. These machines were also marketed as auto-change models and they seem to have sold quite well. Another, rather sad, product of Regina was the Reginaphone, which was a combination of a disc musical box and a gramophone. Many different models of this peculiar machine were made, and Polyphon made a similar type of combination machine. Yet another attempt to keep in the automatic-music field was the production of various types of mechanical pianos. Later still, Regina sold, if not manufactured, a printing press. In 1922, finally beaten, Regina was bankrupt, after making the last disc musical box in 1919, and so ended a period during which over 100,000 disc boxes had been supplied, the best of which were without equal anywhere in the world.

RARE TYPES OF DISC MUSICAL BOX

Before discussing rare disc boxes, we really ought to decide what is meant by 'rare'. In fact, what the collector means when he talks of rare machines is not simply rare, but wanted. To give an example, a small disc musical box, played manually, with say a 6-inch disc and only one of these, with a name no one has any knowledge of, is rare. It is rare, but its value is limited to that of interest. It has no meaning to people outside of a small circle of dedicated collectors, and very few of these will be more than mildly interested. The question of rarity in this case is academic. Of prime importance with musical boxes, is that they play well and be attractive within the concept of their design. If the design is good and the machine is rare because it was either expensive in its day, or because it was possibly too good and so too expensive to make in quantity, it then falls into the right category. There are exceptions to this rule as will be seen. One of the main delights of collecting disc musical boxes is the possibility of, at some later date, acquiring more discs for a particular machine, either by finding some originals or by purchasing new discs from a specialist dealer. Unfortunately in this respect, the rarity of a disc machine can have the serious drawback of having too few discs for the instrument, and no probability of obtaining any more. In the case of a machine rare because of its original value this is not so bad a situation since often discs can be borrowed for copying. Where the machine is of the type of which a small manufacturer made and sold few, then the chances of finding discs are, to say the least, remote.

Bearing in mind the possible disc situation, we have two main categories for machines which are rare; one of these is rarity of design or arrangement of the music—a good example of this is the three-disc Symphonion. The other category contains those machines which are rare because few were sold—in Europe the ordinary Regina falls into this class for the simple reason that few were sold there. Of course, there are

THE PRINCIPAL MANUFACTURERS

some which are within both categories, like the Stella, which had a short manufacturing life but which has a beautiful sound and interesting mechanics. In this chapter we confine ourselves to those musical boxes which have more to them than mere rarity. We are looking at machines which in themselves would be pleasant to own. That rarity makes them interesting and more valuable, is only a part of the total.

The addition of bells

The addition of bells to disc movements was in the old tradition of mechanical music, the use of bells going back to the early barrel organ, and beyond to the carillon. Unlike the bells of many cylinder movements, which often tended, particularly in the later stages, to be an excuse for poor music, those on disc movements tended to be added to an existing size of comb. These machines, which often used tuned metal bars or tubular bells instead of the classic hemispherical shape, used discs on which the tunes were arranged exactly the same as for the normal machine, plus the arrangement for the bells on the outer edge. In this case, the discs were larger, the comb(s) remained the same size, but extra levers or possibly small sections of untuned comb were added to the end of the star wheel assembly to play the bells. These levers can usually be depressed so as to take them away from the projections on the disc and so cut out the bell accompaniment.

Many different companies used the bells on some sizes of their machines. The smallest had tiny hand-turned movements with the bells concealed beneath the bed-plate, and the largest were huge machines such as the 27-inch disc Symphionion and the $33^{3}/_{8}$-inch monster Komet. The largest Polyphon to use bells was the 22-inch disc machine, which had the normal $19^{5}/_{8}$-inch set-up on the combs plus an extra band for the bells round the periphery of the discs. A table disc-box with tuned tubular bells is a rarity, but Lochmann Originals are of this type. Tubular bells were usually confined to upright machines, and the classic hemispherical bell normally used for table models. The Emerald, a very rare 22-inch disc Polyphon with bells is a table machine on which the lids, which meet in the centre of the case, flap back to form supports for the disc to run on. The case of this model is too narrow to allow the disc to be played in any other way. This type of case was also used for a $24^{1}/_{2}$-inch Polyphon movement, the relatively more commonly-found

20. Interior view of a 22-inch disc upright, coin-operated Polyphon. (Graham Webb).

20¾-inch and 27-inch table Regina case of the same design was probably copied from the earlier Polyphon models. Several auto-change disc machines were fitted with a series of bells, the most likely to be found being the 22-inch Polyphon with either tubular bells or tuned metal bars. In general, any of the various machines with bells added are a good find. The variety of sizes allows even the most cramped quarters to house one. The bells make for a more attractive sound, and the rarity of such pieces adds considerably to the value.

Organ accompaniment

21. The most rare 'Fortuna Marvel' disc musical box with drum, triangle, and reed organ accompaniment. The case is in process of restoration. (Grace Thompson collection).

In 1900 the firm of Adler made a machine they named 'Fortuna' which used a 26½-inch disc to play tuned steel combs with an accompaniment of a 14 note reed organ, a drum, and a triangle. This machine, with a change of management of the firm, gave its name to the whole range of machines previously known as 'Adlers'. It was an upright instrument. The tone of the organ and combs combined is very sweet, but from a musical point of view the drum and triangle add nothing. The case of the machine has double doors (usually) which are either carved or fretted and backed with material. It is found with or without a disc bin base. The machine is vary rare so that care should be taken that a good supply of discs is available. Later a double disc version of this machine was made but none are known.

22. Interior view of the Fortuna. The reed organ pallets are situated below the combs, the bellows and reservoir to the lower left.

Symphonion brought out their 'Orchestrion-Automat', a machine using a vast 30-inch disc to play 120 tuned steel teeth, 26 harmonium reeds, 10 bells, 2 drums and cymbal. As the term 'Automat' indicates, the instrument was coin-operated. No examples appear to be extant.

Having left Symphonion in 1900 and set up as Lochmann Original, Paul Lochmann later came out with the 'Concert Original', using a disc just a shade smaller at 29¾-inches to play 160 steel teeth, 12 tubular bells, bass drum, snare drum and cymbal, again in a large upright, coin-operated format. This machine is not to be confused with his 'disc piano orchestrions', which see under that heading.

RARE TYPES OF DISC MUSICAL BOX

Automatic disc-changers

The automatic disc-changing musical box can truly be called the first juke-box. On this type of machine the disc title is selected, a coin inserted or a lever moved, and the disc is lifted from a rack, placed in position on the playing mechanism, plays the tune, and is then returned to the rack. One can imagine what an innovation the auto-changer was, and how welcome it would have been in places where, up to then, the disc had either to play the same monotonous tune over and over, or the owner of the establishment continually change the disc.

The auto-change mechanism was first patented on behalf of Polyphon by Paul Riessner in 1896, the patent being taken out in the United States by Gustave Brachhausen, of the Regina Music Box Company.

The three major companies: Polyphon; Symphonion and Regina all made auto-change disc boxes. Those most likely to be found in Europe being Polyphon, which were made in the disc sizes 15½-inch, 19⅝-inch, 22-inch (with bells), and 24½-inch; the most common, though all are extremely rare, being the 19⅝-inch model.

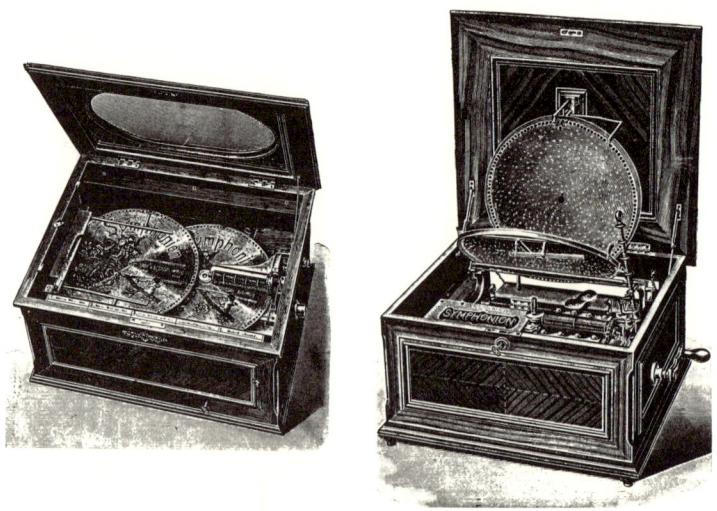

23. Two examples of the only table model autochange machines known to have been made, by Symphonion.

RARE TYPES OF DISC MUSICAL BOX

In America as is natural the indigenous Regina is most likely to be seen, made in the disc sizes 15½-inch, 20¾-inch, and 27-inch.

Though Symphonion made several models, very few appear to have been sold, since only a handful survive. Two upright models are known to have been made, and, more interestingly, two table models. No other manufacturer had made use of the horizontal design. One table model

24. A domestic model of a 27-inch disc Regina autochange. The case is veneered in flame mahogany, with carved dragons as decoration. (Grace Thompson collection)

took a disc from a stack of eight, played it and then replaced it, while the other, after playing the disc, ejected it from the machine.

For home use, Regina used the normal upright format, allowing the whole series of discs to be played through one by one instead of the commercial method of selecting one disc to be played upon the insertion of a coin. Of the Polyphon auto-changers, the 22-inch disc size, with

25. Interior view of the extremely rare 21½-inch disc autochange Symphonion with bells. As with the Polyphon in Plate 16, the bed-plate assembly is upside down, but in this case the discs are titled both ways. (Don Mudd Auctions, Houston, Texas).

RARE TYPES OF DISC MUSICAL BOX

bells added, is sometimes found, as is the 19⅝-inch size, with a base to contain extra discs: the addition of this base gives a fine regal look to the whole machine. Prettiest perhaps is the bow-fronted model of Regina, using a 15½-inch disc, which is set on cabriole legs. Queen of them all however must certainly be the 27-inch Regina, with a quality of tone which is unsurpassed.

Makers of note in other musical box fields made disc auto-change instruments, though very few are now known. F.G. Otto & Sons of New Jersey brought out the Criterion disc box after their success with the Capital 'Cuff' box. In the Criterion range was an auto-change machine. We learn from Chapuis (*Histoire de la Boîte à Musique*) that a report by Louis-Phillippe Mermod, of the firm of Mermod Frères, on the Paris Exposition of 1900, mentions that both Hermann Thorens and E. Paillard & Cie. exhibited auto-change disc movement boxes. B.H. Abrahams, also of Ste-Croix, was another maker of both disc and cylinder boxes who at least patented an auto-changer.

Multiple-disc machines

A most interesting and rare type of disc musical box is the type using more than one disc to play a tune. These discs are generally arranged to play in harmony with each other. Several examples of machines playing two discs together are known. Apart from Symphonion, who made the famous double-disc and triple-disc machine, at least one model was made by Paul Lochmann after his move from Symphonion. The particular model known is a Lochmann Original in a large upright case, complete with a base containing two sets of slots for spare discs. The machine is some 5 feet long, and the movement is constructed by setting two bed-plates end to end across the case with two spring barrels controlled by one governor in the centre. The discs are 24½ inches in diameter and are viewed through two round 'portholes' in the front of the case. The machine uses tubular bells. Another double-disc model was made by Monopol. Termed the 'Gloria', not to be confused with a series of disc boxes of the same name manufactured by a Swiss company (see 'A List of Disc Musical Boxes'), the model known plays two 25½-inch discs. The mechanism is driven by one central motor and one large drive wheel. The drive wheel is in the centre of the case, and one bed-plate extends vertically above the drive and one vertically downward below the drive. The case at first glance appears to have a disc bin below, but in fact the lower bed-plate extends into this area. Almost all of the top disc is on view through the glass of the door, but only about one third of the lower disc is visible. The two pressure bars extend from a bar in front of the drive wheel to the centre of each disc.

Polyphon is among those who made a double-disc movement, using the 24½-inch size, but no example is known. A double-disc machine was manufactured by Zimmerman, the makers of Fortuna, but little is

26. Another very rare machine, the 'Eroica' triple-disc Symphonion. (Keith Harding Antiques).

known of this machine. There were probably other makers who attempted similar machines, but none was really successful on the marketing side of this field, with the possible exception of Symphonion, who must have made and sold a number of their double-disc machines, made in both upright and table models. The cases of double-disc table models are enlarged versions of the better quality cases which house the more ordinary models. The lids have a good inlay of flowers and the case is complete with handles. The discs are turned by one motor which drives two large toothed wheels. At the centre of each wheel is a spindle which drives the discs from the centre. The discs are of the 11⅞-inch size.

By far the most frequently found of multiple-disc boxes is the Symphonion 'Eroica' triple-disc machine. This is found in upright models

27. Interior view of the Eroica, showing the 3 bed-plate assemblies.

RARE TYPES OF DISC MUSICAL BOX

only, but there are several variations of case including hall-clock styles with the appearance of long case clocks, these last being very rare. The more normal type of case is tall and slim, and originally had a glass picture, or a wood carving, in the door. The three discs are driven by two motors complete with two governors. The bed-plates are horizontal and one motor is between the top and the centre bed-plates, the other lying between the centre and the lower bed-plates; the discs overlap each other. There is normally a disc bin as an integral part of the case below the movements. The disc size for the Eroica is 13⅝ inches. The discs, marked A, B and C, are each arranged differently, so as to play together, with an orchestral sound. The 3 bed-plates are each with 2 combs of 50 teeth, arranged in the 'Sublime Harmonie' style.

28. The Eroica with overlapping 13⅝-inch discs in place.

29. A view of the almost unknown double-disc Symphonion, showing the large wheels driven from the single central motor. (Keith Harding Antiques).

A large, upright, version of the twin-disc Symphonion was made, or at least sold, both by the German company and its U.S. offshoot, in a distinctive 'piano' case; the model used 25¼-inch discs, set side by side on horizontal, opposed-comb, bed-plates. There were also 4 bells for each disc.

A 3-disc version of this machine was also made. In this, the more classic Symphonion 'Sublime Harmonie' comb set-up was used, housed in a similar case.

Disc-playing clocks

Many clocks were made containing some sort of disc movement which often played its tune on the hour. Examples still exist of a variety of sizes and movement makers, from a small mantel or table clock playing a tiny 4½-inch disc to a large case clock with a 24½-inch movement in the base. All of these clocks are rare, but obviously the larger clocks are more important and so more valuable. Though a larger number of Sym-

RARE TYPES OF DISC MUSICAL BOX

30. A Symphonion disc-playing 'Bracket' clock. The disc movement, driven by the clock movement, is within the hinged top of the case. (Graham Webb).

phonion and Monopol hall clocks are found today, with movements set into clocks made by clockmakers, often of Lenzkirch, Polyphon is credited with making some three times as many of this type of clock movement as Symphonion. The discrepancy in the number found being accounted for by the fact that clocks with Polyphon movements were made mainly for the Russian market and for sale in Germany itself. Styles of clocks may be separated into four main types: small table clocks, wall clocks, hall clocks, and large-case clocks. The small table clocks generally, but not always, used a movement that was an integral part of the clock movement to drive the disc. Many of these were by Symphonion who used a particularly attractive table clock with the bedplate assembly in the hinged dome top playing 4½-inch discs. Jung-

RARE TYPES OF DISC MUSICAL BOX

31. An exceptionally interesting and rare Polyphon disc-playing clock in the form of a Vienna regulator. It plays an 11-inch disc. (Don Mudd Auctions, Houston, Texas).

hans, a well known large German clockmaker, made many styles of table clocks using a bed-plate assembly obviously of Symphonion design but often having a disc with their own trademark, there having been a link between the two companies. Disc clocks with integral movements may rightly be termed musical clocks; while other styles, since the musical movement is completely separate, being connected to the clock only for the purpose of tripping the mechanism on the hour, should strictly be termed clocks with music. Hall clocks, though having the exterior appearance of a long-case, with their tall trunk with the clock movement at the top, are in fact short-pendulum clocks having the musical movement in the trunk. These having movements using discs from around 9-inches to 19⅛-inches, some of them also being coin-operated. True long-case disc clocks are occasionally found which have their pendulum and weights in the trunk while the disc movement is placed in the foot of the trunk. These are generally using a 15½-inch Polyphon or Regina movement, but very occasionally a huge clock with a 24½-inch Polyphon movement is found. This was a late addition to the range. In America Regina made disc-playing movements for clocks and apart from marketing their own movements set into clocks by Seth Thomas and other makers, made movements to be incorporated into clocks sold under various other names. The rarest of these particular rarities must be the delightful 15½-inch disc playing Regina auto-change movement set into the foot of a fine long-case clock, though a rival is the Symphonion triple-disc clock, obtainable in two distinct case styles.

Two tunes per disc

Shortly before the auto-change disc machine was patented, an attempt was made to overcome the need to change the disc each time a new tune was required. In 1896 two men of whom very little is known, Bortmann and Keller, patented a machine which played two tunes on each disc, each tune playing for a full turn of the disc. The change of tune was made by shifting the centre spindle of the movement to bring a new set of projections into play. The 'shifting-disc' method could also be used to play a longer tune in two halves. The patent for the design was assigned to Mermod Frères of Ste-Croix, Switzerland and the mechanisms were used for a machine called 'Sirion' in both table and upright models, and also for an upright model of the New Century series of machines. Another 'shifting-disc' machine is the 'Tannhauser', of which only two examples are known to exist. Made by *Tannhauser Musikwerke*, Leipzig, Germany, under a patent granted to T. Alwin Plessing in 1897, this machine appears to have been short lived.

Case design

Many disc musical boxes are rare because of the design of the case. A good example of this is the Symphonion 'Gambrinus' machine in the

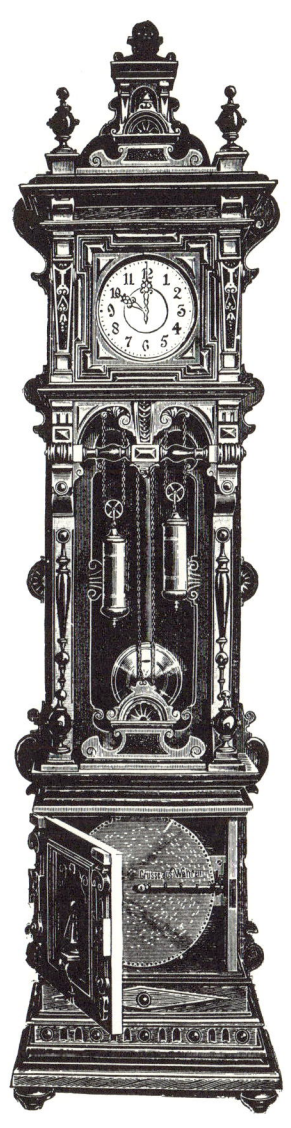

32. A cut of the classic 15½-inch disc-playing Polyphon 'Geisha' hall clock. A true longcase clock, complete with weights and pendulum. (Drs. L. Goldhoorn archives).

RARE TYPES OF DISC MUSICAL BOX

shape of a jovial man sitting on top of a wooden cask. The man is in coloured clay and holds a stein of beer aloft. The mechanism is inside the barrel and is coin-operated. It uses the 11⅞-inch size disc. The machine was intended for use on the bar of a beer cellar or somewhere similar. Another unusual type of case, also by Symphonion, is the 'Rococo', cleverly simulating heavy carving which is, in fact, gesso with a thin veneer of wood. The effect is very pretty, and is continued on the interior where the inside of the lid is lined with velvet and has a silk picture of a couple in eighteenth-century costume. The movement of this model also uses a disc of 11⅞-inch size.

Regina used many cases that are different in various ways from the norm. A design shared by Polyphon is that used for larger disc sizes to

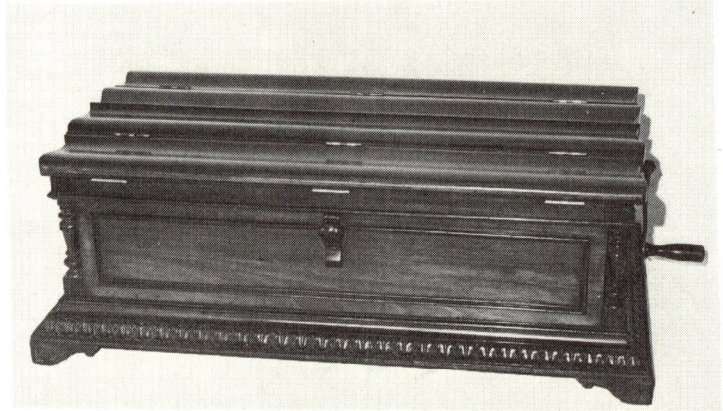

33. The case of a table model 27-inch Regina. (Dr. Peter Whitehead Collection).

allow them to be played horizontally for home use. Variously known as 'accordion', 'casket', and 'folding top', the case is narrow for its length, with double lids. These fold back on themselves to allow support for the large disc. An interesting Regina case is a 'library table', a desk-shaped case on cabriole legs with bucolic scene decoration. On lifting the lid one half is seen to hold the movement while the other is a writing surface. A pretty upright cabinet with similar country scenes imitating embroidery is another, while a third is a china cabinet with triple bow front, housing a 15½-inch auto-change mechanism. Apart from the folding top models, Polyphon used a case in the form of a

34. A rare Regina disc machine in the form of a drum table. (The Music Museum, Wiscasset, Maine).

street barrel organ to house a movement which was sold either with or without a terra cotta figure seeming to turn the handle while it played, known as the 'Savoyard'. Another version housed not just a movement but automaton figures too. Mermod Frères movements, because of the propensity of the makers to sell the mechanisms to be housed by the various wholesalers in each country, are found in several interesting and pretty cases. Among these are the beautiful English 'Art Nouveau'

35. An 11-inch disc Polyphon in the form of a barrel organ. With the addition of a figure behind this became the 'Savoyard'. (Graham Webb).

cases, found with or without a stand, with their finely inlaid woods. Very popular is the 'Smoker's Cabinet' style of case used for the Britannia (B.H.A.) of Switzerland to house some of their 9-inch and 12-inch disc movements. Daddy of them all, in both sizes and rarity, must be the case used by Polyphon for a 24½-inch disc model—a piano!—As the advertisements had it: "an Iron Framed, Full Trichord Piano, 7 Octaves, with brass Sconces and brass Pedals . . . It is tuned to the Piano, so that some charming effects can be produced by accompanying the Polyphon on the Piano." The whole double instrument, with gallery, was a massive 4 feet 6 inches by 5 feet 2 inches by 2 feet 6 inches. It cost £100 (c.1905).

Monopol housed their movements in many different cases. A nice unusual pottery piece is that depicting a gnome automaton seated on an outcrop of rock, who points to his cup for a coin to be dropped in. The wrong coin makes him shake his head, but at the right coin he nods and the machine plays. The firm also used a case in the form of a chalet, fol-

36. View of the most rare Monopol 'Gnome' automation disc musical box. (Graham Webb).

lowing the cylinder movement in this respect, and made movements for many disc-playing Christmas tree holders.

The firm also made a series of toys with disc movements, most of them of the hand-crank variety—or at least not motorized, as in the 'Motor Car', 'Mail Cart', and 'Motor Bus', which played the disc by means of a chain and sprocket as the toy was pulled or pushed along.

RARE TYPES OF DISC MUSICAL BOX

37. The Monopol 'Mail Cart'. The disc-playing mechanism, situated under the seat, is driven by a chain from the axle of the cart. (Graham Webb).

The Kalliope range of machines were also used for a variety of novelties, but these were of a more adult nature in the main. Best known is the 'Panorama', which sports below the disc a race-course with moving, racing horses. An automaton clown, following closely the original French design, was used above an upright instrument, where he stood holding a fan which he placed before his head, which disappeared only to appear in a box by his side. Other automata were used in a similar way.

Vending and gambling machines

Many disc boxes were made which also served as vending machines for chocolate or cigarettes. All of these are rare and interesting to the col-

RARE TYPES OF DISC MUSICAL BOX

lector. Also of great importance are the various forms of automata used in conjunction with a disc movement—from little cardboard cutouts of kittens which move while the music plays, to large automaton figures which carry out intricate movements.

Several types of gambling machines were made incorporating a disc musical movement in both the United States and Europe, though the majority tended to use cylinder movements. The addition of a musical movement had the effect in some areas of making an otherwise illegal machine acceptable to the authorities. Combinations of this type are extremely rare today.

Disc piano orchestrions

The inclusion of disc orchestrions in a book dedicated solely to the comb-playing disc musical box is excused by the fact that a disc is used, and the manufacturers involved were also makers of the classic disc musical box. Apart from these considerations, the machines are of considerable interest. The disc orchestrion can be described as a machine playing various instruments by means of a metal disc. Main manufacturers were Polyphon, Regina, Symphonion, and Lochmann. The machines are all upright models and each manufacturer used the same basic instrument, the piano; added to this were various drums, tuned bells, triangles, etc. Polyphon is believed to have been first with the new machine, closely followed by Lochmann Original in Europe, and Regina in the United States, Regina first selling the Polyphon orchestrion before going on to their own machine. The possibility exists that Regina later marketed the Polyphon machine under the name of Regina. The largest of the disc orchestrions used a disc 32 inches in diameter. The piano had eighty notes, and was augmented by drum, triangle, and glockenspiel. This model could be obtained as an auto-change machine. The Lochmann Original model played a disc of 25½-inches in diameter and had a most pleasant sound, mainly because of the tubular metal bells it contained. The discs had no projections. Neither did a smaller version of the Polyphon orchestrion, which had a disc of 28½-inches.

With its well established multiple-disc musical boxes, it is not surprising that Symphonion made a twin-disc orchestrion among others. Known as the 'Symphonion-Duplex-Orchester No. 98', this weight-driven giant used 2 side-by-side projectionless 25¼-inch discs to play a total of 52 double strings; 36 organ pipes; 10 tuned metal bars (metalo-

RARE TYPES OF DISC MUSICAL BOX

38. A print of the Lochmann disc-playing 'Original Concert-Piano'. It plays an 80 note double string piano; ten tuned metal bars; bass drum; snare drum and cymbol.

phone); bass drums; snare drum, and cymbal, with automatic forte and piano.

Lochmann made at least two models of disc-orchestrion. One used 25½-inch discs to play strings and tuned tubular bells; the other, larger version, with a 32-inch disc, played 80 double strings, 10 tuned metal bars, bass drum, snare drum, and triangle. Dampering, forte and piano were automatic. According to advertising material, a version of this instrument was sold with a horn gramophone attachment.

Disc machine-gramophone

Perhaps the saddest rarities of all are those heralding the passing of the age of the musical box. Among these are early twentieth century models combining a disc movement and a gramophone. Examples are extremely rare, though rather more plentiful in the United States than in

RARE TYPES OF DISC MUSICAL BOX

Europe. Gramophone attachments were used by several companies including Mermod Frères, with their 'Mira' and 'Empress' machines; Lochmann Original, with the disc orchestrion; Polyphon, with both upright and table models, disc sizes being 11¼-inch, 15½-inch and 24½-inch; Symphonion; Regina, whose 12¼-inch, 15½-inch, 20¾-inch and 27-inch disc sizes were all obtainable with the attachment, and Kalliope.

39. A cut of the 'Polygraphon' disc musical box/gramophone. (Drs. L. Goldhoorn archives).

Names were coined for the combination. 'Polygraphon' gives itself away, as do 'Reginaphone' and 'Miraphone'. At first exterior horns were used but later, certainly in Mira and Regina models, interior horns were introduced beneath the bed-plate of the machine. The same motor drove both mechanisms, gearing being used to produce the different speeds required. When the gramophone was not in use the turntable was removed, as was the exterior horn, and sometimes the tone-arm. Regina and Mira were both obtainable in console models, where in a cupboard beneath the movement slotted compartments were made to take both discs and records. Later, ironically, most of these companies entered the previously despised gramophone market more completely in an attempt to survive.

HOW TO CHOOSE A DISC MUSICAL BOX

Whatever the reason for buying a disc musical box, more than blind luck is needed to protect the buyer from what might well be an expensive mistake. It could be said that the best advice would be to seek the aid of a specialist in the field. The problem is, however, that specialist dealers are few and far between, and we must prepare for the time when we are confronted with what, at first sight, appears to be the bargain of the year. It is necessary to judge for one's self, simply because if the dealer is not a specialist it has to be assumed that he has no more knowledge of musical boxes than one's self. The dealer can only pass on what little information, possibly erroneous, he has been given, as well as what little he has picked up over the years. What he firmly believes to be true in this respect, however honest he may be, is not necessarily so. The purpose of this chapter is to point out what might conceivably be wrong with any particular machine and to help you decide whether the faults—if any—can be rectified.

Disc or cylinder

Perhaps before deciding upon which disc musical box the choice should fall, it might be better to decide if, in fact, it compares favourably from your point of view with the other classic design of instrument, the cylinder musical box. Basically, the cylinder musical box has as an advantage the fact that generally it has a shape and design more readily assimilated into the decor of the home. The disc musical box, if a table model, was designed in the late nineteenth century and has all the characteristics of the period; the upright with a coin box was not designed for home use at all. The major drawback of the normal cylinder machine is that whatever tunes are available with it are immutable, and one might feel that there is a limit to the times one can listen to *Home, Sweet Home* with equanimity. On the other hand, the disc musical box has the not inconsiderable advantage of the possibility of a further supply of discs to replace or supplement those bought with the machine. This brings us to a point regarding rare machines.

Rarity values

Rare disc machines have been discussed at length in the previous chapter and further information on different boxes can be found in the chapter 'The Principal Manufacturers'. What may not readily spring to mind is the unfortunate fact that a machine which is rare, by virtue of either the maker or the type of machine, almost invariably has discs which are equally rare. Such are the oddities of fate that often the machine is found with few or no discs available with it. Where the machine is so rare as to be the only one you can ever hope to find, and has a few discs with it, it becomes a straightforward decision as to whether the price of the machine compensates for the possibility of never finding more discs. In the case of a machine with good tone of an unknown or unusual make, I think one must say that an absolute minimum of six discs is necessary, with ten or twelve being a reasonable number, before one should buy. Of course, it is always possible to contact the specialist dealers before buying the box in the hope that they have spare discs available. If one has a friend with a machine of the same make and size then his discs may be borrowed and new copies ordered, but here again the price comes into the decision. The availability of new copies of discs has made it more of a possibility to obtain a reasonable number of discs. Although this is fine for most common discs—and even for unusual rare machines such as those with bells—the advantage tends to lessen with the more uncommon machines of which not many were sold, since they are not so readily found in collections. They are not sought with dedication for the very reason we are discussing—lack of discs.

Approaching a musical box

It may appear self-evident that the most important single feature of a disc musical box is the sound, but much mystery, after many years of popularity, still surrounds the musical box, and many people do not

HOW TO CHOOSE A DISC MUSICAL BOX

know just what to expect in the way of music. To put it simply, the music should ideally be clear and sweet, of the right tempo, and free from metallic noise. The disc should start at the beginning of the tune and continue to the end before stopping even if, being a table model, it is turned off at some time during the tune, though some smaller models do not. It is rare, unless buying from a specialist, that all the above conditions combine in a machine being vetted with a view to purchase. We must know exactly what is wrong with the machine to judge whether it can be put right. If it can, we must also know what time, and extra cost, is involved before putting money down. Although discs can be examined later, it is as well to hear several played, to ensure that we are not listening to the only disc which plays well. It is possible for one to play well even when the others play badly since a particular tune, especially a simple one such as a hymn, may not play on parts of the movement which are damaged or in a poor state. If the dampers are badly damaged or even missing, a slow tune may make it unnecessary for some dampers to come into play, the vibration of the tooth being allowed to die naturally before the tooth is plucked again.

The comb(s)

It is fairly common for the prospective buyer of a disc musical box to completely forget to examine the teeth of the comb(s). Hidden as they are behind the disc, they can easily slip the memory. Remember, although the music may appear perfect, it is possible for quite a lot of teeth to be missing—particularly on a movement with double combs—before the music is noticeably affected. Damaged or missing teeth can be replaced, either professionally or, with some knowledge of metal, by following advice given in the chapter 'Replacing Broken Teeth'. The teeth replaced can be accurately tuned to scale since the scale is the same on all disc musical boxes of the same make, size and type of comb. Even so, the cost in work or money must be counted when agreeing on a price to pay.

Lead tuning weights

There is a propensity in disc machines for the lead tuning weights to suffer from a disease which causes the lead to deteriorate into a white crumbly powder, decreasing the weight of the lead and causing the bass notes of the comb to rise in pitch. In severe cases the lack of bass and the accompanying dissonance are clearly heard while the disc is playing, but often the disease is in the early stages and is only detected by examination of the leads and the area immediately surrounding them or beneath the comb. This disease is a serious problem. The chapter 'Replacing Lead Tuning Weights' deals in detail with the work of replacing them, but the job is not easy, and it might be better to decide against buying an infected machine. It is one thing to discover the defect in a machine already owned; it is another to buy this type of work knowingly.

Dampers

Individual dampers on most disc movements are usually easy to see once the disc has been removed. The dampers should be visible between the tips of each of the teeth of the comb. The end of the damper rail or bar should also be in view, fixed to the bed-plate at the end of the comb nearest the centre of the movement. Should there be an excessive amount of metallic noise as the teeth are plucked while the disc is playing, the dampers probably need adjusting. If the damper rail(s) are missing the only machine for which damper sets are made at the moment is the Polyphon—even then, only dampers for the larger sizes are supplied. This being so, it is not advised that any other type of machine is bought without dampers unless the machine is so rare as to make the considerable amount of time, trouble and expense involved worth while. To make adjustments or repairs to dampers, or to fit new sets, see the chapter 'Damper Problems'.

Other causes of metallic noise

The dampers of a disc movement, although more often than not the culprits, are frequently blamed for noises caused by other parts of the machine. Should the noise be fairly constant, it could possibly be caused by the grating of the edges of the disc hole against the centre dome, or the need for oil on the axles of the dishing wheels fitted to the case. A rattle can often be traced to the coin chute of an upright machine, and this can be checked by pushing the chute(s) firmly toward the back of the case while the machine plays. Should the coin chute(s) be blocked by a bent coin, the coins resting above it could be rattling as the notes vibrate. The wrong setting of the pressure-bar on the centre dome can cause the disc to crackle as it revolves; this same crackle can also be caused by the disc having been placed in position *under* the dishing wheels instead of resting on top of them. This last case is a fairly common fault with the uninitiated. If the dealer has made this mistake, any information from him regarding the machine is suspect owing to his seeming lack of knowledge of the subject.

Discs

Examine all discs carefully to see they are in good order. The projections should be not only present but in good upright position. The periphery drive holes, if any, should also be in good condition. General appearance is important, but of course this should not make the difference—everything else being right—between buying or not buying the machine.

Non-running

Many defects can only be discovered when the machine is playing. If, for some reason, the machine is not in working order, other means must be found to revolve the disc; if the spring is broken but the governor mechanism is intact, the disc can be turned by hand, making sure to complete the tune before taking the disc from the machine. In this case, the governor will act, as it usually does, to regulate the speed of turn. If the governor is broken and the spring is intact take care not to wind the machine since this would cause damage. The best that can be done is to again turn the disc by hand, keeping the speed as steady as possible, to get some idea of the sound of music. If both the spring and governor appear to be in good order it may be that some of the teeth of any one or more of the wheels of the movement have broken or bent so as to inhibit normal running, in which case the machine cannot be played without repair. Take care in this circumstance, since the chances are that the spring has been fully wound during attempts to get the movement running.

Another cause for non-running, although the machinery appears sound, could be that the endless screw of the governor assembly is clogged with dirt and grit, or that the jewel or bearing-plate necessary for the free running of the escapement is broken or missing from the governor bracket. If the endless screw is clogged, a temporary measure could be the use of petrol or paraffin to allow it to run by freeing the endless screw. Yet another possible reason for the machine not running is that there might be no power in the spring and no winding handle. In this case, with upright machines, it is possible (but dirty) to remove the motor cover and turn the crown-wheel of the winding mechanism by hand so as to get at least enough power to get some idea of the sound of the music. Other means may also be found to wind a movement. An upright Symphonion may be wound with a large screwdriver, and so on.

Jewel

When the jewel is missing or broken, a small piece of safety razor-blade may be substituted by loosening the screw holding the jewel-plate on the governor bracket, and sliding the piece of razor-blade between the jewel-plate and the bracket over the hole through which the top of the endless screw protrudes. This, again, is temporary and a jewel should be obtained as soon as possible. In this case too it should be remembered that the spring is probably fully wound.

If, after all, the machine will not run, make an examination as thorough as possible in the circumstances. Should all seem to be in good order with the bed-plate assembly, the machine may well prove a desirable piece (with a little attention). Of course, the price is a factor in deciding whether to buy, remembering the risk in buying an untried machine.

Casework

Should the case contain marquetry, this should be in good condition, as should be most of the veneer, since any work which cannot be done at home must only mean more expense. Woodworm, unless causing much disfiguration to the case, need not be a cause for concern, although it should be treated with a good insecticide as soon as possible.

A coin-operated machine should possess a motor cover, a coin drawer, and a surmount, the last-mentioned missing more often than not, since it was never fixed to the machine, simply relying on two dowels to keep it in position.

For a wider choice of instruments, or a machine that is fully overhauled, it would naturally be better to go to your specialist dealer in automatic music, whose name will give the full protection of experience.

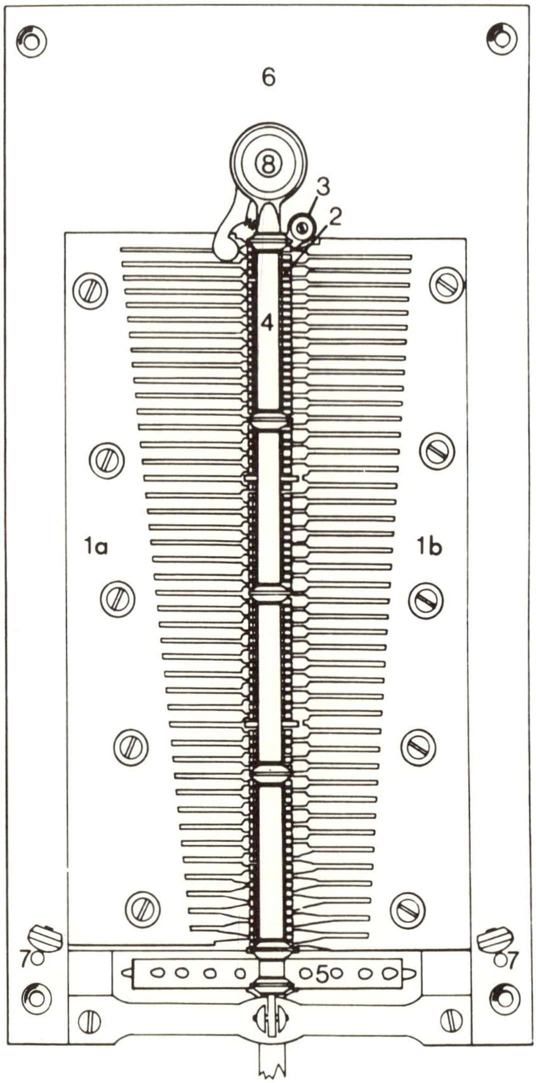

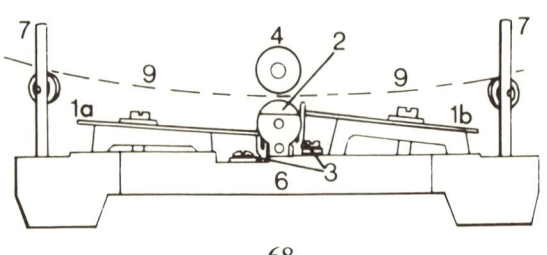

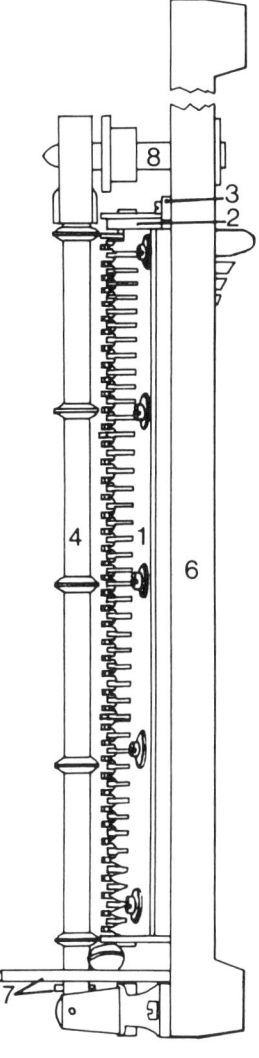

Dwg. 1. A Complete Bed-plate Assembly for an Upright Machine

1a lower comb
1b upper comb
2 star wheel assembly
3 damper rails
4 pressure-bar assembly
5 drive wheel (attached to motor assembly)
6 bed-plate
7 steady rollers
8 centre dome
9 disc

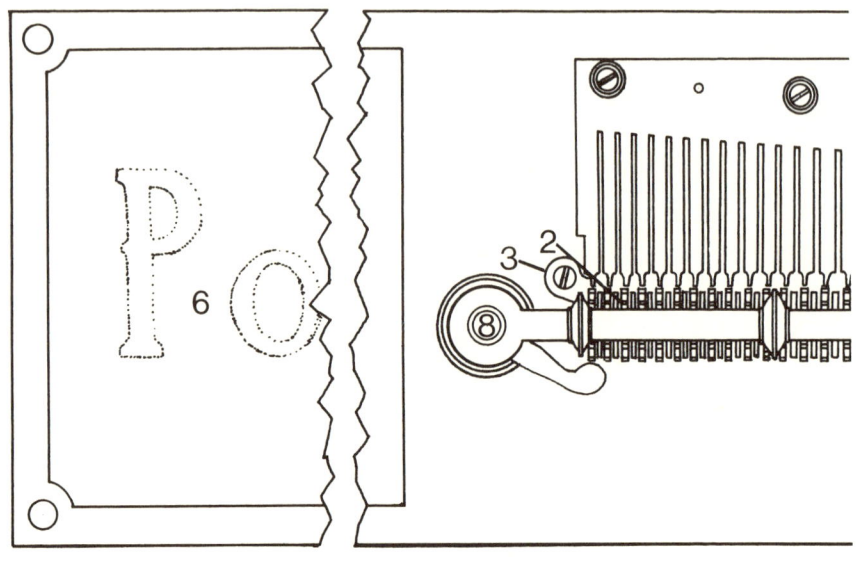

Dwg. 2. A Complete Bed-plate Assembly for a Single Comb Horizontal Machine

1 comb
2 star wheel assembly
3 damper rails
4 pressure-bar assembly
5 drive wheel (attached to motor assembly)
6 bed-plate

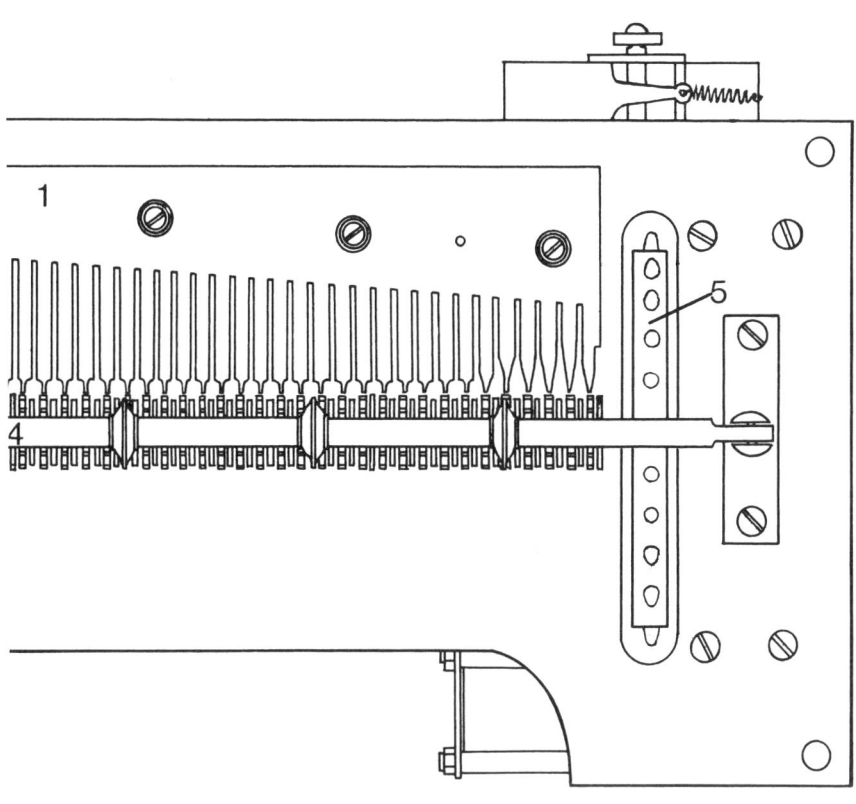

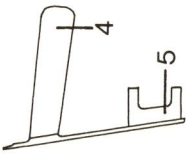
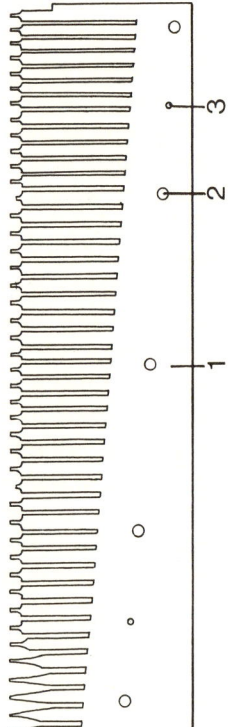
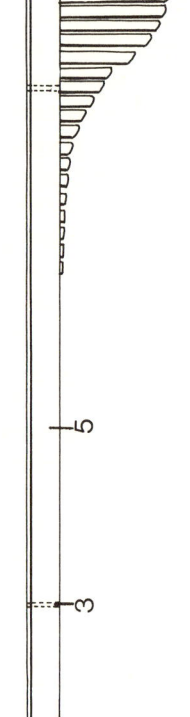

Dwg. 3. Comb Assembly

1 comb
2 comb screw holes
3 dowel pin holes
4 lead tuning weights
5 base of comb

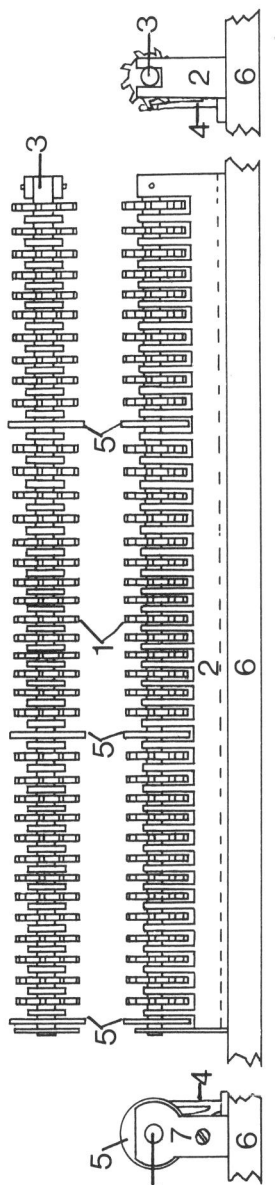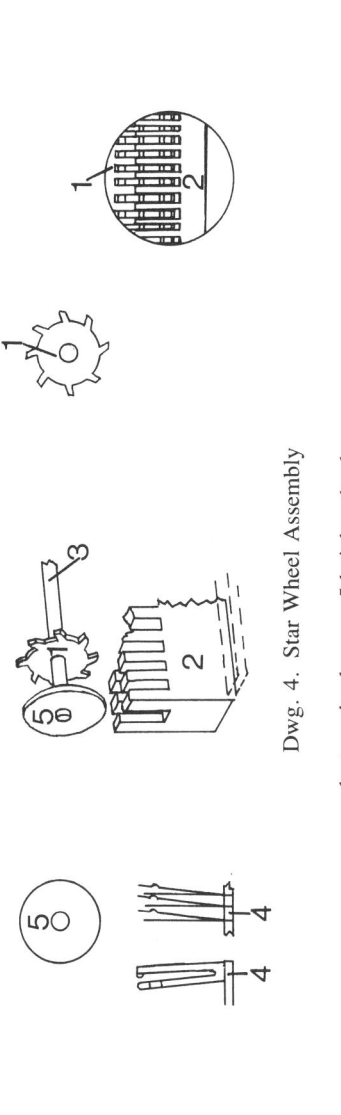

Dwg. 4. Star Wheel Assembly

1 star wheels 5 height wheels
2 gantry 6 bed-plate
3 star wheelrod 7 gantry end-plate
4 dampers

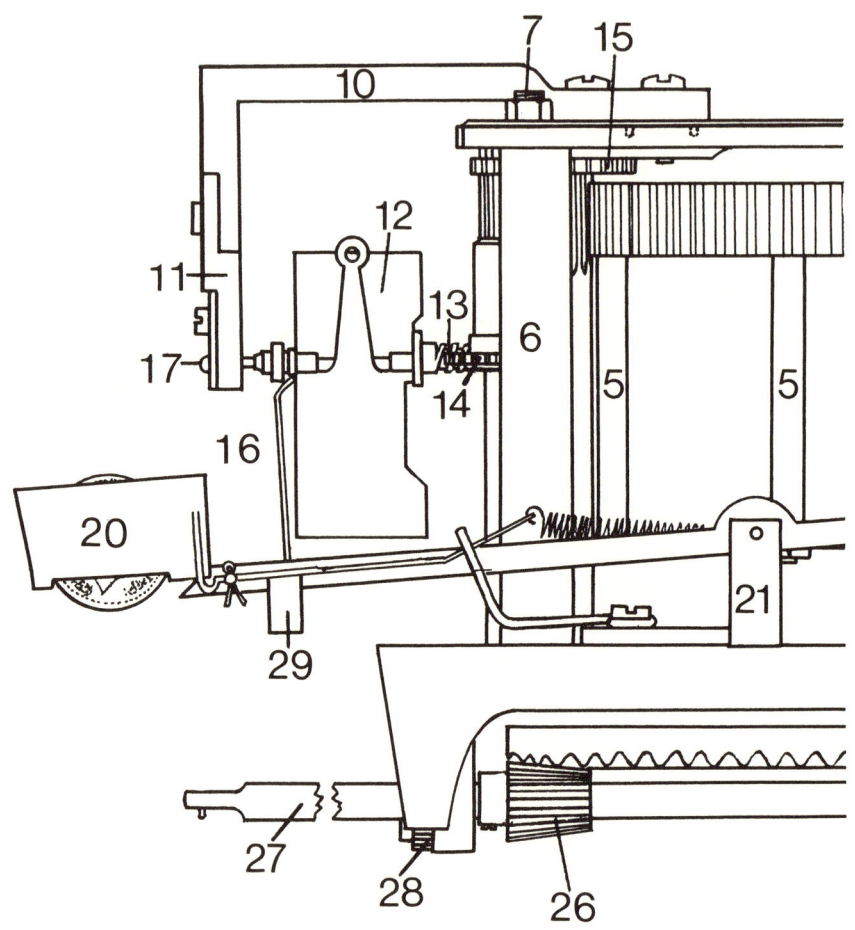

Dwg. 5. Motor Assembly for Upright Machine (*rear elevation*)

1 drive wheel	7 pillar nuts	13 endless screw
2 drive shaft	8 top plate	14 middle or leaf wheel
3 drive domes	9 spring arbor	15 2nd wheel
4 spring	10 governor bracket	16 stop sprag
5 spring cage	11 governor cock	17 end stone
6 motor pillars	12 air brakes	18 big wheel

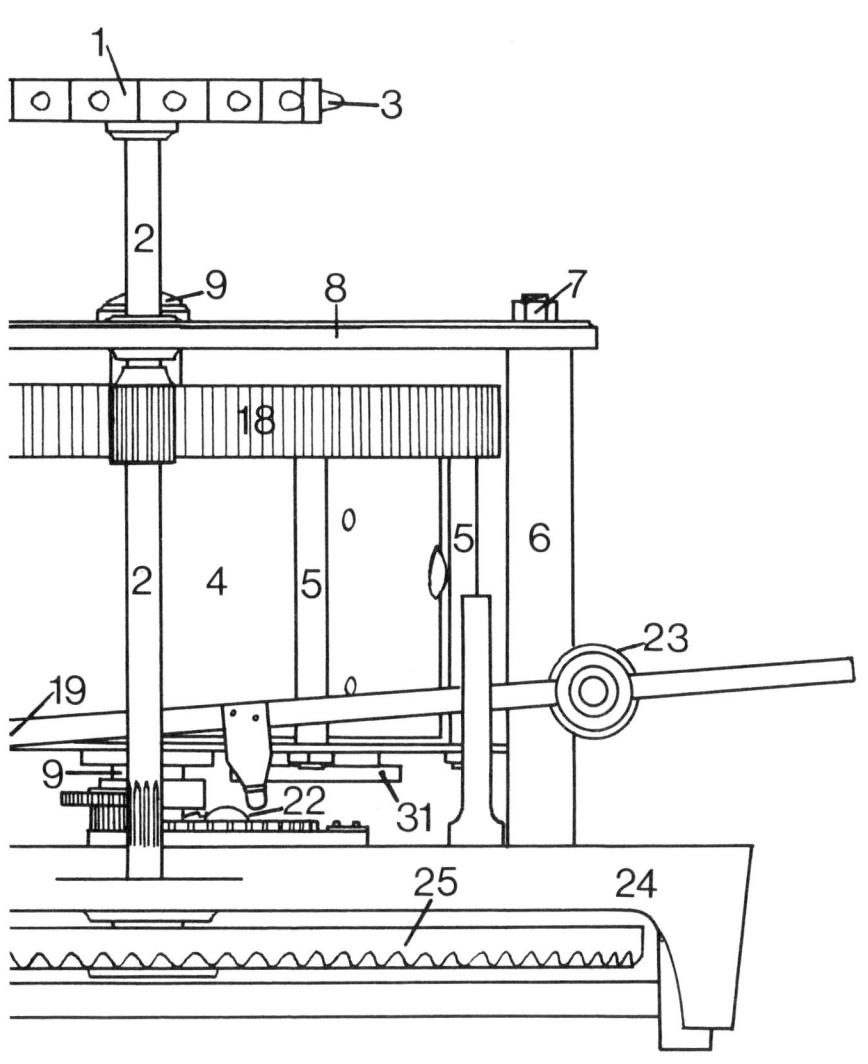

19 balance arm
20 coin pan
21 balance arm bracket
22 timing assembly
23 counter weight
24 bottom plate
25 crown wheel

26 bevelled wheel
27 winding spindle
28 ratchet assembly
29 stop arm
30 timing lever
31 female Geneva stop

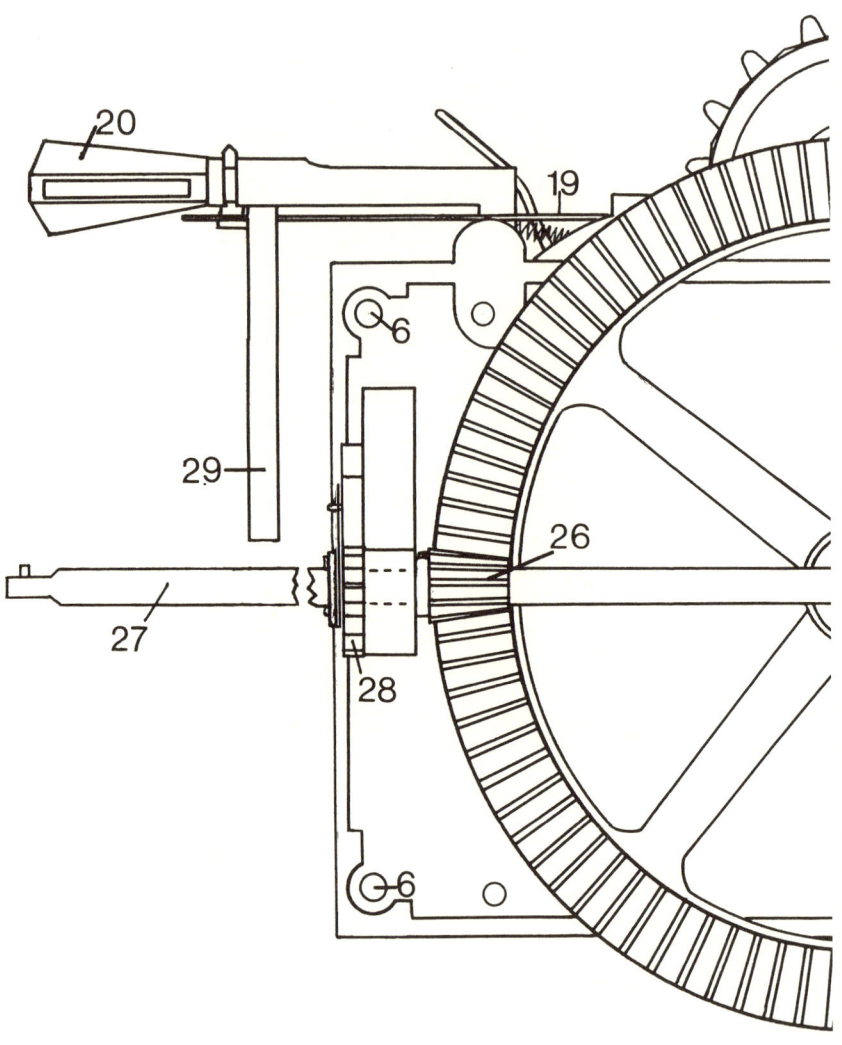

Dwg. 6. Motor Assembly for Upright Machine (*worm's eye view*)
See Key on drawing on page (74–75)

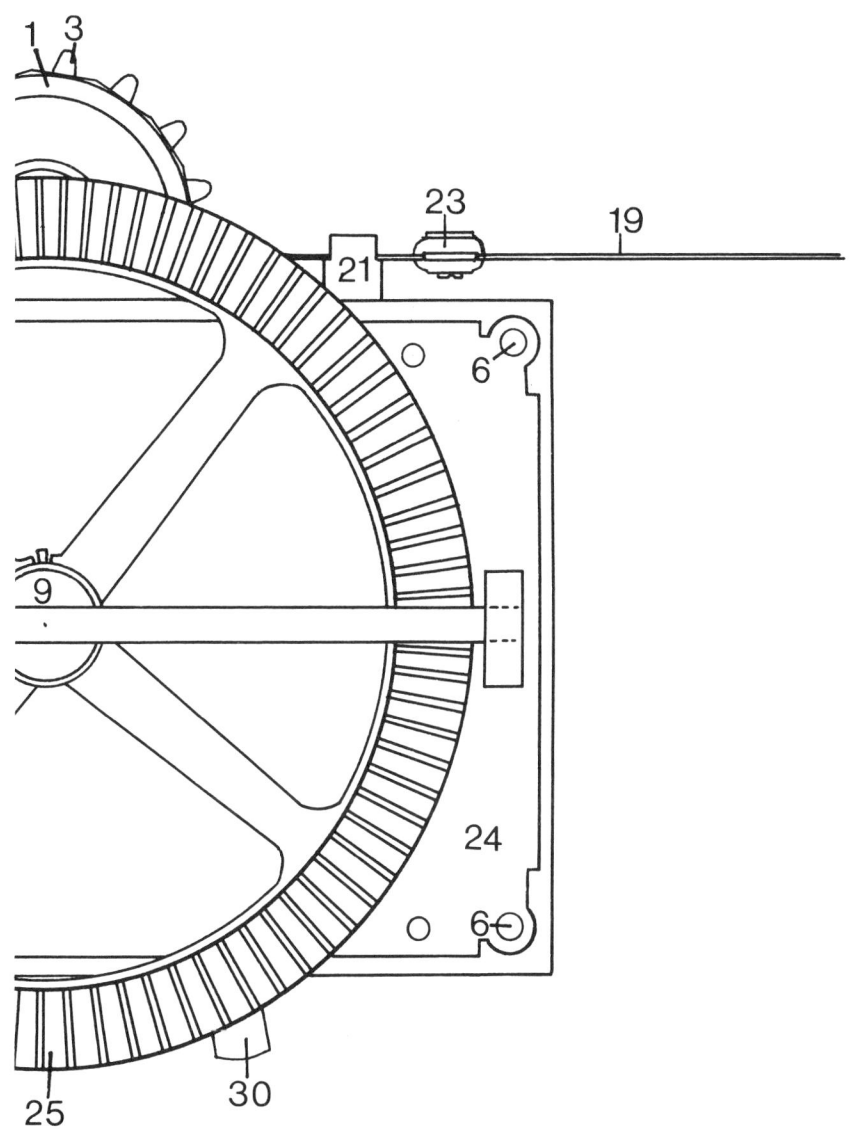

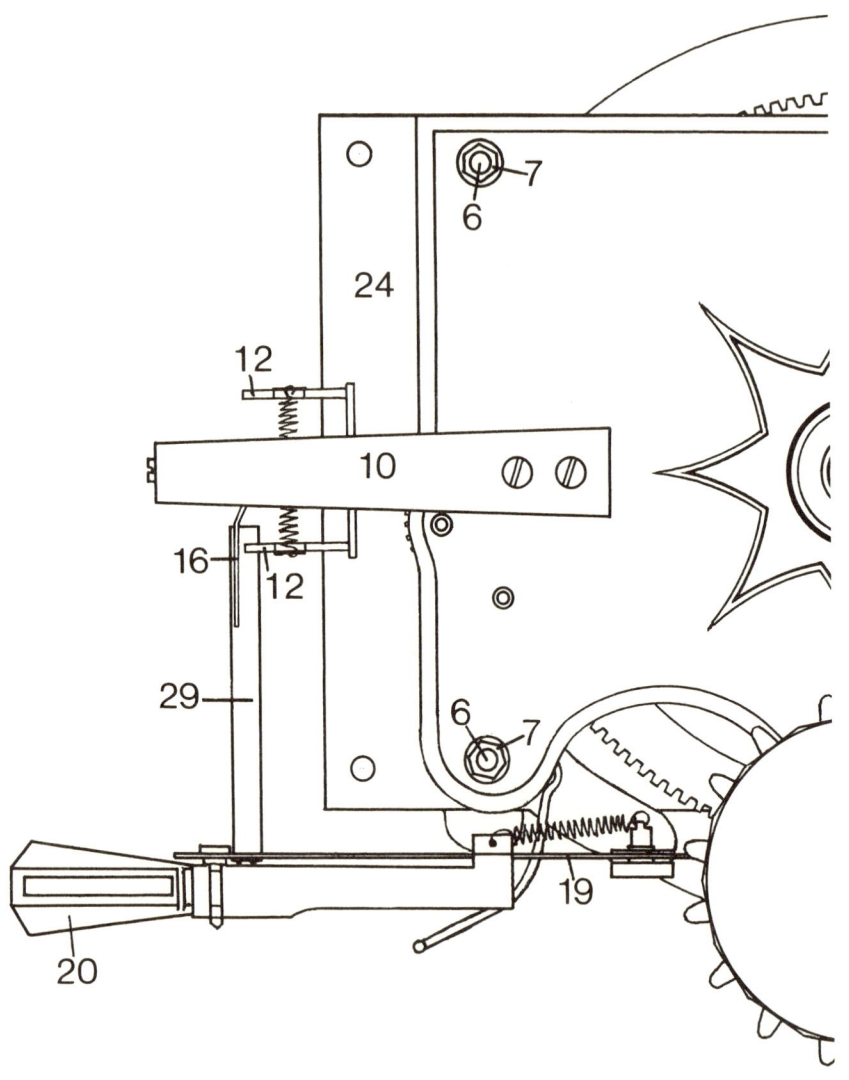

Dwg. 7. Motor Assembly for Upright Machine (*bird's eye view*)
See Key on drawing on page (74–75)

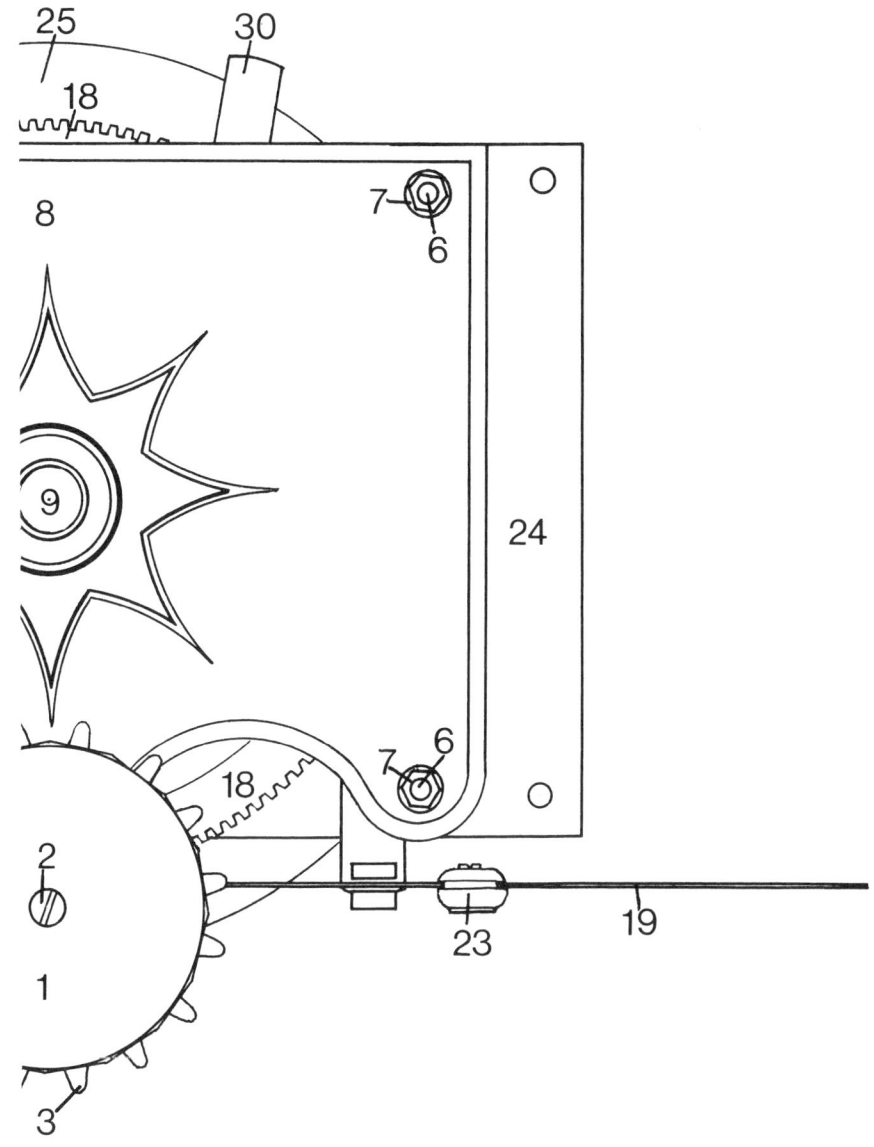

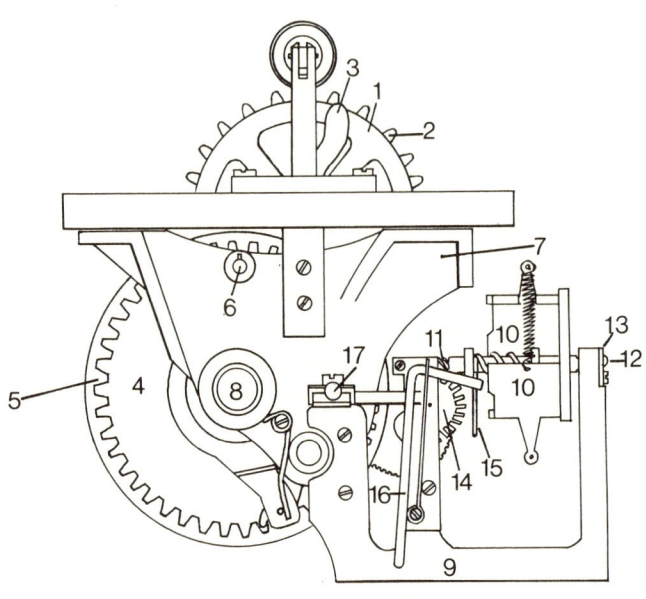

Dwg. 8. Motor Assembly for Horizontal Machine (*front and side views*)

1 drive wheel	8 spring arbor	15 stop aprag
2 drive domes	9 governor bracket	16 stop arm
3 stop lever	10 air brakes	17 stop/start
4 end-plate	11 endless screw	18 end-plate
5 winding gear	12 end stone	19 spring cage pillars
6 winding spindle	13 governor cock	20 big wheel
7 spring cage bracket	14 middle or leaf wheel	21 female Geneva stop
		22 2nd wheel
		23 spring

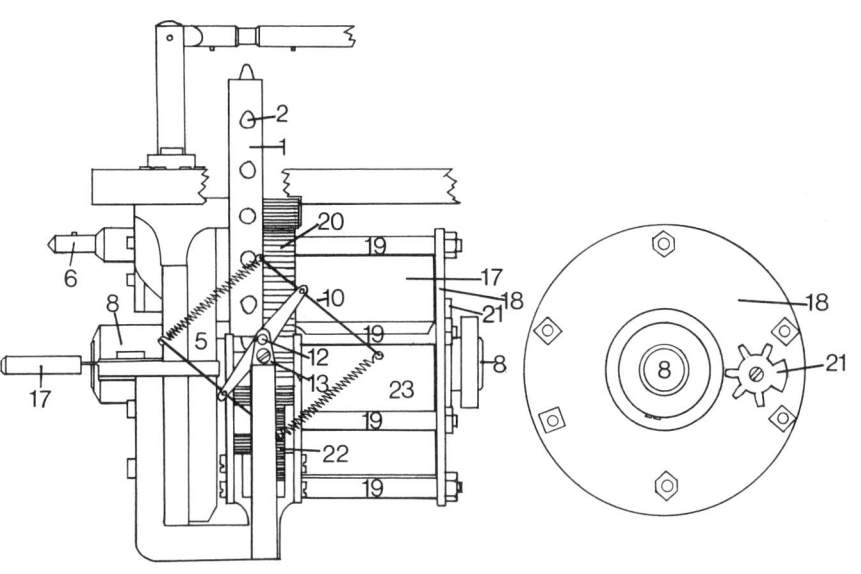

Dwg. 9. Basic Drive and Winding Mechanism for Horizontal Machine
See Key on drawing on page (80)

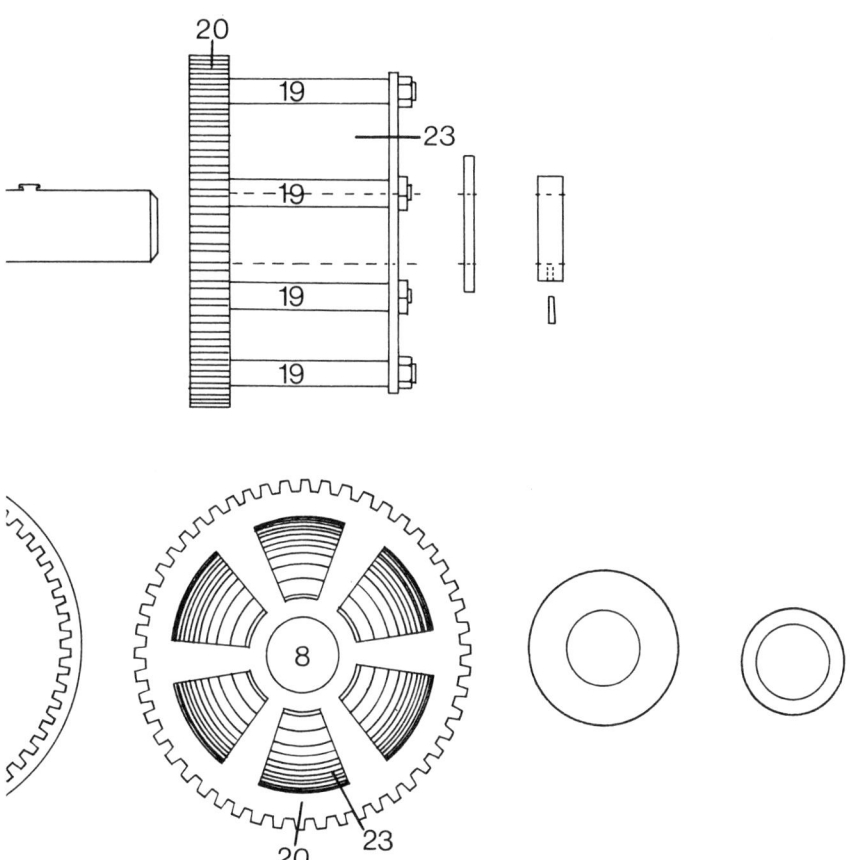

CLEANING A DISC MUSICAL MOVEMENT

This chapter is intended to deal with the problems of cleaning the movement of a disc machine in such a way as to make it possible for anyone, with a table and a few tools available, to do a job which will greatly improve the machine. To avoid confusion, the machine referred to in the cleaning will be a 19⅝-inch Polyphon, since from this machine it is an easy step to transpose the instructions to fit either a table model or an upright machine of this or almost any other make. Since we are using an upright machine we can split the cleaning into two entirely separate operations: first, the bed-plate assembly, and then the motor assembly. It will be necessary to strip each assembly into its component parts and treat them separately and completely. We shall need a table to work at, adequately covered to protect it from the dirt and grease to be removed from the movement. A good light is essential.

Here is a list of tools and materials to be used:

Medium hammer
Large, medium and small screwdrivers
Drill
Pair of good medium pliers
Pair of long-nosed pliers
Fine emery cloth
Punch
Orange sticks
Bristle brush
Wire brush
Pair of tweezers
Several small boxes to hold screws, etc.
Black paint

CLEANING A DISC MUSICAL MOVEMENT

Old gold paint (or silver paint) and paint brush
Very fine paint brush
Metal polish
Bottle of Thawpit or carbon tetrachloride (C.T.C.)*
Soft brush
Penetrating oil
Fine clock oil
Clean old paint brush
New grease

Taking the bed-plate assembly from the case

To remove the bed-plate assembly from the case of a Polyphon, it is necessary only to remove the four wood screws holding it in position. With an upright Symphonion, key-headed bolts with square nuts at the back of the case are used, and a further two screws unite the bed-plate assembly and the motor. These of course must also be removed. In some cases the lead tuning weights of the combs protrude below the four bracket feet of the bed-plate, and two blocks of wood may be necessary upon which to rest each end of the bed-plate to avoid the weights pressing against the table top when the assembly is placed flat. Where the weights are this long, shallow depressions are drilled into the wood of the back of the case to take them.

Dismantling the assembly

To make a good job of the cleaning it is necessary to take each part from the bed-plate, with the exception of the centre dome and the gantry which holds the star wheels. We do not remove the gantry since its position is *absolutely critical* and should not be altered by so much as a millimeter unless it is really essential. It might also be added that if, after everything else has been removed, the star wheels upon examination appear to be in good order and no rust is apparent, then they may also be left in position and cleaned *in situ*.

Removing the comb

After removing all comb screws and washers, take two of the screws and using one at either end of the comb to form small levers, bring the

---

*Carbon tetrachloride is considered a hazardous substance, and the publisher recommends using an alternative material. Consult any clock repairman.

CLEANING A DISC MUSICAL MOVEMENT

comb gently backwards, taking the teeth up and away from the star wheels. In general, the comb is fixed in position by two metal dowel pins which run through both bed-plate and comb case, and position the comb exactly. In some machines, notably Symphonion, the dowels are fixed in the bed-plate and the leading edge of the comb is butted against them to give the correct setting. The comb must be gently maneuvered from its playing position. Take care not to injure the comb, the star wheels, the dampers or the weights while carrying out this operation. The comb should be laid to one side, upper side down.

Star wheel guard

The star wheel guard is a strip of metal which runs along the top of the gantry over the star wheels. When a disc is placed on the movement, the guard is pushed to one side and stays there while the machine is playing. When the disc is removed, the guard is pulled into position once more by a small spring. To remove the guard, take out the screw which fixes the small spring to the bed-plate, and lever the ends of the guard off the centre bar of the star wheels on which they are fitted. Place the bar to one side and be sure not to lose the spring screw.

Damper bars and brakes

Warning: There are a great many disc musical boxes having to squeak their way through tunes minus damper bars, or brakes, or both. These were in many cases taken off by well-meaning amateurs who fully intended to replace them properly but found the task too much for them. To a man who understands elementary metal work, the job of replacing and adjusting the dampers of a disc movement would seem to be fairly simple; however, the amount of time and patience in fact required by the novice for this operation is far greater than would normally be expected. It is suggested that before touching the dampers, the chapter 'Disc Musical Box Dampers' should be studied. With patience and some degree of skill, the job can be done exactly, but don't forget that it is one that cannot be hurried. Rather than make things worse, if there is any doubt in your mind as to your capabilities, do not remove the damper bars, but do an extra good job of removing all the dirt and grit from between and around them, realigning the odd one as required.

The damper bars are removed by taking out the two screws holding

CLEANING A DISC MUSICAL MOVEMENT

each bar in position. There are washers between the heads of the screws and the damper bar surfaces, but much more important, there are height washers *under* the bars which it is most essential to keep *exactly* as they are in order to return the bars to the correct position. Before removing or even loosening the screws holding the damper bars, make a mark with a sharp tool at each end of the bar to show exactly the position in which they must be replaced. Remove the bars carefully and put the screws away in such a way as to keep each with its washers as it should be returned. If your memory is not good, write down the information. The importance of the positioning of the dampers cannot be overstressed. A sketch might well be made of the positions of all washers as they are removed.

Steady rollers

There are usually two steady rollers which are positioned on the bed-plate on either side of the bracket holding the pressure-bar. These rollers are attached to bars which are usually bolted through the bed-plate with a nut on the underside. Undo the nuts and remove the rollers on their bars.

Pressure-bar and bracket

The pressure-bar, which holds the disc in position while playing, is hinged to a bracket which arches over the drive wheel when the assembly is in position. The other end of the pressure-bar ends in a casting, the centre hole of which pushes over the centre dome. The bar is held in place on the dome by a brass spring-catch which enters a slot in the side of the dome. Remove the bar and its bracket by taking out the two screws which hold the bracket to the bed-plate. Watch for any packing which may be between the bracket and the bed-plate, and keep it carefully so that it may be replaced with the bracket (if necessary).

Height wheel

The height wheel is a cast-iron disc on the centre dome. The purpose of this wheel is to give a height to the centre of the disc which, when playing, moves round between the height wheel and the casting on the end of the pressure-bar. The height wheel is usually held in position by a grub-screw, which should be loosened to allow the wheel to be drawn off the dome. It may be necessary to clean off the dome to allow the height wheel to be freed. This can be done with fine emery paper or, if the dome is really rusty, then penetrating oil can be used. Take care not to lose the grub-screws. If the dome appears particularly clean, it may be necessary to mark the position of the height wheel before removal, but normally there is a distinct ring-mark where the wheel has been fixed which will not completely disappear even with thorough cleaning.

Star wheels

We now have everything off the bed-plate with the exception of the star wheels, the centre dome and the gantry. It is time to examine the star wheels most carefully, one by one, turning each through its full circle several times. In examining star wheels, we look for two main possible defects. On some of the wheels, one or more of the teeth may be bent out of alignment. This will become apparent if it is found to be particularly difficult to turn a wheel through a complete revolution, the wheel sticking each time at a particular spot. If this is so, then it may be possible to straighten the wheel where it is, rather than dismantle the whole assembly. Having examined all the star wheels and found possibly two or so bent teeth, attempt to straighten the tooth with the long-nosed pliers. Make sure the wheel revolves freely before considering it fixed.

The other possibility is that some of the star wheel teeth are worn or even (very rarely) broken. If this is the case, dismantle the assembly and do the necessary repairs. Should the whole star wheel assembly be rusty, we must again take down the assembly in order to clean all the star wheels individually. For these operations, see the chapter 'Minor Adjustments and Repairs'.

CLEANING THE MOVEMENT

Bed-plate

The bed-plate is of cast iron and was originally painted gold or silver. Assuming the star wheels have been found to be in good order apart from dirt and old oil, the bed-plate will also contain the gantry assembly with the star wheels in position. The whole of the bed-plate can now be freely brushed with the bristle brush to remove all loose dirt and fluff. When this is completed, use the paint brush to apply carbon tetrachloride liberally to the whole of the bed-plate surface and the gantry. Brush well between the star wheel and around the base of the gantry. When all has been thoroughly soaked, allow to dry, which does not take long. The grease and dirt are now in the form of dry grit and dust, which must be removed by a good stiff brushing with the bristle brush. Cover the whole of the bed-plate in this way, taking care to keep the wood of the brush from contact with the teeth of the star wheels. Brush the star wheels well, the strokes being carefully made in the direction of the wheels and across the gantry. Use a pin to pick out any pieces of grit in the slots of the gantry.

With any luck, the star wheels should now be clean and the bed-plate ready for painting. If there is any loose paint on the bed-plate, a wire brush should be used to take it off. In cases where the star wheels still do not have the cleanliness required, it may be necessary to use the wire brush here to brush carefully across the gantry *with* the wheels. This treatment, although it sounds harsh, is used by most experts on disc machines, without any ill effects to the star wheels, always provided that sufficient care is taken to brush *with* the wheels. Clean the centre dome with *very* fine emery cloth. When all is as clean as possible, the first coat of paint may be applied. The bed-plate is tackled first so that the paint can be drying while the cleaning of the other parts is going on. Note the drying time on the tin and apply the second coat as soon as possible. When painting the bed-plate, make sure none of the paint is allowed to get on to the centre dome, the gantry, or the star wheels. Take great care not to allow any paint to settle into the gully which holds the lower damper rail, or where the upper damper rail rests, as this will affect the setting.

Height wheel

While the paint is at hand, it would be as well to prepare the other pieces which require painting, and give them the first coat of paint. A piece which is normally of cast iron (although not always) is the height wheel, which fits over the centre dome of the movement. Clean out the centre hole in the wheel so that it will go easily over the dome. Make sure that the grub-screw is in good order and moves well on its thread. Place the wheel in a vice, face up, and brush well with a wire brush so that it is clean, and paint whatever parts were painted before. Should the height wheel be of brass it should be cleaned with metal polish.

Pressure-bar and bracket

The pressure-bar also holds two pieces which generally require painting—the bracket, and the casting top of the bar which fits over the centre dome. The bracket is held on to the pressure-bar by a pin, which can be knocked out to allow first the bracket to be removed, and then the pressure rollers and the brass distance pieces to be drawn off the bar itself after any other pin has been removed. Take note of the positions of all the rollers and distance pieces so that they may be returned to the same places. There is no need to remove the top casting from the bar, so this should be cleaned and painted after rubbing down the bar itself, taking care not to get paint on to the spring which operates the catch holding the bar in place during play. Paint the bracket after cleaning, and place it to one side to dry, together with the bar.

To finish the parts of the pressure-bar so that it can be reassembled when the paint is dry, examine the pressure rollers for wear (new ones can be obtained for Polyphon), clean them with wire wool, and then polish them with a little wax polish. Clean also the distance pieces with wire wool and polish them with metal polish. Lastly, polish the heads of the screws which attach the bracket to the bed-plate. Place all the pieces together, keeping them in order.

The combs

Clean the combs by first cleaning away dirt or old oil from between the lead tuning weights. If the leads are badly corroded it may be necessary to follow the instructions in the chapter 'Replacing Lead Tuning Weights'. If all is well with the weights, clean the comb surface with *very* fine wet-and-dry paper. Always polish in the direction of the teeth.

Comb screws and washers

To polish the washers, hold a flat pad of fine wire wool on the table top with the fingers of one hand, and rub the washer across this with a finger of the other hand. Use the same method for the tops of the screws, making sure to rub the way of the slot. To polish the sides of the screw head, twist it through wire wool held between the fingers.

Damper bars and brakes

The damper bars should be wiped clean of old dirt and grease. Straighten all bent dampers or brakes so as to conform with the rake of the others. Any broken or missing dampers or brakes must be replaced. For this, see the chapter on dampers.

If the painted parts need a second coat, now would be a good time to apply it.

Star wheel guard

Clean the star wheel guard with fine wire wool, making sure the spring is in good order. Clean the screw which holds the spring. If the plate on the guard is peeling, use fairly coarse wet-and-dry paper (dry) to remove the rest of the plate, and finish with polish.

Steady rollers

For a really good job of cleaning the steady rollers, the rollers can be detached from their bars. They are held by the axle of the rollers, which is pushed through a hole in the bar, and burred over on the other side. This burr can be removed with a file, and the rollers removed so as to leave a straight bar which can be polished more easily. When the whole is clean it can be reassembled, using a centre punch to make the axle secure once more. Should you feel that it is not necessary to go to these lengths, the whole can be cleaned in one piece.

Before commencing to put together the bed-plate assembly, clean and polish the heads of the screws or bolts which hold the assembly in the case, using the same method as for the comb screws.

REASSEMBLING THE MOVEMENT

All of the parts of the movement should now be gleaming, and ready to combine to form a whole which will not only play good music but look really beautiful. This is the time to check the parts, one by one, and de-

CLEANING A DISC MUSICAL MOVEMENT

cide whether in fact anything can be done, with the means available, to make them more perfect.

Dampers and brakes

Replacing dampers and brakes is not an easy job and takes a good deal of patience. The importance of these being correct, however, cannot be over emphasized. The clean sound necessary for good music is dependent on the steel tooth being still when plucked, and the star wheel tooth in the correct position for the disc projection. Complete instructions for setting dampers can be found in the chapter 'Disc Musical Box Dampers'. Before replacing, apply just enough oil to the star wheels to make a very fine film. Only replace the top bar first on a double comb machine.

Comb(s)

Replacing the comb(s) is done at the same time as the setting of the dampers, since the top comb is set in place before the lower damper bar is positioned, to test the setting of the top dampers. Before putting the comb(s) in position make sure that the surface of the bed-plate is quite clean and free from grit or lumps of paint which may prevent a true seating. Examine the base of the comb for the same reason. Clean out with an orange stick any paint which may be clogging the dowel or screw holes. If the machine is of the type which has dowel pins which do not actually go into holes in the comb, make quite sure the teeth are replaced in the exact positions as before on the star wheels. The teeth and star wheels will have developed wear, and need to keep the same wear position. If the teeth show excessive wear, see 'Minor Adjustments and Repairs'. Do not replace all of the screws until you are certain that the dampers are in correct position and working well, and that the comb is in the best possible place for the work it has to do.

Star wheel guard

Having made certain that there is no more to be done to the star wheels, the dampers or the combs, the star wheel guard can be replaced. Fit the hole in the top of the guard on to the top of the centre rod of the star wheels at the end of the gantry, and lever the angle of the guard carefully over the centre rod so that the hole here also fits on to the end of the rod. Making sure the guard moves freely, replace the screw which holds the spring and test to make sure the guard is acting as it should. Apply a touch of oil to both holes.

Height wheel

Slide the height wheel on to the centre dome and when it is in the correct position, tighten the grub-screws well to hold it firmly.

The pressure-bar and bracket

The bracket of the pressure-bar can now be fixed to the bed-plate. The easiest method is to place the top casting over the dome and clip it in position. This should automatically bring the bracket into place, it can then be fitted on to the dowel pins and the screws replaced to hold the whole assembly in position. If there was packing between the bracket and the bed-plate, it may be that it was put there in error. It is a good idea to replace the packing, but remember it is there! When testing the whole movement it may be found that the machine plays as well, or even better, without the packing.

Steady rollers

Last of all for this part of the musical box come the steady rollers. Place the bars of the rollers in position and tighten the nuts on to the threads protruding from the underside of the bed-plate. Before tightening fully, place a disc in position and make sure that the rollers are correctly set (the axis should point towards the centre dome).

Dishing rollers

The dishing rollers are two wooden rollers fixed to either side of the interior of the case. The object of the rollers, as the name suggests, is to dish the disc as it revolves, and so present the projections to the star wheels in a good bold line. Being attached to the case, these rollers would normally be treated in the chapter on case restoration. It may be, however, that the interior of the case is considered to be in such good condition as to require little more than brushing out. If so, before replacing the bed-plate assembly, some attention should be paid to the

CLEANING A DISC MUSICAL MOVEMENT

dishing rollers and their rods. In most upright Polyphons the rollers are positioned on a length of thick brass wire, one end of which is shaped to an eye to allow a screw to attach it to the side wall of the case. After passing through the roller, the wire is bent and finally pushes into a hole made in the wood of the back of the case. There is a washer brazed to the wire to keep the roller in position.

To remove the rollers, simply take out the holding screw and gently and carefully maneuver the wire from the hold in the wood. Often this wire becomes brittle with age and may need renewing, in which case brass wire of a similar thickness can be made up to the exact shape. If this is done, it would be best to replace both wires at the same time, both for appearance and also to save another job at a later date, since both may be affected, although one more than the other. The shape of the original wire must be followed exactly, since the position of the roller is critical. If the brass wire is sound, it can be cleaned with fine wire wool, and polished. The same may be done with the wooden roller. The roller is then treated with wax and polished, the holding screw cleaned and the whole returned to its place.

CLEANING THE MOTOR ASSEMBLY

Having made a good job of the bed-plate assembly, we are now more than half-way through the cleaning of the whole machine. Whereas with the bed-plate assembly there are parts which you must handle with great care so that they are not damaged, the motor assembly has the spring, which must be carefully handled so that no harm befalls you. Legend has it that a spring from a large Polyphon has been responsible for at least one death by disembowelling!

Most important: *Never* remove an integral part of the motor assembly unless the spring is *entirely* run down.

TAKING THE MOTOR ASSEMBLY FROM THE CASE

With the upright Polyphon, it is best when removing the motor assembly from the case, to first take out the bed-plate assembly by removing the four screws which hold it to the back of the case. This being done, the next step is to remove the scutcheon on the right-hand side of the

CLEANING A DISC MUSICAL MOVEMENT

case which houses the winding spindle and into which the winding handle is inserted. This scutcheon is usually held on the case by a small nut and bolt at the top and a screw at either side. Taking these out will enable the scutcheon to be removed completely. Before actually removing the motor assembly, release tension from the spring by gently wedging something suitable under the weight-side of the coin arm on the left of the back of the movement. This will prevent the motor stopping at what is normally the end of the tune, and allow it to run down as far as the 'Geneva stop' will allow. The Geneva stop is a piece which stops the spring before it has run down far enough to allow the hook on the end of the spring to disengage from the centre arbor—this is explained more fully later in the chapter. When the spring has fully run down, check that there is no tension by turning the drive wheel both ways. It should be slack and able to move a little either way without pressure. Take out the four screws which hold the movement to the base of the case, one in each corner of the bottom motor-plate. When these are out, it will be found a simple matter to remove the entire movement by lifting it from the bottom with both hands, pulling it over towards the left to draw the winding spindle from its hole on the right. In a great many cases it will be found that the bridges for the winding gear are lower than the bracket feet of the movement. This will make it necessary to stand the movement on two lengths of wood, so that it will be upright with no strain on the parts. It is not recommended that the wood be fastened to the movement, since this may make the dismantling of the winding mechanism more difficult.

DISMANTLING THE MOTOR ASSEMBLY

Before attemping to dismantle the motor assembly, it is necessary to understand the workings of two parts of the mechanism: the 'Geneva stop' and the governor or endless screw assembly.

Geneva stop

The Geneva stop is found on all good musical boxes and most good clocks. Its function is to regulate the winding of the spring. The stopwork consists of two parts, the 'male' and the 'female'. The male is attached to the centre shaft of the spring assembly on the outside of either the upper or lower plate. The female is attached by a shouldered screw to the same exterior plate and is roughly similar in shape to a rather stumpy fat hand with thick fingers. The male turns with the centre shaft when the spring is being wound, and on each complete turn engages between two of the fingers of the 'hand', pushing the female round so that the division between the next two fingers is presented for entry when the male has performed a further revolution. This process continues until the part of the female which has no gap is presented to the male, which can then go no further, so that more winding is prevented and the machine cannot be overwound. While the spring is unwinding, the reverse of this process takes place, and when the male comes to the other side of the 'hand' it is again stopped. Thus the spring cannot run down too far.

It will be understood from this that, if the stop-work is in good order and in the right position, there will still be some tension in the spring although it has been fully run down. Where the stop-work is in a place where it is possible to take out the screw holding the female stop, it is recommended that this be done and the female removed, so as to let *all* of the tension out of the spring. Wind the movement a little to release the male stop. There is normally a friction spring ring beneath the female stop. Take care not to lose it. If the Geneva is in such a position as to make removal for the time being impossible, wind the movement a little to back the male stop off the female, and turn the female stop round so that two or three extra entries are offered to the male. This will allow the spring to be released fully. The Geneva can be removed for cleaning when the motor is dismantled.

Warning: At no time should the Geneva stop-work be removed from a dismantled spring cage unless care has been taken, while the spring was in the movement, to let *all* of the tension from the spring, including that tension held by the stop-work. If you are not sure, do not attempt to do so.

Governor assembly

The governor assembly is an arrangement of usually two wheels and an endless screw, which is fitted with an air brake in the form of two 'wings'. The job of the governor is, as its name implies, to govern the speed of the motor. Should any part of this assembly be removed while the spring still retains tension, the spring will be released at *high speed* and may cause serious damage.

Balance arm

Remove the balance arm first, complete with its bracket, which is normally held to the bottom motor-plate by one or two screws.

Drive wheel

Next to be removed is the drive wheel, which is held in place on the drive-shaft on the back of the motor by a grub-screw, or possibly two. Often this shaft has a key-slot down from its top into which a pin is slotted. The pin passes through both sides of the collar on the drive wheel and so the wheel can be removed with the pin still in position, but if there is a lot of corrosion it may be necessary to tap the pin out. It may be advisable in this case to apply a little penetrating oil to the shaft.

Governor bracket and endless screw

After once more checking that the spring holds no tension, remove the governor bracket which holds the endless screw. The bracket is generally fixed to the top motor-plate by two screws. There should also be positioning dowels. Take great care with the endless screw since this part is most delicate; place it somewhere safe until needed.

Winding assembly

The lower end of the spring shaft is held by the crown wheel of the winding assembly which is underneath the bottom plate. To be able to separate the spring cage from the bottom plate we must remove first the winding spindle and then the crown wheel. The winding spindle runs in two bridges which are cast on the underside of the bottom plate. On the inner side of the right-hand bridge is to be found a bevelled gear which meshes with the crown wheel. This is held in position by a tapered holding-pin through a collar on the gear and through the spindle. When the holding-pin is knocked out *very gently* with a punch, the gear should push along the spindle, allowing the spindle to be drawn free of its bridges. It is very important to remember that all of these holding-pins are *tapered* and so have a right and wrong end to work from. To attempt to remove a taper pin by tapping the thicker end will do no good. To attempt to replace a taper pin the wrong way round, or into the wrong side of the hole, may cause damage to the assembly—or at least to the pin. In particular, the crown wheel is held by a taper pin which slants upwards through the collar and the spring shaft. This pin is removed by striking the small end *gently*. When the crown wheel is replaced, the pieces must be in the same position as before removal. Take great care when knocking out holding-pins—a blow in the wrong place can cause cast iron to crack or break. When the spindle is removed, the ratchet wheel will be easily accessible. Depending on the type of machine, there is either a pin right through the ratchet wheel, or a pin through the spindle protruding either side into a slot across the ratchet wheel. Whichever is the case, the ratchet wheel may now be removed, followed by an ingenious shaped spring washer which pushes off the pawl while winding is in progress and pulls it on to engage with the ratchet wheel when winding ceases. A washer follows, and finally the split-pin is removed to clear the spindle completely, except of course for the pin at the winding end for the slot in the winding handle.

Top motor-plate

The top motor-plate provides the bearings for the spring, the two wheels for the governor wheel train, and the drive-shaft. To remove it, take off the nuts and the washers from the four pillars holding the two motor-plates together. Lift the plate gently, keeping it level so that all the parts which enter it are left standing in the bottom plate, or one or more of the arbors may fall, possibly damaging a wheel or a pinion. Place the top plate to one side, and carefully remove from the lower plate the two governor wheels on their shafts, the drive-shaft and the spring cage. Place these on something soft to protect the teeth in the wheels.

Motor-plate pillars

The four pillars which hold the plates together sometimes have the same thread at both ends, one to thread into the bottom plate and one to take the nut on top of the top plate. It is necessary not only to keep these pillars the correct way up, but also to make sure that they return to the original holes. The pillars were often threaded into the bottom plate first and then bent to line up with the top plate. It is fairly easy to differentiate between the upper and lower ends of these pillars since while the lower end has simply the thread, the upper end has a collar before the thread and the end of the pillar is domed. Mark and remove the pillars.

Timing wheels

If the machine is of the type which can be altered by means of a lever to play either two tunes or one for the coin, the two wheels necessary to do this will be seen together with their lever and the carriage upon which they move. These can now be removed.

All other attachments can now be removed, such as the ratchet pawl, the balance-arm bracket and, if fitted, the trip for the coin drop, a piece of shaped metal which tips the coin-holder to release the coin.

CLEANING THE ASSEMBLY

The motor-plates

The cleaning of the assembly starts with the pieces which also need painting. First of all we take the two motor-plates, the governor bracket, and any other piece which was originally painted. The two plates and the bracket will also require lining out in gold so that it is even more important to get them cleaned and the first coat of paint on if we are to have them ready when the rest of the movement has been done. A good scrub in detergent, followed by rinsing in very hot water, will take off the old oil and dirt. Follow this by brushing with a wire brush to take off any flakes of old paint. As soon as possible apply the first coat of paint, which should be a good quick-drying, oil resistant, matt finish. Do not apply the paint too thickly, since the finish of the metal will be obscured. Take great care not to allow the paint to enter any of the bearing holes of the plates. When painting the governor bracket do not paint the part which seats on to the top plate, since this may change the setting of the governor. Place the pieces to one side to dry, and note the drying time from the paint tin so as to be able to apply the second coat as soon as possible. Clean and polish the pillars which hold the two plates in position, together with their nuts.

Spring cage

Often the spring has been oiled from time to time, and this use of oil instead of grease tends to cause the spring spirals to stick together—until the tension is so great as to make them release with a bang. Even where grease has been used, there is a good chance that it is a great many years since it was changed, if ever. To remove the old grease with its dirt and grit is not simple while the spring is in the cage, but the best method is to soak it in C.T.C., and use an old paint brush to push as much as possible of the liquid into the spiral of the spring. Carry on with this treatment until the spring and its surrounds are as clean as it is possible to make them. When you are satisfied you have done the best job possible —and this job is worth spending time on for the future—set the spring, in its cage, to one side to dry. When it is quite dry, the outside of the spring can be cleaned with metal polish. Pay particular attention to the bronze rivet to make it shine. Clean and polish also the pillars of the cage, the top and bottom, and the Geneva stop-work. Do not attempt to grease the spring at this stage as this will be accomplished much more efficiently when the spring cage has been returned to its place in the assembly. If the paint on the motor-plates, etc., is dry, now is a good time to apply a second coat.

Governor assembly

The governor assembly on most upright disc machines is made up of the endless screw, which runs inside a separate bracket, and two spindles on which are the wheels necessary to gear the power of the spring down to even out the energy flow. The endless screw will have been taken from its bracket, so that the bracket may be painted. This screw with its fans should be cleaned and polished. Take great care not to weaken the small spiral springs holding the wings of the fan together, since these springs regulate the speed of the movement. When the movement starts from a stationary position there is a considerable amount of inertia to overcome, and the springs are holding the wings in the fully closed position. While the machine is running, the fans are opened by centrifugal force, but if extra friction is caused by many star wheels being struck at the same time—as in a chord—the springs immediately return the wings to the closed position to allow the speed to remain fairly constant. In a Symphonion, the method often used is to make the fans of thin, springy, curled steel sheet. In this case, the curl is taken out by centrifugal force when the machine is playing at speed, but the natural curl acts in the same way to lessen the surface exposed to the air when more speed is required.

Make sure that the wings of the fan are working properly when the cleaning is finished. Ensure also that the stop-tail, a piece of wire which is friction fitted to the endless screw immediately under the fan, is

CLEANING A DISC MUSICAL MOVEMENT

firmly in place and not loose. Try not to disturb the setting of this stop-tail since the engagement of the stop arm with the tail is critical. Clean and polish the two spindles and their wheels, paying particular attention to the teeth of the wheels. Clean these with the orange sticks. Remove the cock from the bracket and make sure the jewel surface is polished.

Drive wheel

The drive wheel is normally made of brass, with the studs, which engage the holes in the periphery of the disc, of steel. Clean and polish the wheel, and ensure that the grub-screw(s) is turning well and has a good slot for the screwdriver. Be sure the centre hole of the wheel is free from grit so that it fits on to the drive-shaft easily.

Winding assembly

All other parts of the motor assembly can now be cleaned including the winding assembly. While cleaning, examine all of the various pieces for damage, so they can, if necessary, be repaired before the machine is rebuilt. Take care all wheel teeth are clean and all bearings free from dirt and grit.

When all is done, examine each part again to ensure that there is nothing more to be done to make the mechanism look and run well.

Gold lining

The lining-in of the gold paint is best done when the assembly has been rebuilt, so as to keep the handling of the movement to a minimum once the paint is on.

Screws and nuts

Make sure that all screws, nuts, and washers of the assembly are cleaned. To clean and polish a screw head, make a pad of fine wire wool and hold it on the surface of the table with two spread fingers. Take the screw and rub the head rapidly to and fro against the wire wool. The sides of the head of the screw can be polished by revolving it in a pad of wire wool held in the hand. Washers can also be treated in this fashion, as can nuts.

CLEANING A DISC MUSICAL MOVEMENT

The cleaning of the parts being completed, we can now proceed to the reassembly and testing of the movement.

REASSEMBLY AND TESTING

Bottom motor-plate

The work of reassembling the motor is really the reversal of the dismantling. The bottom plate is placed on the table and pieces of wood to be used as a stand placed within easy reach.

Timing wheels

First to be attached are the timing wheels on their carriage, together with the lever for setting the wheels, and the bracket for the lever. The lever should look nicely polished against the black of the paint. Make sure these pieces move freely.

Geneva stop

If the stop-work was removed from the spring cage after the movement was dismantled (simply for cleaning) it may now be replaced, not forgetting the spring. When the motor is fully assembled again, it will be possible to move the female into its correct position.

If it was possible to remove the stop-work before dismantling the machine, it will not be necessary to replace it at this time—unless it would be more awkward to do so when the movement is complete. In either case it will need to be adjusted when the assembly is running.

Spring cage and crown wheel

Before replacing the spring cage, check the big wheel at the top of the cage to see if there are any signs of bent teeth. Often with commercial machines there was a practice among those who used them to make the machine go faster by winding the spring fully, and then continuing to apply pressure to the handle. This sometimes resulted in bent teeth on this big wheel. Should there be evidence of this type of damage, see the chapter on 'Minor Adjustments and Repairs'.

If all is well, the spring cage can now be replaced by first placing the packing pieces on the shaft protruding from below the cage. Enter the head of the shaft into its bearing on the bottom plate and fit the crown wheel to the part of the shaft which is on the underneath of the plate. Locate the holding-pin in the collar of the crown wheel and tap it home firmly but gently. Remember that any packing washers removed when dismantling *must* be returned to their original places. Now is the time to place the four motor-pillars in position on the bottom plate.

Drive-shaft

We can now replace all the spindles which enter both the top and bottom plates. The drive-shaft carries two wheels—the lower wheel engages with the time wheels, and the upper wheel with the large-toothed wheel which forms the top of the spring cage. Place the lower pivot of the drive-shaft into its bearing on the bottom plate, making sure the two wheels are engaging properly.

Governor wheel train

Place both of the wheel train spindles in position so that the first wheel engages with the large wheel of the spring cage, and also with the second wheel. Be careful to do nothing which might cause a knock to either of the spindles.

Top plate

With great care place the top plate over the ends of all the pieces now in the bottom plate and gently maneuver the plate on to the four pillars, making sure that all the pinions enter the top plate correctly. Since the drive-shaft is the longest piece it will enter its bearing first. Before replacing the nuts and washers which will hold the top plate in position, check that all the wheels are correctly meshed. The large-toothed wheel forming the top of the spring cage should mesh with both the drive-shaft and the spindle of the first wheel of the governor train. This first wheel should mesh with the spindle of the second wheel of the train. The teeth at the bottom of the drive-shaft should mesh with whatever time wheel is in position. Upon turning the spring cage by hand, all of the pieces should mesh and move smoothly. If the top plate is of the type which has no access holes to the spring, it will be necessary to grease the spring as well as possible before replacing the top plate. To do this, use a screwdriver to pry the spirals of the spring apart and pack the grease down as far as possible into the spaces.

When everything between the top and bottom plates is in good order, replace the washers and nuts which hold the top plate in position. Before tightening the nuts, make sure that the top plate is level and well seated on the collars of the motor-pillars.

Winding gear

We can now replace the rest of the winding mechanism, which consists of the winding spindle, the ratchet wheel, ratchet pawl, ratchet spring, and the bevelled wheel which engages the crown wheel already in position. Before positioning the winding spindle, attach the pieces which must go on from the end which enters the left-hand bridge under the bottom plate. Put the retaining-pin in its hole and slide on the washer, then the spring washer which engages the ratchet pawl, and finally the ratchet wheel with its pin. Enter the spindle into the right-hand bridge and slip the bevelled wheel, collar first (and any washers belonging there), on to the spindle while the spindle end is between the two bridges. Carry the spindle on so that it enters the left-hand bridge. Fix the bevelled wheel in position by tapping the pin back through the hole in the collar. Finally, return the ratchet pawl to its place, making sure to engage it with the spring washer.

Before finishing completely with the winding assembly, remember there may have been a good deal of wear between the various components. This may not have been apparent when the assembly was being dismantled and it is necessary to check the moving parts before we continue. The most obvious place for wear is between the crown wheel and the bevelled gear or pinion. These two parts should not be tight, but at least a good fit. If there is any slack between them, there are two places where shims or washers can be set, to make a better mesh. The easiest place to get at is behind the collar of the bevelled wheel on the spindle. A washer here may be enough. If the wear is really bad, it may be necessary to adjust the mesh by both this method and by putting a shim or washer above the collar of the crown wheel—this of course means dismantling the winding gear again. The probable cause of the trouble will be wear on the washers already in position, if so these can be replaced.

CLEANING A DISC MUSICAL MOVEMENT

Governor bracket

The winding gear now being complete, all that remains to be returned to the movement is the governor bracket and the endless, complete with fans and stop-tail. Place the bracket carefully into position on the dowels, making sure that the endless screw is meshing properly with the middle wheel of the gear-train, before tightening the screws. When the governor bracket is fully attached, it is possible to test the running by applying pressure on the big wheel at the top of the spring cage in the direction in which it would normally drive the disc. With a little such pressure the endless screw should run freely. If it does not, it may be possible to find the reason and a cure in the chapter 'Minor Adjustments and Repairs'.

Drive wheel

Replace the drive wheel. Make sure its position is correct, and it is firmly held. If the positioning pin was removed, replace it.

Balance arm

When fitting the balance arm and its bracket, ensure the arm has complete freedom up and down and very little side play. Make sure the fit of the arm on the bracket is snug. The pin on which the arm is balanced should be firm. If the small metal finger, which drops into a hole to allow the coin-end of the arm to rise, is bent or damaged this must be made good before returning the arm to the movement. For problems with the balance arm, see the chapter 'Minor Adjustments and Repairs'.

Gold lining

If all is found to be well with the running of the endless screw, the job is nearly finished. It will be seen that there are lines cast into the surfaces of the plates. Normally the top plate has straightforward lines and the bottom plate some form of decoration in relief within a depression in the cast iron. With a *very* fine brush it is possible to line these castings in gold to match the gold of the bed-plate. Great care is needed to give the impression of professional finish, but it can be done with a little patience. Should your first try look untidy, paint it out in black and try

CLEANING A DISC MUSICAL MOVEMENT

again, this time being more careful and perhaps using a finer brush. The result is well worth a little trouble.

Though it is not recommended, you may decide to paint other parts of the movement if the metal has become too discoloured. It is necessary to remember, if this is the case, that paint should never be used on moving parts, and in particular that no paint should be applied to the interior surface of the coin pan, since it will possibly stop the penny dropping from the pan at the required time.

Greasing the spring

Before the motor assembly is returned to the case, the spring must be greased if this has not already been done. Test the working of the motor by winding the spring approximately two turns of the winding handle, making sure that the motor is free of the surface of the table, on its supports. Allow the motor to run, and watch to see that all the parts are doing their job and that all the wheels are meshing nicely. While doing this, prop the coin balance arm so that the stop arm does not interfere with the governor. When satisfied that all is running well, apply the grease. When the spring is fully unwound, the centre of the coil is relatively open; press grease into this part of the spring. Wind the spring slowly and it will be seen that as the spring tightens, the coil opens towards the outer end and closes towards the centre. If grease is applied as the spring is gradually wound, pushing it well down into the gaps as they appear, the whole spring can be greased. The grease is further distributed by the action of the spring being wound. This operation can be carried out, the spring being allowed to unwind each time, as many times as are required to put a surface of grease on the whole of the spring. Any surplus grease can be wiped off. Take particular care to keep the outside end of the spring clean and bright. Before finishing with the grease apply a very little to the teeth of the crown wheel.

Oiling the movement

To finish the job, we must apply a little oil to the movement. Into each of the bearings on both top and bottom plate, place *two* drops only of oil; on the pin holding the balance arm place one drop of oil, one drop also on the bottom bearing of the endless screw, and one on the teeth of the middle wheel which engages the endless screw.

CLEANING A DISC MUSICAL MOVEMENT

RETURNING THE ASSEMBLIES TO THE CASE

Now we have both assemblies ready to be returned to the case. Should it be considered necessary to re-finish the case, this must be done before the final fixing of the movement. See the chapter 'Restoring a Disc Musical Box Case'. When the case is ready and deserving of receiving this beautiful array of steel and gold and black, the motor assembly is first to be entered. Slide the winding spindle through its hole on the right of the case and fit the four feet of the movement snugly within their brackets, making sure that there is no movement in any direction. While maneuvering the assembly into position take care not to interfere with the device for overriding the balance arm. This device is found in many upright machines and is usually operated from the side of the case by a key. It consists normally of a piece of metal which pushes the balance arm down to cause the machine to play without inserting a coin. Before entering the motor assembly, make sure that the metal piece is in the 'off' position, and out of the way of possible damage. Do not replace the motor assembly screws at this stage. Fasten the bed-plate firmly in its original place on the back of the case. When returning this assembly to its position remember that, where the lower end of the bed-plate is fixed to the back of the case, there are two small positioning-pins. These pins, which are simply headless nails knocked into the wood, hold the bed-plate in exact position. It is possible by being careless to disregard these pins and place the bed-plate on top of one of them. If the bed-plate is screwed tight down, the pin can be pushed right into the wood and the bed-plate would be in the wrong position. At the place where the upper end of the bed-plate is to be secured, there are, or should be, small brackets similar to those at each corner of the position for the motor assembly. These too are there to take the bed-plate between them and so keep it exactly in position. If nothing has been altered, the two assemblies should now be exactly in relation to each other, coming together at the drive wheel and the pressure-arm bracket. The holding-screws of the motor assembly can now be entered and secured.

By placing a disc on the machine it will be possible to ensure that the drive wheel is at the correct height and depth; the depth should be exact, since nothing will normally have occurred to put it out, but the height may have been altered from taking off and replacing it when cleaning. If the height is wrong it is simple enough to turn the motor sufficiently

CLEANING A DISC MUSICAL MOVEMENT

to bring the grub-screw which holds the wheel on the shaft into view and adjust the height. It may be necessary to adjust the counter-balance weight of the balance arm if it was removed for cleaning. As a final test, wind the machine and allow it to run until the stop position is reached, put a disc in position and place a penny in the slot. Now ask yourself, was it worth it?

RESTORING A DISC MUSICAL BOX CASE

Cabinet-making practices of the turn-of-the-century were in many ways different from those of some thirty years before, when the best of the cases for the cylinder musical boxes were made. Mass-production methods were very much to the fore when it came to the disc musical box. In particular, machines intended for commercial use, and table models of the cheaper and smaller type, were made to a design which originated as much for ease of manufacture as any other consideration. This design included a finish to the wood which could be easily and speedily applied. The basic method of polishing the cases was the use of spirit varnish, applied with a brush, and finished with a polisher's rubber. The varnish used was, in fact, a thick type of French polish, and was probably made up in the factory before use. The basic ingredient of the varnish was shellac, which is easily soluble in spirit. The same still pertains today, of course. We make varnish in a similar way, but now more ingredients are added for cheapness of manufacture and for ease of application. The method of varnishing used in manufacture makes re-finishing of the cases much simpler for the layman than full French polishing would be. Once more, most of the steps involved are covered if we use an upright machine as a model; even the better quality table machines have cases which can be finished in a similar way. The extent of the work to be done depends partly on the state of the case and partly on what is considered to be a suitable finish. If the case is in fairly good condition but dirty, and a bright finish is not required, the use of the method described below will, with a couple of hours work, give a clean and workmanlike appearance to your machine, ridding it of any surface dirt.

RESTORING A DISC MUSICAL BOX CASE

A quick semi-matt finish

Dissolve a good wax polish in some turpentine to make a thin paste. With a small pad of *very* fine wire wool dipped in this paste, rub the surfaces of the case *with* the grain. Take care to rub evenly all over the entire surface, and do not be tempted to bear more heavily upon the worst parts. Continue until all the dirt is removed, then polish with a clean soft cloth. Should a wax polish be required, it is possible to use this surface as a basis to make a good 'antique' shine by waxing regularly when polishing the furniture of the room in the normal way.

Preparing the case

Before commencing any work on the case other than a cursory cleaning, all removable parts should be taken off the carcase. The winding hole scutcheon, the coin slot scutcheon, any metal or wooden instruction or name plates and any other piece which is not an integral part of the casework, should be removed. The columns which frame the glass window at the front of the case are fixed to the door by screws from the inside, and can easily be removed. The frets which square off the top of the window are sometimes screwed on, but more often are pinned and glued; take them off if they are held by screws. Any surmount on top of the machine is probably only push-fitted on to wooden dowels, and should be easily removable. Mark any pairs of pieces removed, since they are not necessarily identical.

The interior of the case should be cleaned if a thorough job is to be done. Even if the interior wood is clean, it will be necessary to paint the metal parts and this is best done with the parts out of the case. The coin chute(s) can be removed by taking out the holding screws; remove also the dishing rollers on each side on the interior by taking out the screws and maneuvering the wire, on which the roller is set, from its hole in the back of the case, or, where the rollers are on cast-iron brackets, these can be removed in the normal way. If there is an instruction paper fastened to the back of the case, this should be removed carefully. The paper will be brittle, so place it somewhere safe. A medallion with the trademark is often found in the centre of the back of the case. It is not really necessary to remove this since it can be cleaned when the woodwork is rubbed down; it is often made either in pressed brass, or in 'brass-plated' pressed tin, and attempting to remove it may result in damage.

RESTORING A DISC MUSICAL BOX CASE

Examination

When the case has been fully stripped, make a thorough examination and note all faults found. The interior of the case is usually veneered in oak over softwood, except for the ceiling and the floor which are not veneered. Things to look for inside the case are woodworm holes and missing or damaged veneer. The veneer on the interior of the door is susceptible to damage, especially at the bottom, where the veneer is often caught and pulled away by the shelf at the base of the door opening. The exterior may have woodworm holes, the veneer may be damaged or raised by dampness, some of the mouldings may be damaged or missing, and even some joints parted. The veneer of the exterior of the case is usually in walnut, the mouldings and all other pieces, such as frets and columns, being in solid wood. The solid wood used is normally walnut, but is sometimes found to be spruce or birch. Any feet which may be on the machine are usually in birch or a similar wood.

Woodworm

The treatment of woodworm is no longer the problem it was. There are several preparations on the market which will speedily kill the pest and at the same time treat the wood to avoid further infestation. Should evidence of woodworm be present in the case, apply the woodworm killer with a paint brush, soaking the wood completely. Leave for three days and apply again. The case should be left for a further three days before any other work is carried out. If there are only a few worm-holes visible it may only be necessary to inject the liquid straight into these holes, with the injector provided, so as not to disturb the rest of the case finish.

Parting joints

If any of the joints of the case have parted, it is necessary to fix them together before going further. The open joint should be parted as much as possible without damage to the other joints. Use an old sharp knife to scrape out all the old glue and dirt. Remember that even a small piece of hard glue left in the joint will prevent it closing properly. Using a good cold glue, coat the surfaces of the joint and bring them together under pressure. If clamps are available these can be used; if not, then a piece of soft rope may be used in the following way: Make up four pads of newspaper, one for each corner of the case, to protect the surface of the wood from the rope. Tie the rope loosely round the case in the correct position to apply pressure to the joint. Find a suitable piece of wood or a hammer shaft to insert, and apply a tourniquet firmly enough to draw the surfaces into contact. Leave the job sufficient time for the glue to dry thoroughly.

Raised veneer

If veneer is raised on the case, it will be necessary to refit it firmly in position before any more re-finishing work is done. If a large area is lifted, it may be possible to raise it further with an old knife, apply glue, press it back into its original position, and weight it down so that contact is maintained between case and veneer until the glue is set. Where veneer is lifted in a bubble, and it is impossible to insert the blade of a knife without causing damage to the wood, use a hypodermic needle filled with glue. Push the needle home until the point is between the veneer and the case and press the plunger until the bubble is filled with glue. Apply pressure so that any excess glue can escape through the hole made by the needle. Wipe the surface clean and apply a weight as before.

Replacing veneer

Where tiny pieces of veneer are missing it may not be necessary to re-veneer; instead, it would be better to use 'Brummer' stopping, of the appropriate colour, to fill any small gaps in the finish, such as woodworm holes. To replace larger areas of veneer, first remove any old pieces of veneer still in place on the surface to be re-finished. For this use one of the following methods. If an old flat iron is available, it can be heated and applied to the veneer to be removed. This heats the glue, melting it and enabling it to be removed easily with an old knife. Another method is to prepare a thick wad of newspaper and place this on the surface to be removed. Pour boiling water upon the newspaper and this will melt the glue in the same way as a flat iron. The pad should be kept in position while the knife is used to remove the veneer, so that the surface heat is retained for as long as possible. Veneer must now be obtained from a stockist. Thoroughly rub down the surface to be re-veneered, finishing with a coarse paper so as to provide a key for the glue; key the back of the veneer at the same time with coarse paper across the grain. Use a straight edge and a razor blade to cut the new veneer exactly to size and apply glue to the surfaces to be joined. When the veneer is in position, cover all joints with adhesive brown paper and apply weight evenly over the entire surface. When the glue is dry, the brown paper can be removed carefully with medium and fine sandpaper.

Preparing for finishing

When all of the major woodwork has been done, or if, luckily, none is required, prepare the surfaces of the case for finishing.

Metal parts

The metal parts of the case which are to be painted require two coats. Before commencing work on the rest of the case prepare these parts for painting by rubbing down or wire brushing, and give them their first coat of paint. Any brass parts should be polished.

Worm-holes, etc.

Having cured the case of woodworm it is necessary to fill the holes, and any holes caused in other ways. The best type of filling to use for this purpose is probably 'Brummer' stopping, which is a preparation available in many different wood colours—there are three shades of oak alone. The stopping can be thinned with water and where a great many holes are to be filled it is better to use it as a fairly thin paste and apply it to the whole area, working it into the holes with a thin knife. Choose a colour to match the wood being prepared—do not be guided necessarily by the name given to the colour (for instance, it may be found that 'dark oak' will suit for the walnut finish of the exterior). Do not worry too much about any of the stopping which may remain on the surface of the wood; it is easily removed when the job is rubbed down. Leave the stopping to dry for at least two hours before carrying on. Perhaps the metal parts are dry enough to be given a second coat, or it might be a good idea to examine and clean the screws which fix the metal parts.

The interior

With all renovations done, the interior, which should have suffered less damage than the exterior of the case, can be rubbed down, with the grain, with cabinet-grade flour paper. The rubbing down is mainly to provide a good key for the spirit varnish while any dirt or lumps of old

RESTORING A DISC MUSICAL BOX CASE

varnish are removed. It is not necessary to rub down to the original wood.

When the rubbing down is completed, brush out the interior carefully so as to make a good clean surface for the finish. Brush on a thin coat of spirit varnish, with the grain. Make sure that *all* of the surface is covered as quickly as possible. The varnish should be applied so that any joints between brushes of varnish should be along the grain rather than across it. In other words, it is better to apply the finish in thin strips for the length of the surface. Make sure that there are no runs to mar the job. One coat on the interior should be sufficient, but if another coat would be of benefit, allow the varnish to dry, rub down gently, and apply a second coat. The interior, of course, includes the motor cover, and this should be done at the same time.

The exterior

The exterior of the case can be treated in very much the same manner unless there have been repairs or fillings, in which case these may have to be coloured in to match the rest of the finish. To match in the repairs, it is only necessary to prepare a little colour varnish by mixing into a small quantity of the varnish enough colour to make a match. If no spirit colour is available a little water colour from an ordinary child's paint-box may be used. Rub the surfaces down as before, then coat the new surfaces with colour, keeping to the new surfaces only, and using a small brush. Allow to dry for two hours and rub down the coloured parts. The whole may now be treated as the interior, except that two coats will be necessary. When applying a second coat, leave the first coat overnight, and remember to rub down.

Carvings

The carvings, including the two front pillars, are best rubbed down with grade 0 wire wool because of the surfaces, which are difficult to get at in the ordinary way. Otherwise, they are treated in exactly the same way as the other parts of the case. Take extra care when applying the varnish to prevent runs.

Missing turned parts

It may be that a part is missing from the case, possibly as small as a key-hole scutcheon or as vital as a foot. In the case of a scutcheon or a similar small piece, it is often simpler to make another piece from some other material than to attempt to copy the original. A scutcheon may fairly easily be cut from a piece of brass sheet with a pair of metal shears. It can then be cleaned up and polished, and screwed into place. The shape of the original wooden scutcheon need not be followed, and the size may well be dictated by any damage which might surround the keyhole caused by the drawer or door being pulled open with things other than a key.

Where a foot is missing, it must, of course, be replaced; and it will need to look original. For someone with an adventurous nature, it is possible to make a simple lathe with the aid of a power drill, a large screw, and a good vice. All that is required apart from this is a piece of suitable wood, and two or three chisels. To prepare the makeshift lathe, mark a centre on the block of wood to become the new foot, and use the drill to make a hole in which the large screw can be fixed. When it has been fixed well into the wood, cut off the head of the screw. Take down the corners of the wood to a little oversize of the widest part of the foot to be copied, and mark up the block for shaping. By placing the shank of the screw in the chuck of the drill and fixing the drill firmly in the vice, the wood can be made to rotate at speed. By using the chisels very gently to shape the wood as it rotates, it is possible to copy the existing foot. Should the foot appear to be of too complicated a pattern, it is possible to make a simpler pair by this method—and so save having to make a difficult copy. When the foot is shaped as well as possible, use sandpaper (while it is still revolving) to make a smooth finish. Finally, the foot can be fixed in position, if possible by the method used originally, or if not, by some other means. In many cases, the feet were dowelled to a square shank on the case; if the shank still exists, the hole made by the screw can be made large enough to take a short length of dowelling, the other end of which can be entered into the square shank. The 'lathe' can also be used to make small feet for table model cases. For many of these a piece of broom handle can be shaped and used.

Door and drawer locks

The keys to drawer and door locks are so often missing that it may be necessary to find a replacement key. A tour of the local junk shops, *with the lock*, may well produce a key which will fit and at least start to turn the lock, with a little filing here and there it may be possible to make the key work properly.

RESTORING A DISC MUSICAL BOX CASE

Opening the door of a locked upright machine is often easier than one might think. In many cases the lock tongue is of the hook type which, when the key is turned, moves forward and down to hold the door closed. If so, a thin knife can be used to lift the hook upwards and release the door. There is usually a bar below the hook which keeps the door at the right level—the knife must be inserted between this and the hook.

Replacing metal parts

When the cabinet is fully finished, the metal parts can be fixed to the case with the exception, on an upright Polyphon, of the scutcheon for the winding spindle. It is necessary to leave this off, since often the motor cannot be replaced with the scutcheon in position. Should any of the metal parts be missing, they are frequently available as reproductions.

CARE AND REPAIR OF DISCS

Any disc musical box, however grand, is completely useless without good discs. With this in mind it is incredible to see the way in which discs are almost universally mishandled. Like any tool, a disc must have a reasonable amount of care and attention to ensure proper working, and, like any tool obtained in a poor state, it must be brought to good condition, and kept that way. If discs are in very poor condition, before attempting to carry out some of the more difficult or time consuming steps below, see if it is not easier to obtain either original discs, or copies of new discs for your instrument.

There are surprising numbers of original discs of many sizes and makes available. Contact all the specialist dealers you can find; study the advertisements in the *Musical Box Society Journals*, or even put an advertisement in yourself.

New discs have both advantages and disadvantages. They are, if made well, perfect, and so should play well on your machine. They are also clean and bright, though some might feel they are too bright for a period instrument. The main disadvantage is that they come with either a very plain and simple title, or none at all, though the title will be known. This can be overcome by following the advice on titling. A further problem is that new discs tend to be expensive, even more so than originals (if they can be found).

Should other discs be found, do not discard your old discs. At the very least they can be used to copy new ones, and, who knows, you may, at a later date, want to recondition them.

Inspecting discs

As a matter of course, all original discs newly acquired should be examined thoroughly for damage. Pay special attention to projections to see they are present, and in good upright order. No discs should be played

CARE AND REPAIR OF DISCS

on a good machine until all the projections are in alignment. Another most important problem is rust. If a disc has not been played for a considerable time it may well have quite heavy deposits of rust in small spots between the projections even if the face of the disc is comparatively clean. Buckling or warping can affect the playing, as can a fold in the metal caused by the disc having been bent at some time. Also, parts of the disc may be dished from constant pressure on a maladjusted machine. Drive holes, whether on the periphery or in the centre of the disc, can be broken or distorted or even simply rusted away. Of less importance but still of some consequence is general appearance. A rusty surface, or even part of the title obscured or missing, will contribute to giving the impression of an unkempt machine.

Something can be done about all these problems and a little work on discs, which after all are as important to the disc box as the cylinder to a cylinder musical box, will be well repaid by improvement in both sound and appearance of your machine.

Straightening projections

Although there are many types of projection, not to mention discs without projections, the most common by far is that used by Polyphon, Regina, and frequently by Symphonion—known as the bridge of D projection. This is formed by curling the piece of metal forming the projection, back upon itself until the tip is resting on the underside of the disc, thus making it strong and firm. The method used is a shaped tool which cuts in the particular way required for the metal to bend just so.

Projections can of course be damaged when played on a movement which is incorrectly set up, or which is itself damaged in some way. Many more are lost, however, by bad storage or handling. To straighten bent projections all that is needed is a pair of long-nosed pliers and good eyesight. The majority will be found to have been forced to one side or the other, so that it is mainly a matter of straightening any which are out of line with the others. Some discs are found whose projections are very brittle and tend to break off almost at a touch. Other discs, even though they may have belonged to the same machine from the start, tend to have much more malleable metal. This is thought to be due to the state of the cutter when the disc was made. If the cutter was sharp then the cut was made more quickly, causing the metal to harden slightly. On the other hand, if the cutter was more blunt it would tend to tear the metal slightly, and stretch it, so making it softer. This would be hardly noticeable in ordinary terms, but in this case it makes a difference. Some projections are sure to break off, but are better missing altogether than damaging your machine.

Replacing broken steel projections

To replace projections which have been lost either by damage or by attempted straightening is not too difficult. It can be done with a reasonable amount of care and patience, together with some small skill in metalwork. In some cases the loss of a few projections is undetectable, and in this case it may be better to leave well alone, since some disfiguring of the disc is unavoidable when replacing even a few projections. If, however, the missing notes come at a particularly important place such as in the middle of a run or perhaps where a single note should play with effect, then the projections should be replaced where possible.

Here is a list of the tools and materials required:

Small soldering-iron
Several small files
Needle files
Pair of side-cutters
Pair of round-nosed pliers
Cored solder
Wire wool
Box of 3/64-inch cotter pins (split-pins)

Before commencing work on the projections, the discs must be free from grease and oil, so that first they must be washed in detergent, using a small brush to clean both sides of the discs. Wash one disc at a time and rinse thoroughly in hot water so that the heat retained by the metal helps to dry the disc. Pat off excess moisture with a soft dry cloth and stand the disc in front of a fan heater or radiator to dry. The disc must be absolutely dry, or it will rust.

Preparing the disc

Prepare a stand on which to rest the disc. If the kitchen table is to be used, cover it first with plenty of newspaper. At one end of the table place two supports side by side, high enough and wide enough apart for

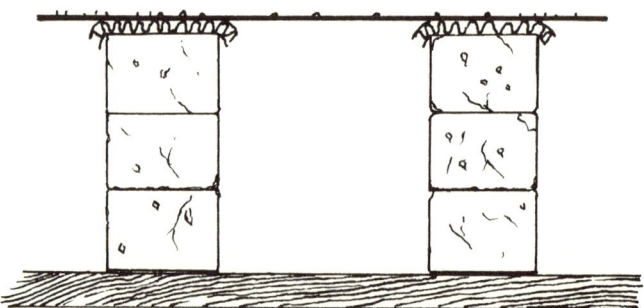

Dwg. 10. The disc on its stand

the arm to enter easily, with the disc resting on top. Three bricks on top of each other on either side would be fine. The top surface of the support is covered with soft card, corrugated paper, or some similar material. The rest of the surface of the table can be used for the tools and the preparatory work.

When replacing projections there is a problem of timing in the music. The point of break is normally where the projection curls round to go under the disc; in this case the tiny portion of metal left means that, if it is not removed, the new projection will be a thickness in front of the original and so sound slightly earlier when the disc is played. This would be less noticeable on the treble notes (outer edge of the disc) than the bass (centre of the disc) since the notes on the outside are travelling so much faster than those in the centre. To put the projection in the right place, it is necessary to file the back of the projection hole, not only to remove the thickness of the old projection but a little more to allow for the thickness of the new projection. Use a needle file to take the metal back on all places where a new projection is to be placed. The next step is to clean the area on the underside of the disc, a little larger than would have been covered by the original projection. In this operation, the whole of the disc can be prepared at the same time. There is lacquer on the undersides of nearly all discs, which must be removed from the immediate area so that the solder can do its job. After this has been done, go over each point again with the soldering iron and tin the metal to take the new projection.

The new projection

To prepare the cotter pin, straighten and clean it thoroughly until the metal on all sides is bright. Turn the end over with the round-nosed pliers to make the same shape as a projection, which is normally the shape of a D lying on its back. We now have a miniature walking-stick. Fill the 'crook' of the walking-stick with solder.

Fixing the new projection

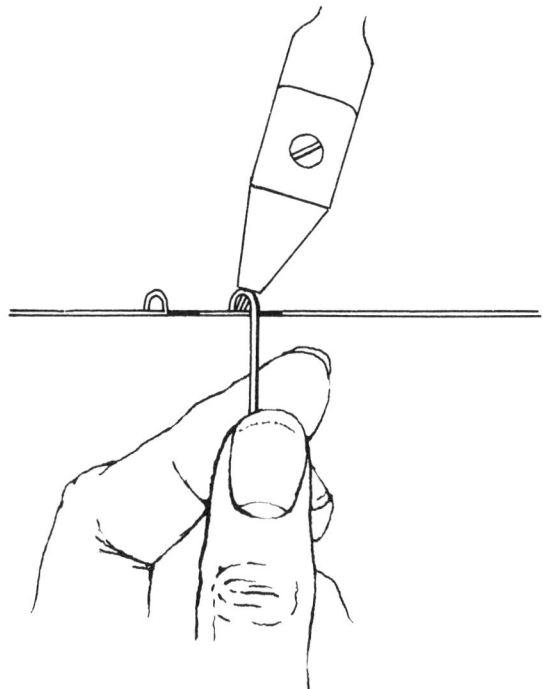

Dwg. 11. Fixing the new projection

By pushing the prepared cotter pin through the projection slot we can now position the 'crook' filled with solder so that it takes the place of the missing projection. Holding the straight of the metal in one hand with the disc on its stand, projection-side up, place the soldering-iron on the crook until the solder starts to move. Take the iron away at once and after testing the join turn the disc over. Cut the excess metal with the side-snips as close to the disc as possible, and file flat, taking care not to mar the surface of the disc. Continue this process, using the same cotter pin, until it is too short to hold either with the hand or pliers. The bending of the top of the pin to the correct shape can be practised and quickly learned.

Repairing zinc discs

The replacement of projections on zinc discs—as opposed to those of mild steel—is more difficult in that we are not able to use solder. To fix the new projections the use of '*Araldite Rapid*' or a similar fixative is recommended. The drying time, of course, is greatly increased, but the problem can be overcome by using a different type of replacement projection. The tools are the same for this method except for the solder and iron, which are no longer required. The main difference between the two jobs is that with the '*Araldite*' we must first increase the area of the points to be joined. This means that the cotter pin is shaped differently, and used in a longer piece. In the drawing it will be seen that the disc is placed flat upon supports with the projections pointing downwards. The new projection is shaped so that it lies along the front of the disc which is uppermost; and enters the hole from which the original projection was cut, ending in the D shape of a new projection.

Preparing the disc

The disc must be prepared first by removing any grease with detergent, and then by scraping the metal free from rust or lacquer with a file in the places where the new projections will be held by the '*Araldite*'. Score the metal quite heavily to give a good key for the fixative. File the backs of the projection holes to allow for the thickness of the new metal. When the disc is finally ready to receive the new projection, make sure it is standing firmly on its supports, none of which should be directly under any of the places due to be treated. If possible the disc should be left where it is at the end of the work for at least twenty-four hours.

Preparing the projections

Straighten and clean the cotter pins in the same way as for soldering. They need to be made into a different shape, however, not like a walking-stick but more like a question mark with an elongated tail, as in the drawing. Shape all of the new projections before attempting to attach them, so the disc is disturbed for as short a time as possible.

Attaching the new projections

Dwg. 12. The new projection in position

Use enough fixative for it to form a shallow dome over and around the 'tail' of the projection, and make sure the new metal is in exact position before moving on to the next one. Take care not to disturb projections already done, and when finished, examine each one to make sure it has not been disturbed. It is most important to leave out any missing projections which come into the path of any of the pressure wheels, which hold the disc down on to the star wheels. The dome of fixative, together with the metal of the tail of the projection, will cause the wheel to push the disc too far in, with the possibility of jamming or damaging the movement. If it is necessary to move the disc when it is finished, take care not to jog it, and when it is placed in the new position make sure that none of the new projections have been displaced by the move.

When the fixative is thoroughly dry, examine the new projections to make sure they are in perfect alignment, and adjust where necessary.

OTHER REPAIRS

Damage to the periphery

Apart from loss of projections there are other forms of damage which may interfere with the playing of the disc. Most important of these is rusting of the rim of a periphery-driven disc so that some of the drive holes are missing. This is mainly caused by the discs having been left standing at some time on a damp floor, so that normally just one portion of the edge is affected. To repair the disc it is necessary to take out the offending portion, and replace it with a piece of new metal with the holes already drilled. The tools and materials for this operation are as follows:

 Sharp tool for marking
 Mild steel sheet—of similar thickness to the disc
 'Abra' file (a patented file with attachments to fit a hacksaw)
 Hacksaw frame
 Hand drill

CARE AND REPAIR OF DISCS

Sheet metal drill-bit of exact size of drive holes
Vice
Soldering-iron
Cored solder
Block of wood (to support work while drilling)

The mild steel sheet may be difficult to obtain, but most large towns have at least one shop where this type of metal is available. The 'Abra' file can be used to cut metal in the same way as a fretsaw cuts wood. The sheet metal drill-bit cuts round the edge of the hold required, taking out a disc of metal.

Preparing the disc

Dwg. 13. Line of cut with Abra file

We must first cut out the bad metal with the 'Abra' file in the hacksaw frame. Place the affected part in the vice after marking a line for the cutting. When making the line, try to position the cut between where the pressure wheel comes near the drive holes and the first of the projec-

CARE AND REPAIR OF DISCS

tions, leaving as much space between the projections and the cut as possible. Set the part to be cut in the vice at the bottom of the disc, hold the disc by the top with one hand and cut round the line carefully. The straighter the cut the better, and take special care not to put any kinks into the metal. If the disc is large, get someone to hold the disc upright while you concentrate on the cutting, giving support with the free hand to the immediate area being worked. When the cutting is complete, clean up the edge with a fine file and remove some metal from an area of about ⅛ inch wide along the length of the cut on the projection side to prepare it for soldering.

Shaping the new metal

Take a section of mild steel sheet larger all round by a good inch than the space to be filled. Place the metal under the edge of the disc at a part where the drive holes are good and clip the two together, making sure there is enough new metal to fill the empty space. With the two pieces firmly clipped together, place them on the wooden block and carefully drill the new drive holes using the sheet metal drill-bit. With the original holes to guide the bit there should be no problem, although again with a large disc it might help to have someone to hold the work firm as you drill.

When the holes are completed and before moving the work, scribe a line, using the edge of the disc for a guide, for cutting the edge of the new metal. Unclip the disc and use the 'Abra' file to cut the new edge. This being completed, we now have a piece of metal which corresponds to the rest of the disc in every way round the periphery. Place the new piece under the gap in the edge of the disc, making sure the holes which come at the ends of the gap are the right distance from those on the disc. Do this by moving the new piece from side to side until it matches.

Fitting the new metal

Mark a line where the cut edge of the disc finishes and, taking the metal away, mark a line ⅛ inch out from this line to allow the overlap necessary for soldering. Cut this line carefully with the 'Abra' file, clean up the edge, and take a little metal off the extra ⅛ inch on the side which will be the *smooth* side of the disc.

CARE AND REPAIR OF DISCS

Fixing the new metal

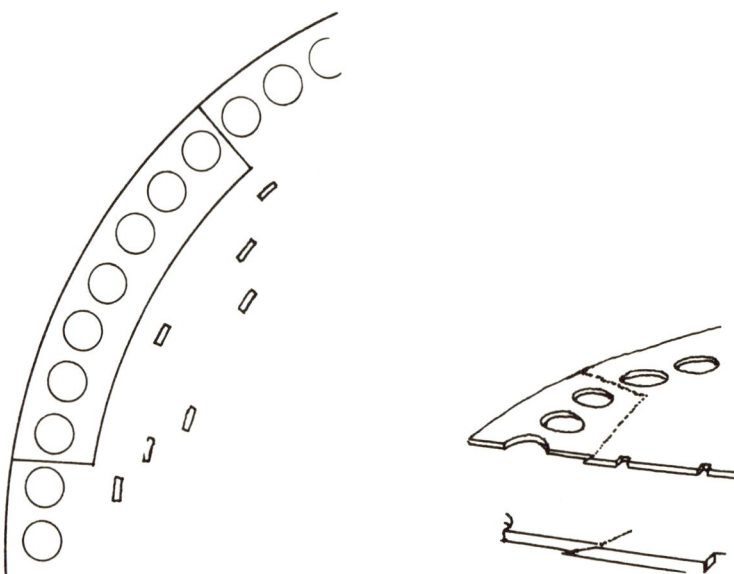

Dwg. 14. New periphery in position

All that remains is to tin the two parts to be joined, lay them on a flat surface and solder them together. At this stage take great care the new piece is in exact position and matching in every way, in particular the drive holes. The join must be good and flat in order to allow the disc to play well.

Folds or bends in discs

When a disc is unplayable due to a severe fold or bend in the metal holding the projections, it is possible to make the fault good. The method given does not necessarily improve the looks of the disc, but it will make it playable in most cases.

Required is a medium screwdriver and a soft springy surface on which to place the disc. A piece of old carpet or a folded blanket will do nicely. Place the disc on the soft surface with the apex of the fold upwards. With the screwdriver, press gently along the line of the crease to make a series of small dents rather like small stitches in a long cut. This

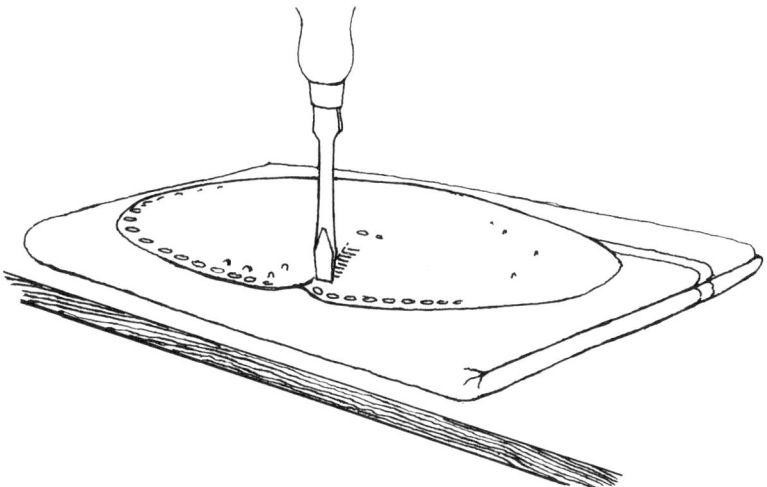

Dwg. 15. First treatment of bent disc

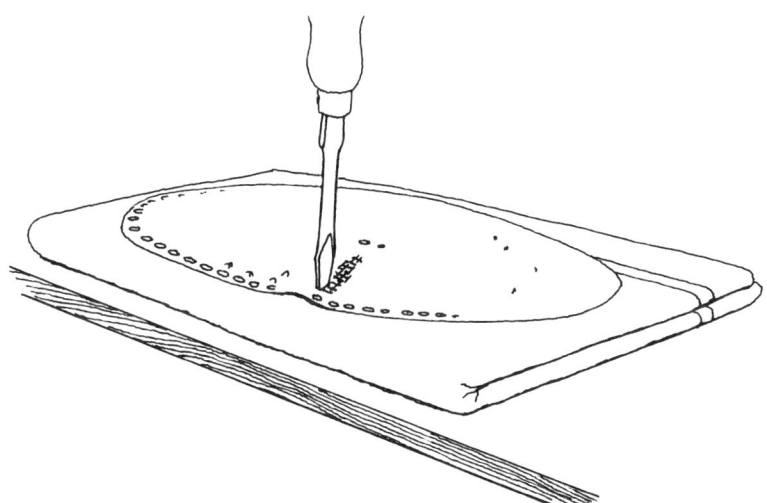

Dwg. 16. Second treatment of bent disc

will have the effect of making many small folds in the opposite direction in place of a large single one. When the line has been fully covered turn the disc over and carefully push down all the small high spots on this side caused by the new dents. Continue this method until the fold has been replaced by a large number of tiny dents on both sides, which will have become nothing more than irregularities in the surface of the disc. Take great care not to press hard on any one place, or to break the metal through careless work.

Torn centre drive holes

Discs of sizes under 15 inches are generally driven from the centre, although there are exceptions to this rule. If for some reason there is more than normal resistance to the drive, damage is often caused to the drive hole(s), which are usually placed on either side of the centre dome, or at the centre hole. The type of damage generally caused is the tearing of the metal at the edge of the holes. It is possible to remedy the damage by covering the whole of the area of the centre of the disc with a metal plate, and in this plate provide a new centre hole and new drive holes. Remember, there is no point in doing a job of this nature unless the cause of damage is removed. A list of the tools and materials required is given here:

Sharp tool for marking
Mild sheet steel—of similar thickness to the disc
A pair of metal shears
Hand drill
Sheet metal drills of a size to fit the holes required
Vice
Soldering-iron
Cored solder
Block of wood to support work while drilling
Metal rule or calipers
Anvil or similar
Small hammer

The pressure rollers on the pressure-bar are set to the thickness of the disc to give an exact pressure to hold the disc against the star wheels. It is essential for this reason that the new metal, making as it does a double thickness, should not be cut so large as to reach the first pressure wheel out from the centre. Cut a piece of the new metal into a disc which is as large as possible without fouling the pressure wheel. Clean both the surface of the new metal and the part of the disc to which the metal is to be applied, which is the *smooth* or upper side of the disc. Use the anvil and the hammer to tap down gently any part of the torn metal which is proud of the surface of the disc. Do not tap so hard as to spread the metal. When you are sure both surfaces are clean, tin each of them and solder the new centre to the old. Make doubly sure that the new metal will not interfere with the first pressure wheel during any part of the turn of the disc when the machine is playing.

When the new centre is nicely fixed, turn the disc over and place it on the wood block to drill the new holes for the centre and the drive. The centre hole should normally still be true, but there are times when it has been made oval by pressure. The drive hole(s), although torn on the leading edge, are usually in good condition at the back of the hole. Should there be a problem with the placing of the new holes, which must of course be exact, it is simple to take bearings from a disc in good condition by placing it over the disc to be drilled and marking the new holes in this way. If the disc is of the type which uses a drive hole cut square and folded over to make a stronger leading edge, there is no reason why this type of drive hole should not be replaced by a round one, if the drive peg to enter it is round. When working on discs of this type remember to take off the fold of metal before fixing the new centre.

Dished centres of discs

A fairly common malady, particularly among discs of the smaller sizes, is that the centre of the disc becomes dished or distorted. This is often caused by the height wheel of the movement being too high. The pressure caused by the downward thrust of the pressure rollers against the disc, which is held up at the centre, results in the metal around the centre stretching to take the shape of the opposing pressures.

The remedy for the stretching is to shrink the metal to something like its original shape. This is far less difficult than may be thought, and a method is given which is both simple and effective. Here are the tools required:

A gas torch or blowtorch
A flat-headed hammer
Large cold surface—anvil, large flat stone, or similar.

CARE AND REPAIR OF DISCS

Heat the centre of the disc until it is dull red, and immediately, with the hammer head, press the centre of the disc, smooth surface down, against the cold anvil or stone. Both the hammer head and the surface should be as cold as possible, with enough pressure applied to push the metal flat against the anvil. Do not beat the metal; the hammer is used simply because it is a convenient tool. This treatment should result in the shrinking required to bring the centre in line with the rest of the disc.

Warped discs

In the case of discs obtained with a particular machine being badly warped or buckled resulting in bad crackling when the discs are played, it is possible to present a better line of disc to the star wheels by increasing the angle of dish applied to the disc by the dishing wheels. These wheels are usually attached to the case of the machine. With table-model machines the carriers of the wheels may be fixed on the furniture boards on either side of the bed-plate; in this case they can be packed up slightly—say ⅛ inch. If the dishing wheels are attached to the side of the case, as in upright machines, they can be moved forward. In no case should they be moved out more than ⅜ inch. Do not do this unless the warped discs outnumber the good.

Disc titles

Although discs must not be re-titled until they have been cleaned, it is necessary to make sure before cleaning that all the data from the surface of the disc is recorded before cleaning commences. If the disc is badly rusted the title will be destroyed during the cleaning.

Missing titles

If the title is already missing, one must either recognize the tune and find out the full title and composer, or look for the number of the disc and hope to locate the particulars in a disc catalogue. Some Polyphon and Symphonion discs had the title applied after the making of the tune, and so had the number of the disc scratched on the centre of the projection side of the disc. Since this side was protected with lacquer it may still be possible to read this number. Regina discs were not only titled before the cutting of the projections, but on both sides, so that with luck the title will still be legible. In the case of most Swiss machines the number was stamped on the centre of the discs, but this may not be of much help since very few catalogues are available to verify the title, though more information is continually becoming available.

Replacing titles

There are several ways to replace a title which has had to be removed when cleaning a disc. The most simple way is to note all the details before the cleaning, and then re-title with letters of the self-fixing type which are readily available everywhere. These can be covered with a spray lacquer to fix them, and the effect is very good.

Reproducing titles

For those who wish to reproduce the art work of the titling more exactly, perhaps to match other discs, the task is more involved and requires some skill in art. The result of this type of work, however, if done well, will please the owner every time the disc is played and may well be considered to be worth the extra effort and time.

Tracing a title

Find a disc of the type to be re-titled with all the titling intact. Take a large sheet of tracing paper and attach it to the disc by folding the corners over the edges of the disc, and secure them with paper clips or similar. With a sharp pencil first mark the centre hole and place where the tune begins and ends. This will fix the position of the tracing exactly on any other disc of the same type. With a sharp pencil trace all the patterns and lettering printed on the disc, with the exception of the actual title and number of the disc. The positioning and general shape of these should be indicated. When the tracing is finished it should be a complete copy of all the decoration on the disc. If some of the lettering of the title is still legible on the disc to be cleaned, the tracing paper can be fixed to this disc and as much as possible of the lettering traced so as to give the maximum amount of information for the eventual renewal of the titling.

CARE AND REPAIR OF DISCS

Marking out the disc

When the disc to be re-titled has been cleaned, the tracing can be fixed as before, but with carbon paper beneath those parts which are to be copied on to the surface of the discs. The carbon can be first fixed to the underside of the tracing paper with a little cow gum on each corner. Make sure the carbon paper is facing the right way. With an instrument with a good point go over the lines of the tracing so that all the necessary outlines are committed to the new surface, including indications of the area and general shape of the title itself and the number. This being done and the papers removed, all that remains is to line in the title.

The chances are that each of the letters required is contained in one or other of the titles of other discs in your possession. Mark straight on to the disc as best you can the area required for each letter. Trace each of the letters required separately from the discs involved and transfer their outlines to the space set out for them on the new surface. Where part of the title was extant when the first tracing was made before cleaning, the task will be a lot easier. It will perhaps be a question of the odd letter, or possibly completing a part of some letters or words.

Writing a title

When you are satisfied that all the wording and decoration is perfectly blocked out, the final step of inking in can be undertaken. For this purpose India ink can be used. An old receipt (recipe) for an ink to mark bright metal or glass is as follows:

> "To write black on glass or bright metal use one to two parts of silicate of soda with 10 parts of India ink".

The ink can be applied with a water-colour brush while the disc is resting on a flat surface. Great care must be taken with all edges for the job to appear really professional. Any gold lines can be added when the ink is fully dry, using any good gold metal paint, and any other colour can be applied. Colours other than gold or black should be chosen from a range of modeller's enamel paints.

Fixing the new title

Finally, spray both sides of the disc with a clear polyurethane varnish, taking care not to make the varnish run or clog the projections.

When trying the above method of giving a disc a new title it is well to remember that should the end result not be as good as was imagined nothing is lost but the work already done. The disc can be cleaned off completely before the final fixative is applied and another try made, either with the same method or using the easier way of ready-made lettering, or even a mixture of both.

Cleaning discs

The casework of a disc musical box can be in immaculate condition, the movement may witness by its perfect sound the many hours spent in adjusting, cleaning, and renovating the various parts, but in spite of all this, if the discs are dirty and look ill-used, a great deal of the effect is lost. A few hours more spent improving the appearance of your discs will be well repaid.

Dirt and grease on discs

Unfortunately we are often in the position of having to do more than is strictly necessary when cleaning discs since it is seldom a satisfactory job can be done on the surface without the removal of the original lacquer, or what is left of it. This, of course, means deciding whether the title can be left undisturbed and retouched later, or if it must be removed with the rest of the surface to make a really good job. Often original lacquer on the face of the disc is discoloured or dirty and, though washing with detergent will take off the surface grease and dirt, the lacquer will remain dingy. We are faced with a job at least as difficult as cleaning the lid of a musical box which has a transfer motif. We cannot remove all of the dirt without removing the titles. After washing and drying the discs the decision can be made whether to leave the title or not. This will depend on the difficulty you would find in replacing the lettering, either because of the intricacies of the design or simply because your skill is not sufficient.

Cleaning by hand

Should you decide to keep what lettering there is on the disc, then the cleaning job must be done by hand. In this way the titling can be carefully left while as much work as necessary can be done to the rest of the surface. The best and most economical way of cleaning the surface of a disc by hand appears to be with wet-and-dry paper used wet. This abrasive paper is the type which is used where ordinary emery paper would get quickly clogged with the material it is removing from the metal. In this case we are removing old lacquer, rust, and some grease, a combination which would quickly clog any dry paper. This idea is economical since the paper will last for a very long time, only diminishing in size as the edges fray. The paper and job are kept wet by continually dipping the paper into water. The cleaning must always be done round the disc so that all cleaning marks run one way. Start with a grade 180 paper and work down to grade 280, finishing with grade 360. A possibly quicker but more expensive way of hand cleaning is the use of silicon-carbide paper, using this in similar grades or fineness and discarding the piece being used as soon as it is too clogged to be efficient.

When the front of the disc is pristine, make sure that the projection side of the disc is free from rust. A wire brush can be used to clean this side, brushing always round the disc so as to get between the projections and at the same time not subject them to any sideways pressure. After a thorough brushing, the edges of this side of the disc can be papered off. The disc is now ready for a final wash, titling, and lacquering.

Chemical cleaning

The cleaning of all steel discs by immersion in the usual rust-removing agencies is not recommended, because of the poor colour imparted to the metal during this process. Where the disc is to be finished in clear varnish we are merely exchanging one bad colour for another. There are, however, many discs which were originally finished with a coloured lacquer—Symphonion, Monopol and Polyphon spring readily to mind as companies using this type of finish on their smaller discs. In these cases the reason for not using a chemical rust-remover such as 'Jenolite' no longer exists, and such a cleaner can be used by simply following the instructions. The resultant colour will be covered by the colour of the lacquer finish, although it is well to remember that no chemical cleaner does more than remove the rust; the rust pattern in the metal will still be visible. Should you feel the coloured lacquer can be used to good effect on discs originally finished in clear, there is nothing to stop you from using it on any type of disc. The coloured lacquer is applied before the titling, and the titling then covered by a clear lacquer.

CARE AND REPAIR OF DISCS

A neat way to clean rusty discs chemically is described by Keith Harding in an article in *The Music Box*: '. . . (for) very rusty steel Polyphon discs, the nearest garage will be very happy to sell you a tin of "Radflush". Try to decipher the title of the disc first, then immerse it in the first solution for an hour or so, having first degreased it if necessary. Scrub in warm water and dry at once, preferably with warm sawdust or a fan heater, and avoid touching the metal with the bare hands. This process should leave the metal clean and bright. Immediately when it is dry enough, coat it all over with polyurethane marine varnish, obtainable from any hardware store.' ('Radflush' is the trade name for a preparation used for clearing rusted water-cooling systems in motor vehicles.)

Projectionless discs

The cleaning of projectionless discs does not present the same problems as the cleaning of those having projections. It is, however, even more important to make sure that these discs are free from rust or corrosion, since the star wheels of the machines on which they play act on springs. If a piece of rust or similar was to turn the star wheel while it is in the down position, it would probably cause the comb tooth, plucked much harder by the star wheel, to break.

Disc storage

Owing to the fragile nature of the projections, it is most important to store discs so that they are kept in good condition, not only while being stored but also while being removed from storage. With the majority of disc machines the question of where to put the discs not being played is a problem. Even with a storage bin there is a right way to store the discs so that they are secure from harm.

Disc bins

Where the machine is of the type which stands on a storage bin, a natural inclination is to put all the discs into the bin. The problem then is of selecting a disc to play without damage to it or its fellows. The ideal number of discs in a bin is two to each compartment. These should be stored with the projections toward each other. This gives a smooth sur-

CARE AND REPAIR OF DISCS

face to present to each side of the compartment and if the discs are always withdrawn from the bin and returned in pairs, carefully, no loss of projections will result.

The discs for your machine can first be sorted, with those most likely to be used being kept in the bin. A little tab with the titles can be stuck to the interior of the bin above each pair of discs. Discs not being used very often can be stored in the attic or some similar place, remembering that discs laid flat do not warp as they tend to do when stood on end. Lay the discs with the projections downward. Ideally, the place for storage should be warm and dry. If there is any possibility of dampness do not store with paper or card between, since this will attract moisture and hold it to rust the discs. A good idea is to wrap the discs in polythene.

Loose discs

Should there be no place provided to store the discs, some sort of protection should be given before settling on a place to keep them near the machine. If the discs are under 12 inches, nothing is more suitable for safe keeping than a record album of the type used for the old 78-r.p.m. records for gramophones.

Making a disc cover

If the discs are large, a cover for each disc can easily be made using card and a stapler. Obtain some stiff card at least two inches wider than the diameter of the disc. Cut the card so that it is two inches wider than the disc one way, and one inch wider than the disc the other. With the stapler join two pieces of the cut card on three sides, half an inch in from the edge. Cut a half moon in the centre of the side not joined, and you have a disc cover. Give it a label for the name and number and it is complete.

If all this appears to be a lot of trouble for a few discs, remember it has only to be done once to protect your discs for many years, and the importance of a disc being in good order when played cannot be overstressed.

MINOR ADJUSTMENTS AND REPAIRS

Major repairs, can, of course, be undertaken by a specialist in mechanical music. There are, though, many small adjustments or repairs which can be done by the amateur without specialist knowledge, with a few simple tools and a degree of patience. If the machine in question has already been dismantled, cleaned, and reassembled, the knowledge gained in this way will be a great help. Always, before commencing work, and bearing in mind the limits of your personal skill, evaluate the particular work to be done. Decide with honesty whether your attentions will benefit the machine or not, and, if in any doubt, seek professional help.

Correct diagnosis of faults

Many good instruments have suffered from well-meaning major 're-pairs', where a little thought and deduction would have saved much hardship for both machine and 'repairer'. There are many parts to disc musical boxes that, once shaped and put into place during manufacture, do not move or degenerate to any degree. Most of the problems we have to deal with are minor, overcome easily with a little thought.

Before changing the shape of some part, putting packing somewhere, or moving something vital, study the problem and make absolutely sure it is really necessary to do so.

MOTOR ASSEMBLY

The governor assembly

Warning. It is most important to ensure, before attempting to do any work on the governor assembly, that *all* tension has been removed from

MINOR ADJUSTMENTS AND REPAIRS

the spring. Even a small and seemingly harmless adjustment to any part of this assembly could cause serious damage if a mistake is made while the spring is under tension.

End stone or jewel

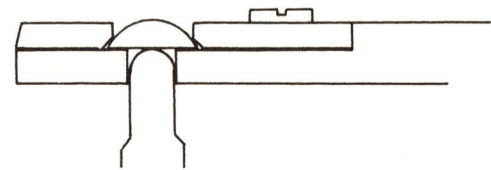

Dwg. 17. The end stone and domed head of endless screw

The running of the endless screw is dependent upon, among other things, a hard flat surface for the domed head of the top of the endless screw shaft to bear against as it rotates. If the surface of the bearing is pitted or rough or the wrong shape, the endless cannot run. The setting of the governor mechanism in a disc musical movement is generally fixed at manufacture so that, if there is no damage to the wheels of the train, not much wear in the bearings, and if the endless screw is in good condition, the usual cause of an endless refusing to run is the jewel. If, upon examination, the jewel is found to be pitted, it is possible to polish the surface flat again. It is also possible to buy a replacement jewel if the existing one is too far gone, or possibly split. If neither of these courses is possible, it may be necessary to use something else in the way of a hard flat surface on which the endless can run. As a temporary measure it is possible to use a piece of safety razorblade as a surface, and even quite permanent results have been obtained by placing such a piece under the pitted jewel to make a new surface. Perhaps a better way is to shape a piece of tool steel to the measurements of the plate which holds the jewel, the copy being exact in every detail except that it does not contain a hole for the jewel. The surface which will form the bearing for the dome of the endless should be highly polished and the steel should be really hard. The original screw can be used to fix the new plate to the bracket.

Running too slow

Should the movement be running too slowly, in spite of all appearing to be well with the endless, it may well be that the two air brakes or fans

MINOR ADJUSTMENTS AND REPAIRS

Dwg. 18a. Normal spiral spring   Dwg. 18b. Stretched spring

Dwg. 18c. Spring which must be replaced

attached to the endless screw are presenting too much surface to the air. The method used in the majority of cases to regulate the speed is the use of two spiral springs between the two fans. When the machine is at rest the springs hold the fans firmly together. When the fans are thrown out by centrifugal force as the movement gathers speed, the springs expand, then contract as soon as the movement is slowed down for any reason, such as a chord using a lot of notes together. In this way the fans are able to compensate and so regulate the speed of the movement.

Ideally, when the machine is at rest the spirals of the spring should be close set. Owing to constant tension the springs may, however, have become sloppy and no longer hold the fans together firmly. This will result in the machine running slowly. To remedy this fault we must renew the tension of the springs, if possible, by shortening them. Remove the governor from its bracket and examine the springs (of course with the spring fully run down); it may be that they have been shortened before, so that it is no longer possible to obtain a good result with this method. If they have been shortened it will be seen that the spirals are so wide apart as to make an almost straight piece of wire with a kink or so in it. If this is the case, new springs must be obtained. If the coils of the spring are simply a little apart from each other, cut a few coils from the end of each spring until a fully closed position is obtained for the fans, and fix the new ends in the same way as the ends were fixed before.

Symphonion used, on their larger machines, a pair of fans of thin metal which were curled over at each end. This has a similar effect of presenting a smaller surface when the machine is starting or going slowly. When the machine gains speed the fans are uncurled by centrifugal force. This type of fan can also lose its tension, and to renew the tension the fans can be curled more tightly. Take a pencil or something similar and wrap each fan round it in turn, rolling the metal tightly. If this is done several times the curls will gradually tighten. Take care to curl both fans to the same degree to keep the balance right. It is also

MINOR ADJUSTMENTS AND REPAIRS

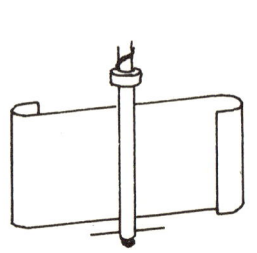
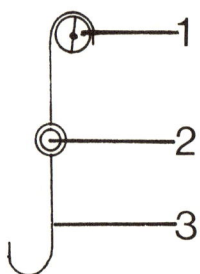

Dwg. 19a. Symphonion-type fan

Dwg. 19b. Renewing tension with a pencil
1. pencil   2. endless screw   3. fan

necessary to make sure that the curl is straight, or the fan may touch the bracket as it rotates and so cause a noise and slow the machine. Should one of the blades of this type of fan be already out of true, the same treatment may well cure the fault. Make sure *both* fans are treated in this case also.

Running too fast

The design of the movement does not allow the machine to run too fast unless something has been done in the past to alter the running speed. The normal cause of a machine running too fast would be that either the surface area of the fans has been lessened, or the springs replaced with others which have too much tension, and which do not allow the fans to fly out in the proper manner. Where the surface area has been lessened, it is necessary to add metal so as to restore the original size, but fortunately this particular fault is rarely found. What is normally the case is that the springs have been replaced. Where the springs have too much tension they must either be replaced or, if possible, stretched. To stretch a spiral spring simply pull gently from each end so as to separate the coils a little, and cut off any excess length gained in this way. If the springs are of much thicker wire than the originals they must be replaced.

Loose stop-tail

On most large disc machines the stop-tail is a piece of wire spiralled on to the shaft of the endless. The spiral is held under tension by two brass

MINOR ADJUSTMENTS AND REPAIRS

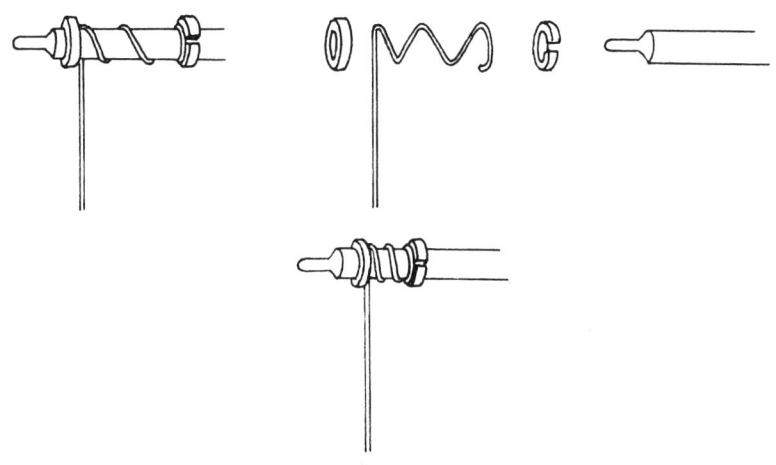

Dwg. 20. Stop-tail

collars; the collar nearer the centre of the shaft is split, and the one nearer the end of the shaft is solid. On occasion, it has been found that the split collar is not holding the spiral of the tail firmly enough, allowing the stop-tail to move round on the shaft, and so not stop the movement when it should. To remedy this, if the split collar is still tight on the shaft, it is possible to ease it down so as to compress the spiral more between the two collars and so hold the stop-tail firm. If the split collar is loose on the shaft from wear, it is necessary to remove first the lower collar, then the stop-tail and then the split collar. The lower collar can be carefully gripped with a pair of pliers and eased off the end of the shaft. The tail and the split collar will follow easily. If the split in the collar has been widened, it may be tapped back to its original shape, and pushed back on to the shaft. If the wear on the collar is so bad as to allow easy movement even after the split has been closed, one or two small lengths of thread may be passed through the collar before pushing it back on to the shaft. When the split collar can be moved only with some pressure, the stop and then the lower collar can be replaced on the shaft. Should the stop still move around the shaft with ease, bring the collars a little closer by moving the split one until the stop moves only with pressure. Last of all, cut off any pieces of thread which are showing on either side of the split collar. Some movement of the stop-tail must be allowed, since this is the reason for the type of friction-fit employed in this part. There is considerable momentum when the stop-tail is hindered, and the slight movement allows a slightly more gradual stop.

Burrs on leaf or middle wheel

It is sometimes found that the middle or leaf wheel of the governor train is the cause of non-running of a movement. The leaf wheel is the smaller of the train wheels and its teeth engage with the worm of the endless screw itself. The teeth of this wheel can become burred through excessive wear; these burrs interfere with the meshing of the two pieces. Using a fine needle file, it is possible to remove the worst of these burrs without changing the shape of the teeth of the wheel. If this operation is attempted at all, great care *must* be taken to take off only metal which is outside the shape of the teeth. Remember that this wheel, if worked on carelessly, can cause a run. Unless there is a good final mesh, and smooth running, the wheel will need to be renewed.

START/STOP PROBLEMS

Lack of winding handle

The first thing required when starting a disc musical box is a handle with which to wind it. The handle, being detached from the machine, is often a piece which gets lost, particularly when the machine is being moved or sent from one place to another. The handle may also be broken and need replacement, or at least repair. A new one can be obtained, and this will be a good copy of the original, or one can be made.

Making a handle for a Polyphon

The simplest beginning to the making of a winding handle is to obtain a handle originally intended for some other machine, and alter it to suit the new purpose. The handle of a wind-up gramophone is ideally suited for the job. It may even be that the handle will fit the Polyphon with no alteration at all. Most handles found, however, are of fairly heavy-gauge solid metal with a male thread. If this is the type then it will need to be worked on to make it suitable. You will need a length of pipe of a size suitable to fit both the spindle of the gramophone handle and the winding spindle of the machine. If the pipe is slightly under-size for either spindle, the spindle(s) may be filed to size. Required in the way of tools are a hacksaw, one used and one new blade, soldering iron, solder and flux, several files, a vice, and a drill. The important thing is for the handle to fit well on the shaft, and not be so long as to be awkward to wind or so short as to foul the casework while winding, while the crank must not be so long as to be awkward.

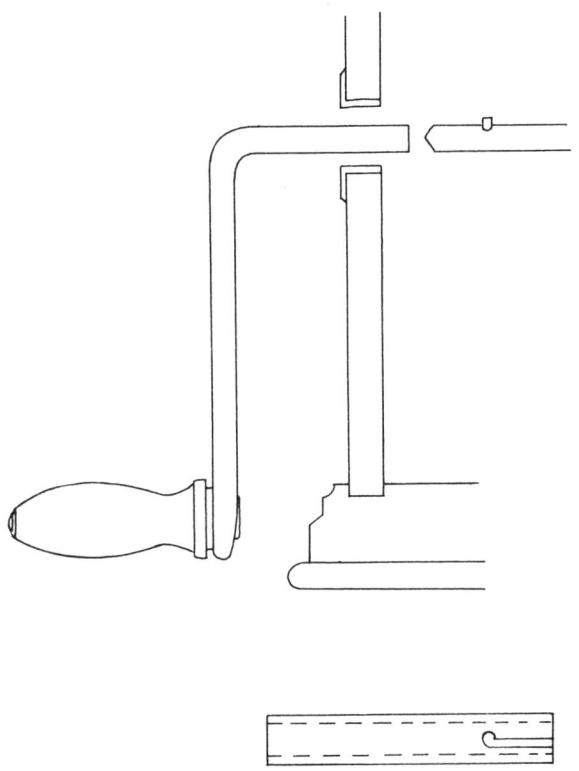

Dwg. 21. The handle cut to size, with (below) the pipe prepared for soldering

Measure the distance from one inch beyond the pin on the winding spindle to where the crook of the handle should be; measure also from one inch beyond the pin to the end of the spindle itself. Cut a piece from the pipe which is two inches longer than the distance from one inch beyond the pin to the end of the winding spindle. Cut also the spindle of the gramophone winder so that two inches of the spindle is left to enter

MINOR ADJUSTMENTS AND REPAIRS

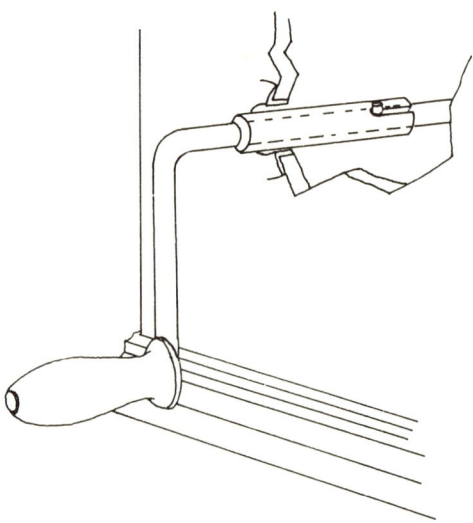

Dwg. 22. The completed handle

the pipe, plus as much as is necessary for the handle to be the right length when complete. Place the piping in a vice, and prepare the hacksaw: first place in position the new blade. Position next to it the old blade. The normal hacksaw has holding-pins for the blade which slant out from the body of the saw; the use the old blade has had will have stretched it so as to make it possible for the two blades to fit side by side on the pins. Using two blades in this fashion will make only one cut necessary with perhaps a little filing to finish the job. Use the drill to make a hole on one side of the pipe at a place ¾ inch from one end. Take the double saw and make a straight cut from the near end so as to join the drilled hole on the right-hand side looking from the other end of the pipe. When the cut is complete, use the file to clean up and smooth off the hole and the slot. Clean off the interior of the pipe at the end which is to take the spindle of the handle and the spindle itself. Flux the parts and solder the pipe firmly on to the spindle. The handle is now complete, all that remains is to polish it up to give the job a good finish.

Making a Symphonion handle

All the advice given for making a handle for a Polyphon applies here, except that the fitting on the winding spindle is a slot instead of a pin,

MINOR ADJUSTMENTS AND REPAIRS

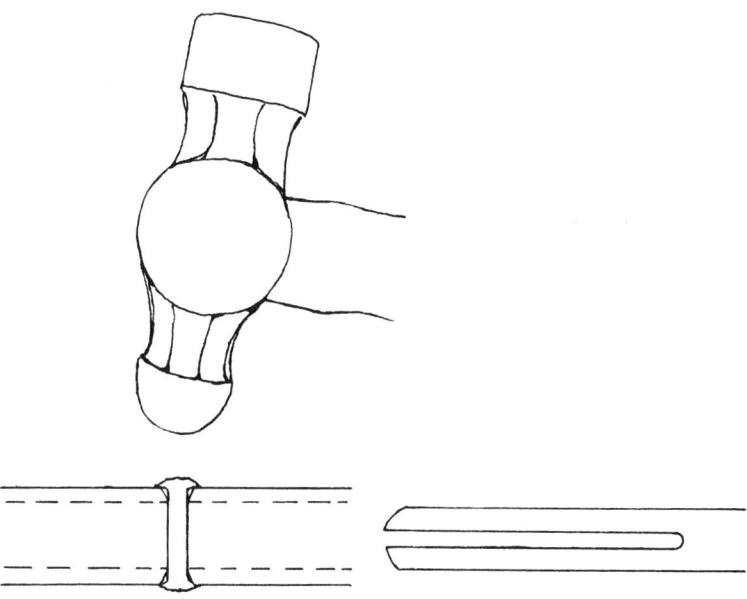

Dwg. 23. Peening the end of the new pin

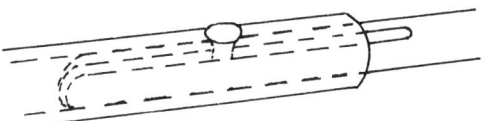

Dwg. 24. The winding handle in position

and so requires a different fitment. Instead of making a slot to fit a pin we must make a pin to fit a slot. The measurements are taken in the same way, except that the measuring is to ½ inch beyond the end of the slot on the spindle. When the pipe has been cut to the correct length, take a nail of a size which will fit easily but not sloppily into the slot of the spindle and drill two holes to this size through the pipe in opposition ¾ inch from one end of the pipe, and countersink them. Cut the head from the chosen nail, place it in the vice, and carefully peen one end with a peening hammer so that when the nail is pushed through the two holes the peened end fits snugly into the countersinking of one hole. Cut the nail to 1/32 inch over the width of the pipe. Push the nail through

MINOR ADJUSTMENTS AND REPAIRS

and, resting the peened end on top of the vice, gently peen the other end so as to make a good fit into the countersink. After the pipe has been soldered to the gramophone handle and polished, the job is complete.

Winding without a handle

While waiting to make a handle for a machine requiring one, or possibly waiting for a reproduced handle ordered from a specialist, it is possible to get a little tension at least into the spring of some machines by other means. With the Symphonion, since it uses a slot on the winding spindle, a large screwdriver can be used to turn the spindle so that a tune may be heard. A Polyphon is a little more awkward, but this, or any other large disc machine may be wound in part by turning by hand the crown wheel of the winding mechanism (see the drawings of all parts). The operation should be carried out with care, making sure each time to check that the ratchet pawl is engaged before releasing the wheel. Remember that the crown wheel is greasy and probably dirty.

Broken pin on winding spindle

To replace a broken pin on the Polyphon-type of winding spindle, make sure that the spindle is supported, and punch out the remains of the old pin. Take a new nail, slightly oversize, and file it *exactly* to the size required. Tap the nail gently into place until $1/32$ inch is protruding from the opposite side of the spindle. Support the nail and peen the end protruding so that it may not easily be withdrawn. Cut the length of the nail to size and the job is done. Make sure that the head of the winding handle will move freely over the peening to properly engage the new pin.

Jammed coin chutes

Where a coin-operated machine is being used by a number of people, it is possible for the coin chutes to become jammed with money. The jamming is rarely caused by bent coins but is far more likely to be caused by coins inserted after the machine has run down. Someone puts a coin in the slot and nothing happens; they either leave the machine or put another coin in and then leave. The next person puts a coin in and from there, since the coins are not being allowed to move on to the coin

MINOR ADJUSTMENTS AND REPAIRS

drawer, a jam starts which, even when the machine is wound, will not clear itself. The chutes must be removed for the jam to be cleared, and this necessitates removal of the bed-plate assembly.

Remove the four screws or bolts which hold the bed-plate to the back of the case and take off the bed-plate. The chutes are held by small screws to the back of the case, the side of the case and top of the back of the motor cover. Remove all screws and the chutes can be taken out. At the back of the chutes is an open slot through which it is possible to reach the coins with a screwdriver. Remove them towards the entry! When all have been removed, check for free passage in the chutes by entering a coin several times at the top, holding the chute at its normal angle, and making sure that the coin runs through freely. Check again after replacing the chutes and before replacing the bed-plate.

Vibration noise of chutes

An annoying rattle during play can often be traced to the vibration of the chute(s) against the back of the bed-plate, or possibly of one chute against another where they join. This can often be cured if the chute is touching the bed-plate by inserting a piece of soft material between the two pieces. If a more workmanlike job is required, the bed-plate must be removed as before and a means found of fixing the chute a little closer to the back of the case. This is done by bending the bracket which holds the chute. When doing this, make sure not to bend the metal of the chute. Where one chute is touching another, a similar method can be used to put them a shade more apart from each other. In each case, test the coin passage before replacing the bed-plate.

Coin problems

There are many small problems which can crop up in the coin mechanism of a disc movement. For instance, if the coin goes into the receiving pan but the machine does not start, it may well be that the counterweight at the other end of the balance arm is too far towards the end of the arm, and so too heavy for the coin to lift. Before moving the weight, make sure that this is necessary by placing more weight on the coin pan—perhaps another coin. If the weight needs moving, there is a holding-screw in the centre of the weight which can be loosened so that

MINOR ADJUSTMENTS AND REPAIRS

the weight may be properly set. The weight should be moved inwards until one coin is just enough to lift it. Tighten the holding-screw when the weight has been reset.

If the machine does not stop at the end of a tune, a possible reason is that the counter-weight is too far in and so too light to hold the balance arm in position when the coin is released. In this case, move the weight towards the end of the bar to add weight to that end. Should the counter-weight be missing altogether, a narrow piece of sheet lead can be cut and wrapped round the arm to provide the necessary weight. Adjust the new weight properly and then pinch it to the arm with a pair of pliers to keep it in position. Another possible cause for the movement not stopping at the end of a tune may be that the stop-tail is loose. The adjustment of this has been dealt with earlier in this chapter under the heading 'The governor assembly'.

Should the coin leave the coin pan before the movement can start, there are several possible causes. If the machine is a Symphonion it may have the type of coin receiver which is made from two separate pieces of metal held together at the base by a spring. Normally when the arm is tilted to release the coin, the two flaps of metal are forced apart and the coin drops. If the spring holding the flaps together is weak, it is possible for the coin to drop straight through. In this case, the spring must either be re-tensioned or a new spring made in the pattern of the old one, and fitted. This can be done fairly easily with music wire. If the machine has either a flat pan for the coin or a slot pan of the one-piece type, both of these are held in position by either a spiral spring or a weight. When the coin is released in the normal way, the pan is tilted against the tension of the spring or against the weight until the coin is dropped. If the spring is weak it will allow the pan to tilt with the weight of the coin and so allow the coin to fall through without activating the machine. If the bracket holding the weight is bent or misaligned this too may cause the pan to tilt too easily by lessening the counter-balancing effect of the weight.

In the case of a weak spring, the same method can be used as for the springs on the governor fans described earlier in this chapter under the heading 'Running too slow'. Where a weight is involved it is necessary to correct the angle of the bracket. It is more probable that some part of the mechanism is interfering with the movement of the weight, rather than that it is not working for its own reasons. The adjustment is a matter of trial and error.

MINOR ADJUSTMENTS AND REPAIRS

Coin-stop bracket

On most upright machines there is a bracket, fixed to the case, with its face at the end of the coin pan. This bracket is there to stop the coin falling out of the pan before it should. It sometimes happens that the coin pan comes into contact with this bracket as it is moving down to eject the coin, and so is unable to complete its movement, thus allowing the coin to remain in the pan. This, of course, affects the stopping of the movement at the end of the tune.

It is as well to remember, however, that normally the bracket has *not* moved, so that the cause of the fault must be looked for elsewhere. It may be that a weak return spring on the coin pan is causing the trouble, or the centre pin (see below) which is the fulcrum of the balance arm is loose. It is not the immediately obvious which is necessarily the real problem.

The balance arm

Some of the problems of the balance arm have been already discussed under other headings. One major problem is that of side play at the centre pin. Symptoms of this ailment might be that the machine does not stop, perhaps because the arm which should enter the stop hole on the time wheel is out of alignment and so misses the hole, or possibly that the stop arm at the coin end does not properly inhibit the governor and so allows the machine to continue play. Correction of this condition depends on whether it is the actual pin which is moving or the sleeve which fits over the pin. If the sleeve is at fault, the chances are that it has parted from the arm where it was joined. If this is the case, it can be soldered back on the arm, making sure that it is at the correct angle. Should the pin be broken, a new one must be of the exact design and measurements of the original. This type of part is best left to specialists to make.

Stop/start devices

Although almost all machines, both upright and table models, use the time wheel method for stopping and starting, there are some table models which use different devices for stopping. In particular, many 15½-inch Polyphon table models use what could be described as a

MINOR ADJUSTMENTS AND REPAIRS

pop-up arm. In this method, the disc has a slot in its surface near the periphery holes and at the end of the tune. When the disc is at rest, a metal arm is raised through the slot from beneath. When the stop/start lever is operated, the arm is lowered at the same time as the governor is released. When the lever is set at stop the arm rises to rest against the underside of the disc; entering the slot on the disc—when it reaches the correct position—to cause the movement to stop. By this method, the disc itself is acting as a time wheel.

There are two main causes for the failure of this method of stopping. One is that the spring which holds the lever pressed upwards against the disc may be weak or broken, in which case it must be replaced. The other reason is that the lever which should enter the disc slot is possibly out of alignment, and so unable to rise up at the right time. In this case it is a simple matter to realign the lever. One more reason of course is that you might well be playing the type of disc, albeit of the same size, which does not have a slot for the lever to enter. Some 15½-inch Regina discs, for instance, do not have a slot, though playable on a Polyphon.

A similar type of stop arm is used in the Stella and other machines of this style. In this case the stop/start lever is at the side of the disc normally, and when the lever is operated, an arm is raised from a position pressing on to the edge of the disc. The disc has a cut-out in the edge at the correct position. When the stop/start lever is released, the arm rides on the edge of the disc and enters the cut-out at the end of the tune, allowing the stop arm beneath the movement to enter the governor. The main cause of failure in this device is lack of spring tension on the arm.

The over-riding device

On nearly all large upright coin-operated machines there is a device for activating the movement without the use of a coin. This device is a piece of shaped heavy wire which runs through two wooden blocks screwed to the back of the case. The arm is controlled by a removable key and operates by pressing down the balance arm when the key is turned. The key is removable for obvious reasons and few, if any, of the original keys remain. It will be found, however, that an ordinary clock key of the right size will turn the arm. The wire arm, being set in blocks of wood and depending solely on friction to keep the action tight, is subject to gradual loosening if used a great deal. If the arm is loose, or one or both of the blocks cracked, it may be necessary to replace the blocks

MINOR ADJUSTMENTS AND REPAIRS

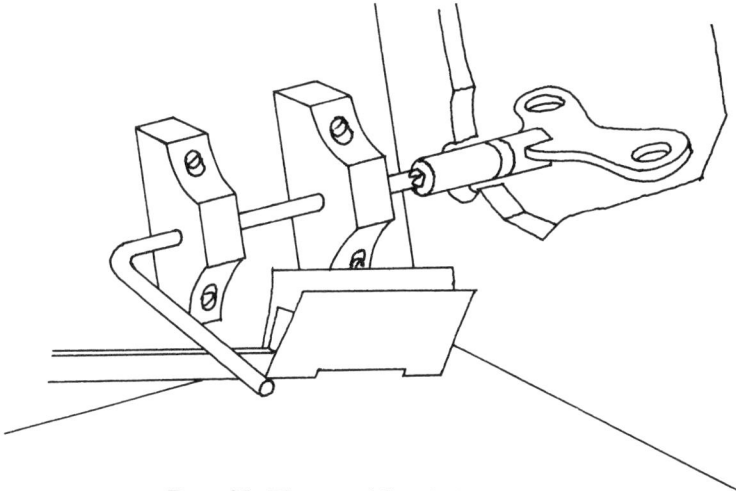

Dwg. 25. The over-riding device in action

entirely by making and drilling two blocks of similar size to the originals. Drill the holes undersize so that the arm must be forced through, but not so small as to risk the new blocks splitting.

Play in the winding mechanism

It is most important that the parts of the winding mechanism do not have too much free play between them. There is always the danger, where there is sloppiness, of a 'run', causing severe damage to the machine. In particular, the setting of the crown wheel and the bevelled gear on the winding spindle should not be allowed to get sloppy. If it is thought that these parts are not meshing properly, it may only be necessary to add a distance washer to the packing behind the bevelled wheel on the spindle. If this is found insufficient, a little more dismantling will enable extra packing to be placed above the crown wheel. Before starting any job of this nature, make sure that *all* pressure is off the spring.

The ratchet wheel

In most disc musical boxes the ratchet wheel is held firm on a round winding spindle by a holding-pin which may go right through both ratchet wheel and spindle, through the spindle and resting in a slot in the

MINOR ADJUSTMENTS AND REPAIRS

top of the ratchet wheel, or possibly through the spindle and resting in a slot running through the centre of the wheel. On occasions this pin may be found to be broken, allowing any tension put into the spring to be released through the winding spindle. On most machines this particular fault can be repaired without dismantling the movement, but of course the movement should be taken from the case and put where it is easy to work on. In general, the ratchet assembly is held in place on the winding spindle by a split-pin. When this is removed a washer may be moved along the spindle so as to expose the spring washer which activates the ratchet pawl and the ratchet wheel beneath. On larger machines there may be two spring washers, and two ratchet pawls. The remains of the holding-pin of the ratchet wheel may now be knocked out, making sure to support the spindle, and a new one made from an oversize nail *exactly* the right size, inserted and knocked home. No play should be allowed between the ratchet wheel and the pin since we are using softer metal than was originally used. It goes without saying that if a replacement pin is available this should be used. When replacing the split-pin, be sure it is firmly in place.

Ratchet pawl

Wear is unusual on a ratchet pawl of a disc machine, owing to the practice of using a spring washer to draw off the pawl when winding to return it when winding is finished. There is however a possibility that either the screw holding the pawl, or the spring washer, may become damaged or loose. In either of these cases, unless one is skilled enough to make replacement parts, it is recommended that the help of a specialist repairer is sought. These pieces are so vital to the machine that only first-class work will do. Should the problem be lack of tension in the washer, it is possible to put more of a kink in the metal and so renew the tension.

Bent teeth in large wheel

Occasionally it is found that a group of teeth in the large wheel of the machine, usually on top of the spring barrel, are bent over so as to make it difficult for the wheel to mesh either with the drive wheel or with the first wheel of the endless train. This is generally caused by the machine having been wound too strongly, so as to jolt it at the end of the wind,

CARE AND REPAIR OF DISCS

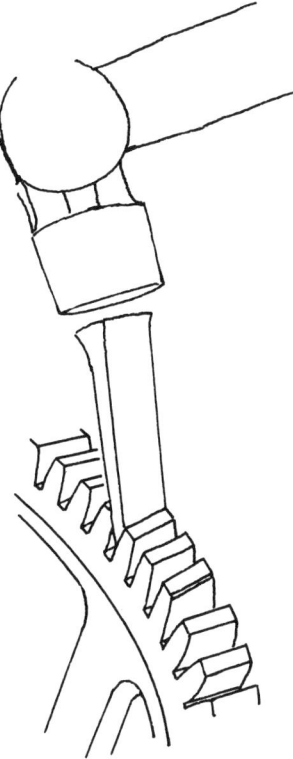

Dwg. 26. Straightening teeth in the large wheel

or possibly by the machine having been 'raced' at some time. Racing is when the machine is fully wound and pressure then applied to the winding handle in order to make the disc play faster. This was a fairly common trick in the days of commercial use of these machines.

If the teeth are not so badly affected that the metal is cracked, though it has to be said that this is rarely the case, it is possible to straighten and clean them off so as to make them nearly as good as new. What is required is to make up a punch of mild steel, filed to a shape at the tip as wide as the teeth and as fine as is necessary to allow entry between the teeth. Using a hammer, tap the teeth *gently* upright with the punch. Make sure all are exactly upright and in line with the other teeth. Clean off any burrs with a file. If any cracks are now apparent, the teeth will need replacing.

MINOR ADJUSTMENTS AND REPAIRS

Replacing teeth

If, for any reason, several teeth in the large or big wheel need replacing, the need for a perfect job in making up and shaping the teeth is so important that it is probably better to admit to limited skills and give the work, at least of supplying a shaped section, to the professional.

Fortunately, particularly with Polyphon, new wheels are available. This does not mean, necessarily, that a replacement wheel should be fitted, though if enough teeth are in a bad state this is an option to be considered. What it does mean is that, through the last few years, damaged wheels have been replaced by repair men, and have been kept for exactly the sort of repair we are discussing. So, because of the availability of new pieces, old sections are available, and not at the cost of cannibalizing a damaged machine that might be repairable at a future date!

Though it may make the work more cumbersome, it is necessary to replace the section of teeth while the spring is in its cage. The reason being that there will be no change of stresses, other than the normal winding of the spring, when the job has been completed.

Offer up the replacement section to the damaged part of the wheel and decide what length it needs to be, to replace all the damaged teeth, cut it to size, so that each end represents a gap in the wheel teeth, and shape up and finish the joining edges for soldering.

Use a clamp to hold the section on the surface of the wheel exactly where it is to go, and scribe round it with a sharp instrument to give the area to be taken out of the wheel edge. The section must enter the main body of the wheel at least as deep as the teeth are long.

If a flexible drive drill and an appropriate abrasive disc is available, use this to take out the section to be replaced, leaving a shade of metal round the edges of the cut to finish with a good file. Offer up the new section continually during the final stages, until the fit is *perfect*. Nothing less will do! The height of the teeth and their spacing at either end of the section must be exact.

When both wheel and new piece are exact and ready, solder into position in the normal way, using flux rather than spirits of salts, because of the possibility of leaving some in contact with the spring. Even so, do not forget to clean up properly after obtaining a good join!

Before putting the whole together again, examine the meshing of the entire wheel carefully to check for binding or slipping. Wash off the flux, clean up the job and all is well. Do not worry about this type of re-

MINOR ADJUSTMENTS AND REPAIRS

pair being permanent; as many as twenty-five teeth have been put into one wheel in this way! Provided the job is well done, it will be as good as new.

BED-PLATE ASSEMBLY

Removing the star wheels

On examination it may be found that the star wheels of the gantry assembly are in need of individual attention. Where they are broken or worn, it is necessary to remove them from the gantry so as to be able to treat them properly. In case of excessive rust, refer to the heading 'Rust affected star wheels' in the chapter 'Rust Affected Bed-Plate Assembly'.

First remove all combs and dampers so as to leave the gantry free from encumbrance, apply penetrating oil to its whole length, and leave overnight. In most cases, the rod which runs through the centre of the gantry to form an axle for the star wheels is held at one end by a plate and at the other by a taper pin. The pin should be removed together with the plate. It should now be possible to grip the star wheel rod at the outside end of the gantry—the end farthest from the centre dome of the bed-plate—and gradually ease it completely through until it is free. If there is any problem, *do not* attempt to push the rod. Take care that there are no burrs worn in the end of the rod by the star wheel guard which may cause difficulty in pulling the bar through. As the star wheels are freed, remove them and keep them carefully *in order*, together with the height wheels. It is most important that the rod be *pulled* through. On no account attempt to tap it from the other end, the brass pieces which separate the star wheels are quite thin and might buckle and jam the rod thoroughly. Should it prove difficult to move, apply more penetrating oil and allow time for the oil to work. A twist of the bar might well free it, but great care is essential. A damaged gantry is difficult and expensive to replace. Should the object of removing the rod be to take off one or two star wheels for work to be done on these only, it is not necessary to do more than pull the end of the rod past these wheels and remove them, leaving it in that position until the work is done and the star wheel replaced. If it is required that all the star wheels be removed, it is essential that they be kept in correct order so

MINOR ADJUSTMENTS AND REPAIRS

that they will go back into their original places in the gantry. To do this something is necessary upon which to thread them, such as a knitting-needle, or a piece of wire. An ideal thing for instance would be a letter spike.

Removing light rust

Should the object of the exercise be to remove accumulated light rust and dirt from the star wheels, dip them first, if possible, into a bath of degreasing fluid, or at least brush them well with the fluid. When all grease has been removed, each of the wheels in turn can be cleaned by rubbing on a piece of very fine emery cloth (180 grade), on a piece of plate-glass, or something similarly flat. The wheels can easily be held on the flat surface with the fingers. Remember always to keep them in order; they should come off one threaded pile on to another threaded pile, and none should be displaced.

The operation of rubbing these wheels on a flat surface will, in effect, also tell whether they are all absolutely flat, or if any of the teeth are bent out of line. When such a tooth is discovered, take time out to straighten it in a vice with pliers so that, when clean, the wheels will also be quite ready to return to the gantry. The cleaning operation is finished by cleaning between the teeth with emery stick or similar, so that the whole of the wheel will be bright. This operation should be carried out in one go, so that there is no possibility of mixing up the star wheels.

Wear on teeth

While the wheels are being cleaned, it is a good idea to examine for wear on the teeth. Should there be much wear on even one point, then the whole wheel is useless, since it will not turn once it has reached this tooth. The wheel must be replaced with a new one.

Replacing the star wheels

Before replacing the star wheels in the gantry, the star wheel rod must be cleaned and examined for wear. If the rod has been worn, it should be replaced, following the relevant part of 'Rusted star wheels'. The gantry must also be cleaned, using fine garnet paper for the slots, and very fine burnishing paper for the top and side surfaces to give a good finish. Lightly oil the rod.

When all is completely ready, the star wheels can be threaded back one by one as the rod is pushed home. As each star wheel is returned to its place, spin it round a few times to test that it is free. If it is not free, find out why, and cure it before continuing. Finally, fix the rod in position and the job is done.

Dampers

The dampers, brakes, and damper bars are dealt with in full in the chapter 'Disc Musical Box Dampers'. This subject is fraught with problems and no attempt should be made to move them without careful study of the chapter.

Slipping discs

Periphery drive discs may slip as they rotate, usually for one of two causes. Either the disc edge is dished and so slips on the drive wheel, or the drive wheel is not at the proper depth to allow the domes which enter the periphery holes to penetrate fully, or not parallel with the holes. Where the disc is at fault the answer can be found in the chapter 'Care and Repair of Discs'. In the case of wrong depth, some way must be found for the drive wheel to come into closer contact with the disc. To make the drive wheel parallel with the holes is simply a matter of moving it along the drive shaft. Under normal circumstances, the motor assembly is fixed rigidly in position, as is the bed-plate assembly. This being so, unless something has been done to alter this permanent setting, there is little possibility of a distance change to cause the depthing of the wheel to be wrong. It will probably be found upon examination that the depthing has been altered, either with a misconceived notion that it was necessary, or by accident when the machine was last put together. In either case, once the cause is found—perhaps misplacing of either of the assemblies, or packing under the bracket of the pressure arm—the remedy is fairly simple. The domes of the drive wheel should enter the disc periphery holes fully, but not so deeply as to cause the disc edge to dish.

In the case of discs slipping on a centre-drive table model, it is probably for one of two reasons. Either the centre wheel is slipping on its

MINOR ADJUSTMENTS AND REPAIRS

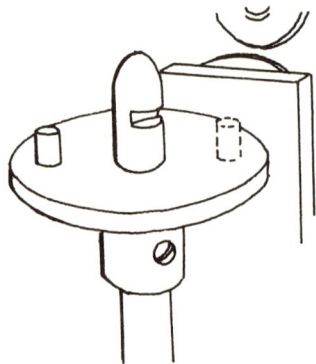

Dwg. 27. Centre drive wheel showing grub screw

spindle, so that the wheel and the disc remain still while the spindle rotates with the motor, or the centre wheel may be too low so that the drive hole(s) in the centre of the disc are being allowed to slip from the drive pin(s). Where the centre wheel is slipping on the spindle, the grub screw(s) which hold it firmly to the spindle are probably loose. It is a simple matter to tighten the screw(s). Be sure when doing this that the drive pin(s) on the wheel are in the correct position so that the disc stops exactly at the end of the tune. A centre wheel which is too low may be put at its correct level by loosening the grub-screw. Bring the wheel up on the spindle so that the top surface of the wheel is in line with height wheels on the gantry. Here also ensure that the drive pins are lined up correctly before tightening the grub-screw.

Crackling discs

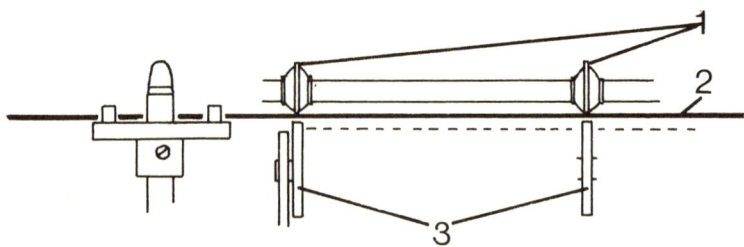

Dwg. 28. Correct position for disc
1. pressure wheels   2. disc   3. height wheels

MINOR ADJUSTMENTS AND REPAIRS

Should the disc make a crackling sound during play, the reason is usually that the disc is rotating at the wrong height. If the projections of the disc are not in good contact with the star wheels, they may often ride over them—making the noise—instead of turning them. The remedy for the crackling is to bring the disc nearer to the star wheels by adjusting the pressure-bar. If the machine is a small one it may be that the centre casting of the pressure arm has been bent out of position so that it does not bring the bar fully into the firm contact with the disc which is necessary. In larger boxes it may be that the bracket of the arm needs adjusting. The ideal position for the disc to play well is for it to be held between the pressure heels of the arm and the height wheels of the gantry without too much room to move up or down.

Loss of some notes

Should the movement appear to be playing less than its full complement of notes, it may be due to the problems described above. It may also on some machines be due to the centre spindle being misaligned. Should the spindle be even slightly out of true centre, it may result in projections missing star wheels. It is sometimes quite easy to examine the playing of a disc by running the movement while out of its case. If this is possible it will be seen whether the problem is caused in this way. The spindle may then be adjusted and tightened.

Honing the teeth

Like other operations described in this book the honing of teeth is work that should only be undertaken if considered absolutely necessary. If it is undertaken then great care is needed to prevent permanent damage. Since it is quite easy to do such damage, anyone who intends to do the work should obtain a second opinion from an expert before the undertaking. The fault may very well lie elsewhere.

The presence of wear on tooth tips is easily verified by removing the comb and examining the underside of the tips with a glass. In severe cases a 'step' will have been worn in the tips. This is a fault more common in coin-operated disc machines, simply because they have had much more use than domestic models. Usually the bass and middle register teeth are more affected because of their extra weight. To remedy

MINOR ADJUSTMENTS AND REPAIRS

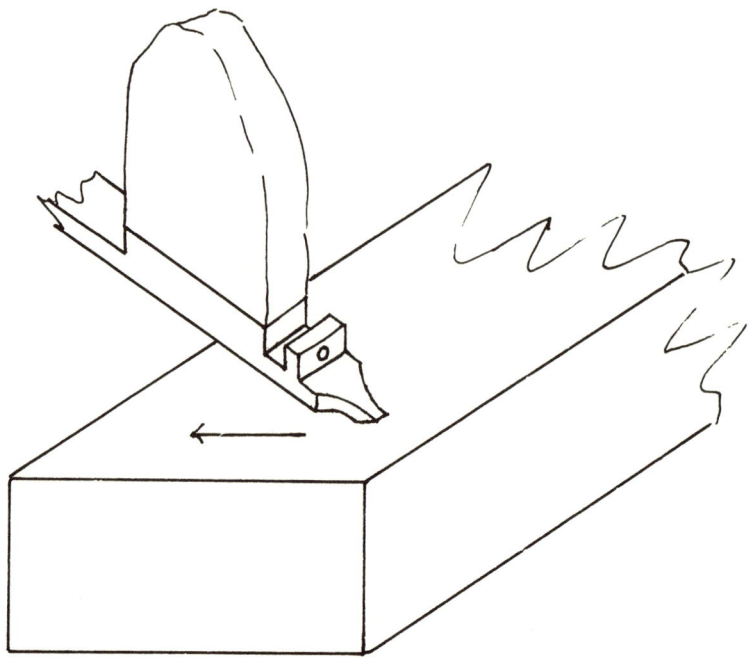

Dwg. 29. Honing the teeth

this, it is necessary to hone the teeth, remembering that afterwards it will probably be necessary to do some tuning.

Before commencing the honing, it is vital that the teeth of the comb are carefully checked to make sure that all are in a straight line, with none of them bent either up or down. Should one or more of the teeth be bent, see the heading 'Straightening bent teeth'.

What is required is to remove the very end of the tooth tips, while leaving the tips the original shape. The shape is that of a blunt chisel, with the bevel at the top of the tip.

Obtain a new 8 inch sharpening stone, and paraffin to lubricate it. Fix it to the bench in some way so that it will not move. Holding the comb, upside down and tilted toward you at the correct angle to match the existing bevel, place the tips at the far edge of the stone and draw the comb toward you. If the comb is longer than the stone, hone the lower part first. Check the tips after each movement, don't forget that the last fraction of wear will disappear when the edges of the tips are slightly

MINOR ADJUSTMENTS AND REPAIRS

blunted. Repeat this movement, taking the comb off the stone before it reaches the edge, so that it does not slip off. Only hone in one direction, toward you. When satisfied that sufficient has been done, repeat the action with the rest of the comb, remembering the treble end has far less metal. With a straight-edge, check very carefully that the tips are all *exactly* in a straight line. Finally hold the comb upright, again exactly, and impart the blunt edge in the same manner, being sure once more to check that all the tips are exactly in line.

It is vital to remember at all stages of this most delicate operation that metal is being removed from the teeth of the music comb. If too much is removed it is irreplaceable, and the whole musical box is spoiled!

Straightening bent comb teeth

Occasionally it is found that a tooth of the comb is bent out of alignment with the rest. It is obvious the problem requires a cure, since even one such tooth will make a difference to the playing of the movement. While one is tempted to say leave it to the expert, there are a couple of ways in which it is possible to cure the problem.

Both makers and repairers of earlier years, aligned or straightened teeth by spreading the metal on the opposite side of the tooth to the direction in which they wanted it to bend. In other words, with a tiny shaped anvil underneath, the top surface of the tooth was tapped just behind the bend. The very slight elongation of the metal caused the tooth to straighten. The same method can be used to bend a straight tongue of metal. This course is not recommended, since it needs lots of practice to do perfectly, and it is easy to break the tooth.

A less dangerous method is the one in general use today. This involves heating the tooth with a suitable soldering iron, while bending it by pushing on the iron gently to take the tooth past the point at which it is required to set. Use the iron as hot as possible. Should this not prove effective, run some solder on to the tooth and repeat the process. The solder forms a good medium for the heat.

Metallurgists say flatly that this amount of heat will not affect the metal of the tooth to any degree. There is no doubt, though, the method works well in practice. The heat will, however, affect a tuning weight, so if the tooth has one, leave it to the expert, unless you allow the weight to unsolder, do the work, and refix the lead.

A friend of the author, who does his own repairs, has described how

MINOR ADJUSTMENTS AND REPAIRS

he straightens teeth. He has made up a mini medieval torturer's finger breaker, a small cramp with a screw. The tool fits over the tooth, and gradual pressure is applied by turning the screw, until it is straightened. This method also works well, and dispenses with the need for heat, leaving no cleaning up to be done.

Where the comb tips are to be honed, the line of the tips must be exact. In this case, near enough will not do. If there is any deviation in the line *at all* do not hone the tips!

REPLACING BROKEN TEETH

The techniques for replacing teeth described below have been well tested over the years. The repair industry has by now split up into a variety of specialists, though some repairers still do the bulk of the work themselves. Above all, toothwork, however fondly the client imagines it being done by the dealer, usually finds its way to a specialist in this department. In one workshop alone, over five thousand teeth have been replaced by this method. It has the advantage of being relatively quick and simple, and it allows the best chance of doing a good job. With top quality work, it is hard to find the new tooth by looking at the top of the comb. This is one aim, the other, of course, is that it cannot be found by sound either. A word of advice: if you have no knowledge of the working of metal, do not attempt to learn by working on a musical box comb!

Remember the comb is the instrument upon which the movement plays. If this is damaged beyond repair, the rest of the movement is useless. There are many ways in which to ruin a comb; a major one is the application of too much heat!

Tools and equipment:

Large electric soldering iron—at least 1000 watts (see below)
Flexible drive drill
1 inch bonded abrasive discs (often known as Carborundum discs)
Half-round diamond file
Several small good quality files
Small smooth-jawed vice
Larger vice
Blow torch
Hacksaw and high speed steel blades
Bar magnets
Engineer's marking blue paint

REPLACING BROKEN TEETH

Scriber or similar for marking out
Length of soft iron wire
Fine oilstone
Old chisel
Electricians' low melting point flux cored solder (see below)
Baker's fluid
Gauge plate (see below)
Thin engine oil (for quenching)

Soldering iron

The aim is to get a large amount of heat to a small area as quickly as possible. A professional generally uses a gas fired soldering iron for this work. If one is available, then use it.

Abrasive discs

These are not easy to get in small quantities. In England Messrs. John Quayle Dental Manufacturing Co., Derotor House, Dominion Way, Worthing, have been found helpful. In the U.S. perhaps one of the many 'Hard to Find' catalogues.

High speed steel blades

This type of hacksaw is by far the best. Ordinary carbon blades will wear too quickly.

Solder

Electricians' low melting point flux cored solder is recommended for several reasons. It has a very low melting point, the lowest of any common solder. It creeps readily into tiny spaces, and is available in small diameters. It is cored simply because this is usually the only way it can be bought, though the author heard from Dr. Frank Metzger recently that he had obtained an even better colour of low melting point solder, matching the comb steel more nearly. If this is available, then of course it can be used. Ralph Heintz, too, has recommended pure indium, available, at least in the United States, as 'Tix', in a tube of 25 sticks. This,

REPLACING BROKEN TEETH

too, has a very low melting point, lower than the solder used for the leads originally, and so very useful. There is a 'Tix' flux to go with it.

Gauge plate

Gauge plate is recommended for the following reasons: it is about the right sort of steel; it is obtainable in a thickness of 3/32 inch, and happily this is about the overall measurement of the thickness required for a normal tooth; its surface is ground to a very similar finish to that of comb teeth.

It is obtainable in sizes from ¼ inch to about 6 inches in width, and is normally 18 inches long.

Preparing the comb

Fix the comb right way up, in the larger vice by dropping two large old screws through two of the screw holes, and tightening the vice up on these, after covering the jaws and top surfaces of the vice with fibre board or similar to stop heat running into the metal of the vice. Take up the slack of the vice jaws, then tap the screws down as you tighten, until the comb is very firmly held.

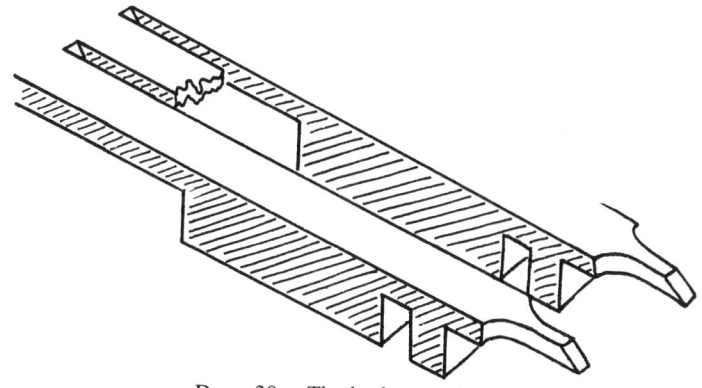

Dwg. 30a. The broken tooth

Using the flexible drive drill and a suitable abrasive wheel, grind a slot into the comb. The slot should be exactly as wide as the original tooth, and at least 1½ times as deep into the metal as the tooth is wide. Take the cut into the comb base as shown in drawing (a).

REPLACING BROKEN TEETH

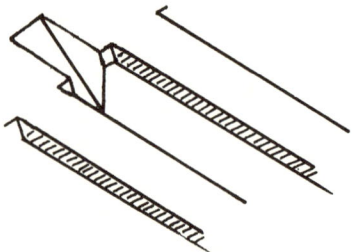

Dwg. 30b. The slot prepared

Because the hand held tool cannot be held at an exact right angle, there will be some slight bias to the slot. Try to keep it as upright as possible, but do not worry. The important thing is that the top of the slot is cut straight and true. The slot will also tend to follow the shape of the wheel. This does not matter either. What does matter is that great care is taken that the wheel does not mark the top surface of the comb, or wander on to any other teeth.

Preparing the tooth

Paint the gauge plate with the engineers blue, and with the scriber, mark out a shape as wide as the tooth and about $1/16$ inch longer than required, including the heel to enter the comb. Use the top of the plate as the top of the tooth, and keep to the way of the 'grain' of the metal-lengthways.

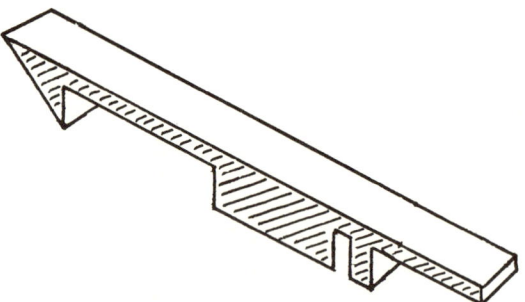

Dwg. 30c. Tooth ready to be positioned

Using the hacksaw, cut out the shape very carefully. With the embryo tooth in the smooth jawed vice, clean up the sides, shaping the size more exactly if necessary.

N.B. If at this stage or any of the subsequent stages, the shape of any part of the tooth is damaged, scrap it and cut another!

Shape up the underside of the tooth to match—exactly—those on either side, except for the heel that is to enter the comb, and the tuning area (vibration point). This latter should be taken down to, say, about 5–10 thou. oversize, to allow for tuning later, unless the tooth requires a lead weight, in which case an exact match is made since tuning will be done with the weight.

When all is done and ready, shape up the heel as shown in the drawings. The sides of the heel are left perpendicular for the depth of the tooth, and then slanted in so that the flat of the underside is about half the width of the topside of the heel. A straight line is taken from the back edge of the tooth to the front edge of the heel. Take great care to make a *very* good fit between the top of the heel and the cutout in the comb.

What you should have now is a tooth which seen from above fits exactly into the top of the cutout in the comb, has a square 'tip', and is $1/16$ inch longer than the other teeth.

Place the tooth in position and hold it there by placing the bar magnet across it and the teeth to either side. The heel should rest exactly in place.

Hardening and tempering

Take the new tooth, finished except for the tip, and the lead (if required), and wrap its body with a couple of turns of soft iron wire, leaving a good nine inches length of wire. Holding the tooth by its wire, take the torch and play its flame on the tooth. Take up the heat until the metal is an overall bright red, and quench it in thin engine oil. Make sure the tooth enters tip first. If it enters the oil sideways it may distort. Clean up the top side of the tooth on an oil stone. Place it top side down on a small sheet of copper and heat again by holding the flame under the copper sheet. Take the heat to mid-blue, and quench in water. Clean off fully. The tooth is now ready to go into the comb.

Soldering in the tooth

Offer up the tooth to its new home. If it is an excellent fit, place the bar magnet in position, and make extra sure the tooth is parallel to the others, the centre line in line for register.

REPLACING BROKEN TEETH

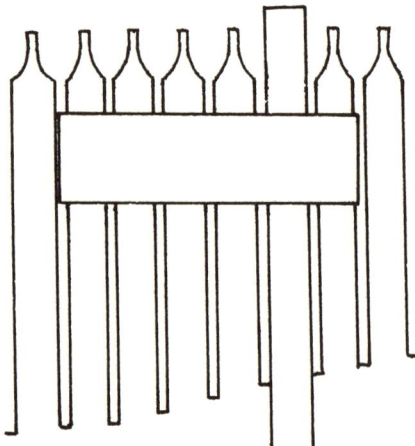

Dwg. 30d. Ready for soldering

Get as much heat as possible into the iron, flood the area with Baker's fluid, and place the tip of the iron about ⅛ inch behind the heel of the tooth, on the surface of the comb. Apply solder to the iron tip to make a pool of solder over and behind the heel. This serves two purposes; it creates a good medium for the heat, and will, as soon as the area is hot enough, creep round the edges of the heel to fill the hole below. Keep an eye on the underside of the comb, and as soon as the hole is filled with flowing solder, remove the iron.

When the area has cooled, clean off the surface solder with an old chisel, finally dressing the heel and its immediate surrounds with a fine oilstone. If the job has been done well, it will be hard to see the join!

Baker's fluid will quickly rust the metal if even the smallest part is left. It is essential to treat the comb. Wash in detergent and rinse. If *'Horolene'* or a similar clock cleaner, is handy, completely submerge the comb in the solution for several hours; if *'Horolene'* is not available, apply a strong solution of bicarbonate of soda to the area. This will react by bubbling up. When all reaction is finished, or when the *'Horolene'* has done its work, wash the whole comb in hot water with detergent, rinse in hot clear water, and dry before a fan heater or on a radiator.

Shaping the tip

The tooth is now firmly in position. The shaping of the tip has been left until now, first because it is easier to match it to the rest when it is in po-

REPLACING BROKEN TEETH

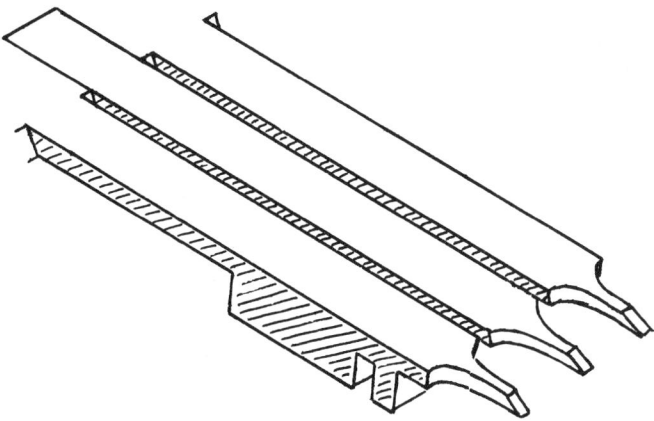

Dwg. 30e. The finished tooth

sition, but, almost more important, also because its shaping will place some strain on the new join. If it is a poor one, it will show up while the work is being done.

With the comb again in the vice, wrap a piece of blotting paper round a small block of wood and press it against several of the tips to find the register—the distance between each tip. Use this measurement to mark the exact centre of the new tip. Hold the new tooth firmly with one hand, and shape up the tip roughly with an abrasive wheel in the drill. Because the work is so delicate, and in so sensitive an area, if you are at all worried about using the wheel, use the half round diamond file. In any case use this to finish the shaping, remembering the underside, as well as both sides.

If preferred, the tip can be shaped up before the tooth is fixed. If so, however, the point must be left proud to allow for slight error in the soldering, and the fitting of the tooth has to be exact in every way, the final shaping of the tip must be to the star wheel position on the gantry.

Tuning weight

If the new tooth is at the bass end of the comb, it will require a lead tuning weight. For advice on making and fixing this, see 'Replacing Lead Tuning Weights'.

Tuning

Finally we come to tuning. Advice on this, for both leaded and unleaded teeth, is to be found below.

REPLACING BROKEN TEETH

Before returning the comb to the movement check that all has been done as well as possible, and make sure the rest of the comb surface is clean. Check once more that the tooth is exactly the same length as the others, and perfectly in register.

Extreme bass tooth

Study of the comb of almost any disc musical box movement will show that the extreme bass tooth is thicker than the rest. It is the one unique tooth in any comb, because its tuning is much lower than that of the tooth next to it. It is thicker to allow for a heavier tuning weight.

The different size of this last tooth on the comb needs to be remembered, since to put a tooth into the comb that matches the next one

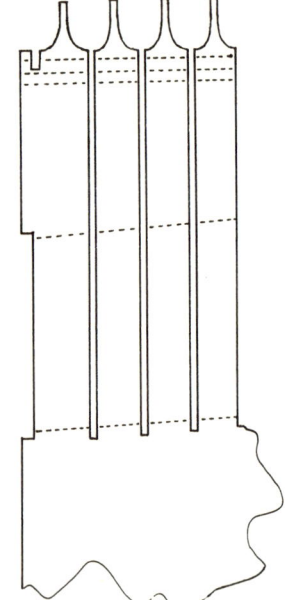

Dwg. 31. Extreme bass tooth

would not only look wrong, but would sound wrong, since it could not be tuned to a low enough pitch.

Not only is the size of the tooth different, but it is also set in the comb differently when replaced. Though it is possible to set it the same as the

REPLACING BROKEN TEETH

others, we have the opportunity, since it is the last tooth on the comb, to set it in a way that, if done properly, will give a better cosmetic result. The tooth is fashioned so that it has, not a heel, but a tongue of steel that replaces part of the actual comb. It is also possible to use this method where more than one tooth is missing from the very end of the comb. A single block of teeth, though, is obviously more difficult to make!

Preparing the comb

Set the comb in the large vice, as already described. Use the engineer's paint and scriber to mark a line exactly in continuation of the inner side of the broken tooth, from front to back of the comb. With the abrasive disc, cut along the line as carefully as possible. Take care only to cut for the depth of the comb, and not into the comb base. On the other hand, be sure to cut right through the steel. Remove the unwanted part of the comb by placing the soldering iron on it until the solder below gives way. With an ordinary file, clean the comb base free of solder, leaving it clean. Use the diamond file to even the cut end of the comb to a perfect line.

Shaping the tooth

Always be sure that the new tooth (or teeth) will look right on its comb, and be a perfect fit. In particular, unless the join is perfect the result will not be so good as if the other method of tooth setting has been followed.

Fitting the tooth

When absolutely sure of a good fit, place the new comb part in position, holding it there with two bar magnets, one across the teeth towards the tips, the other across the back of the comb. Leaving the joint itself dry, apply Baker's fluid to the top of the join, to keep the solder, and round the comb base, front, side and back, to keep them solder free. Place the tip of the iron on the comb itself, about $1/8$ inch or so from the join, and flow a good pool of solder along and over the join. Keep the iron there until sure the solder has moved into the join and below, between new piece and comb base, but remove it as soon as possible. Clean up and rinse as before.

REPLACING BROKEN TEETH

Tuning the tooth

To tune a tooth with a lead tuning weight, providing the thickness of the metal is correct, all that is required is to find out what the note of the tooth should be by testing the tooth on either side of the new one, and remove lead as in the chapter 'Replacing Lead Tuning Weights' until the note is obtained. Should the scale for the particular comb you are working on be contained in the chapter 'Tuning Scales for Combs' your work will be made easier by knowing exactly what the note should be, and the musical interval from the tooth on either side. Since the notes of the comb may not match the stated notes exactly, it is still necessary to tune finally to the comb itself.

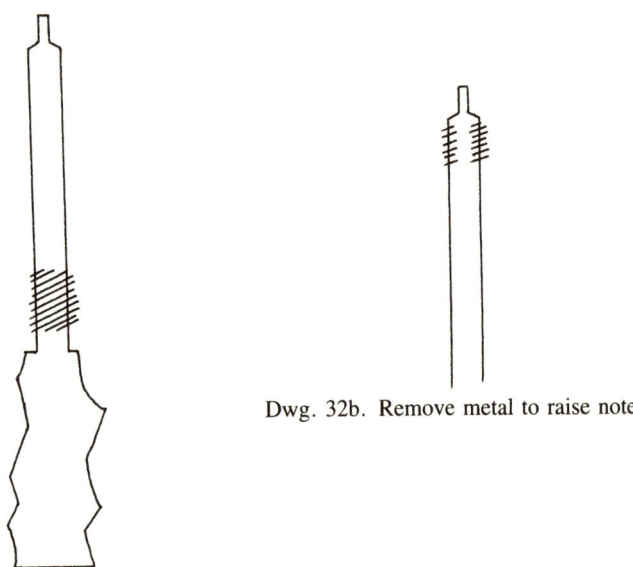

Dwg. 32b. Remove metal to raise note

Dwg. 32a. Remove metal to lower note

To tune a tooth for the middle or upper register of a comb, again compare it as before; however now the tuning is done by removing metal from the new tooth. If the pitch is required to be higher, metal must be removed, with a small flat file, from a point near the tip of the tooth. Take care when attempting this not to file the tip itself. To lower the pitch of a tooth of this nature, metal is taken in the same manner from a point near the base of the tooth at the centre of vibration. Please

REPLACING BROKEN TEETH

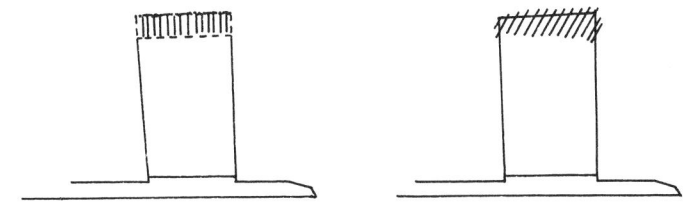

Dwg. 32c. Remove lead to raise note   Dwg. 32d. Add lead to lower note

remember that it is very difficult to correct the fault of removing too much metal. If at all worried, lower the note by adding a touch of solder to near the tip. Constantly test the note until it is as perfect in pitch as you can make it. At this point it is easy to say it is 'near enough'—but nothing short of exact *is* near enough.

REPLACING LEAD TUNING WEIGHTS

Attached to the underside of all musical box combs at the bass end are lead tuning weights. These are pieces of lead, decreasing in size from the bass upward, whose purpose is to slow the speed of vibration of the teeth, and so obtain a lower note in relation to the length of the tooth. This is necessary since to have teeth of the length required without added weight would not be possible in the space available.

The weights of some disc boxes, especially table models where the movement is enclosed and the lead does not have access to a free air flow, are prone to disintegration into a white powder. The loss of weight which results from this phenomenon causes the notes which are affected to become higher, and so make the comb out of tune. The reason for the prevalence of what, in this sense, is a disease of the lead, has been a subject of discussion for years.

Whatever the cause of the problem, the resulting loss of tone has to be dealt with, and in serious cases it is necessary to completely replace the lead on the comb. The job is not an easy one and calls for some skill with metal soldering, and a good ear for music, or at least a friend with a good ear. With patience and these attributes it is however possible, and the result, if well done, will repay with interest the time spent.

The reason for the method

It will be found that even those teeth which are without a tip, because they fall opposite the rider wheels, are leaded. This points to the fact that originally the lead was attached to the comb in a shaped block, and then cut in some way through the gaps between the teeth. Although at the time of manufacture it would have been simple to cast the blocks, set them on the combs, and cut them, leaving only the final tuning to

REPLACING LEAD TUNING WEIGHTS

do, these operations are not a proposition for dealing with the old comb. If the cutting of the lead block were attempted by hand, the saw is bound to run off the line of cut. There is also the danger of breaking teeth or removing metal from them with the saw. With this in mind it is obvious that we must do the job by a method totally different to that used in manufacture. Here is a list of the tools and materials required for the job, all of which are readily available.

Some small lead blocks (see 'Preparing tools')
A panel beater's hammer
A good instant heat soldering gun
Cored solder
Bakers Fluid (killed spirits of salts)
Feeler strip (see 'Preparing tools')
An old tooth-brush
An old chisel (or similar)
Pair of *very fine* end-snips (see 'Preparing tools')
Several small files
Penknife (or similar)
Pair of tin-snips
An anvil (or similar)
A vice
A good comb (from the same make, size, and model) *or*
A tuning scale and a good ear

Preparing the tools

The small lead blocks should be some 2 inches square, and roughly twice the thickness of the width of the teeth of the comb to be worked on. 'Feeler' strip is the metal strip used in the tuning of a motor-car. It is now obtainable in lengths from a motor repair supplier. The thickness of the strip varies, and that required is of a thickness to be a good fit between the teeth of the comb. When buying the strip of this size, try to buy also a piece which is a little thinner, as this may be useful later.

Method to be used

To replace all the weights it will be necessary to take off the original leads. A bench is best for this job, and since it may require more than

REPLACING LEAD TUNING WEIGHTS

one period of work it would be best if it were done in a place where it can be left undisturbed.

Preparing the comb

The comb must first be screwed firmly upside down to a block of wood by using several of the fixing screw holes, and fixed in such a way as to allow complete access to both sides of the teeth to be worked upon. The wooden block may then be placed in the vice with the teeth facing toward you. The vice must first be set in a convenient position to make the work as easy as possible.

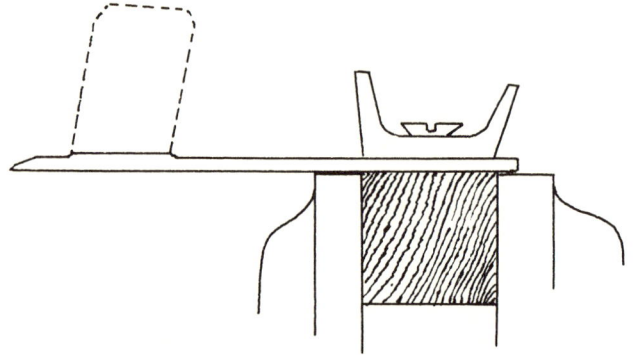

Dwg. 33. The comb on a wooden block and firmly in the vice

It will be found when the comb is in position for work that the weights are not at right angles to the teeth but sloping, and in some cases the weights at the very end are shaped so as to miss some projection on the bed-plate. It is most important to take note of the angle at which the weights come off the teeth, and to copy this angle and any other irregularity to be found so that the comb will fit properly when the work is done.

For each weight there is a small platform on the underside of the tooth, and the old lead must be taken from this in each case by unsoldering with the gun, and scraping with the old chisel so that every part to be soldered is fully cleaned of all material, leaving the platform ready to take the tinning which is the next step.

REPLACING LEAD TUNING WEIGHTS

Tinning the comb

Tin all the platforms by putting a thin layer of solder over each one. Take care to remove any solder which goes on to any part of the comb other than the platforms, and particularly any which gets between the teeth.

Preparing the lead

Although strip lead is fairly easy to obtain in the sizes that we may require, it is proposed to use lead in the region of twice the thickness of that required, so as to allow for work hardening. Ordinary strip lead is too soft for the job in hand, and we must make it tougher in some way, so that it will not bend easily. Using the anvil and the panel beater's hammer, beat a small block of lead so that it spreads and gradually thins to the thickness of the end lead; this will be found to be thicker than any of the others, which are of uniform thickness. Regular tapping will give a better result in the end, and cause less strain, than heavy battering. Care should be taken to keep the thickness as even as possible throughout. When the thickness required for the end weight is reached, use the saw to cut a portion from the lead of the right width and a little extra length. Allow a little more all round, so as to be able to trim the shape with a file to get a good clean look to your new weight. After removing sufficient lead from the bulk to make the largest weight, continue the beating until the whole of the thickness is exactly that required for the rest. Each side of the lead must be as smooth as possible so that there is no chance of the weights fouling each other once they are on the comb.

Cutting the weights

When the lead is of the exact thickness required, it will have assumed the shape of a piece of rolled-out pastry. Strips must be cut from this with the tin-snips to make the weights. Although these are all of the same thickness, they graduate in both length and width (depth along the tooth). Each piece of lead will have to be that much smaller in two dimension than the last, and although we know, or should know, the graduation of width, we may not know the graduation of height. We may not be able to cut more than one resonator at a time—in order to be as

REPLACING LEAD TUNING WEIGHTS

close as possible to the desired height. The less trimming we have to do once the lead is on the comb the better, and the safer.

Preparing the weights

It is necessary now to ready the first (largest) weight for fitting to the comb. If the height of the original is known, then the piece of lead is shaped almost to this, leaving it a little proud, and to the width required. The end which is to be attached to the comb must be cut to the angle required. The angle is critical, as is the perfect fit of the lead on to the platform on the comb, so that great care must be taken at this stage. Offer the lead up to the tooth, and make quite sure of the fit. Scrape the corners of the new weight with the knife so that the job looks as neat as possible. The weight may now be fitted to the tooth. This operation is described later.

Square off the straightest edge of the hammered lead and cut a strip of the right width for the second weight. Although the strip will make several weights which will graduate in width, it is better to cut the strip a uniform width. From the strip obtained, cut a piece to correspond in height to the first weight (now on the comb). Shape the lead as before, and just as carefully attach it to its tooth. This process is continued until all the weights are on the comb. Keep any small pieces of lead for use when the very small weights are required. As the job progresses it will be possible to judge more accurately the length of the next piece of lead needed.

Attaching a weight

When fully satisfied that the new weight is perfect in every way, tin the end to be attached by applying a thin coat of solder. At the same time make sure once more that the platform of the tooth to be fitted is clean and tinned. Cut two pieces from the feeler strip, and push them into the gap on either side of the tooth to be worked on. This will serve two purposes. Firstly the strips form a cradle for the lead to rest in and to keep it in the right position, and secondly they will prevent any solder from getting on to the leads on either side. Place the tinned lead exactly in position and hold it there with the point of the knife. With the soldering gun in the other hand, press the tip against the top of the tooth (which is

REPLACING LEAD TUNING WEIGHTS

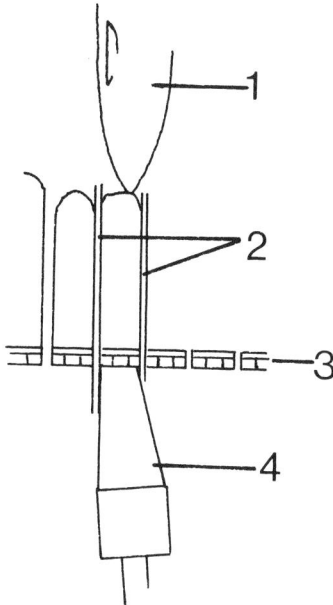

Dwg. 34. Attaching a weight
1. knife 2. feeler strip 3. comb 4. soldering iron

underneath); the part of the strip coming through the comb will help to position the gun. Watch the joining of the lead and the tooth platform carefully, and as soon as a little solder begins to seep from the join remove the gun. Keep the knife in position for a little while longer, making sure not to press so hard as to run the risk of breaking the tooth. Remember to remove the gun at the *earliest* possible moment, since too much heat will affect the fixing of the weights on either side. In the case of the end weight, the process is the same, though using only one piece of feeler strip, and taking a little more care perhaps to make sure the join will be good before using the gun. As soon as the weight is fixed and cool, remove the feeler strips and make sure that the join is good; if necessary, clean away excess solder. The weight is now ready to be tuned.

For the replacing of *very* small weights it may be possible simply to use some solder rather than cut what would be a minute piece of lead. Simply run as much solder on to the platform of the tooth as can be contained before the solder runs off from its own weight. Make sure that none of the solder is left to touch the weights of the teeth on either side.

REPLACING LEAD TUNING WEIGHTS
Tuning a weighted tooth from another comb

The tuning of a weighted tooth, or for that matter any tooth, needs a good ear for music. If you are not sure of your ear, then it is far better to have someone with you who is capable of discerning one note from another, than to attempt to go it alone and possibly ruin your work. It is well to remember that the object of the exercise is to put the comb back into tune, and not to present a pretty piece of metal work. The most beautiful job of soldering will not make a scrap of difference if the notes are not sounding as they should.

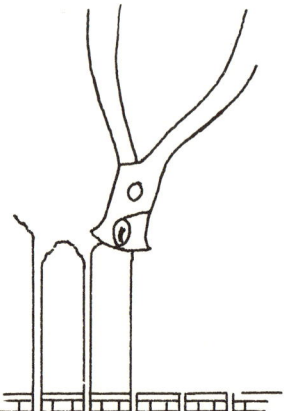

Dwg. 35. Using the fine end-snips to 'nibble'

By far the best way to tune a comb is to find a really good-sounding comb from the same type of movement, and use it as a basis upon which to build the tuning of the releaded comb. The problem which presents itself is that even two combs from identical movements may well be a semitone, or even more, out with each other. In this case, to tune the bass notes to the new comb while the treble end is different, would be of no use. The comb to be worked on must be in tune with itself right through, however much it is out with the other comb.

If you are lucky enough to get another comb, first compare the treble teeth on both combs to find out what, if any, difference there is between the two. If there is a difference then follow this difference right through the comb. The scales set down for various combs in the chapter 'Tuning Scales for Combs' contain many cases where the note of a particular

REPLACING LEAD TUNING WEIGHTS

tooth is a shade sharp or flat. Should the comb to be copied have notes of this nature, then they should be included in the comb to be tuned, especially if the other comb is known to have a very good sound. These seemingly small differences often make a comb outstanding rather than good, although, to take this too far would result in discord.

Fix the comb to be copied firmly, so that it is able to sound a proper note. The comb to be worked on is already fixed, of course. When the tuning comb has been set and is sounding well, a comparison may be taken by ringing with the finger-nail first the tooth of the tuning comb and then the tooth to be tuned. The tooth with the new weight should be lower in pitch than the tuning tooth. Using the very fine end-snips, start to nibble small pieces of lead from the top of the weight (furthest from the teeth), sounding both teeth in turn all the time until they begin to get somewhere near together. When notes are just a little bit out with each other, a warble pulse is heard in the sound when they are plucked together. This is because they are vibrating at slightly different speeds, and this can be seen if the tooth is examined. When this pulse is apparent, the slightest piece of metal removed will make a difference; it is imperative, therefore, that extreme care is taken at this stage, remembering that it is much easier to take metal off then to put it on again. With care, however, the exact note can be obtained so that the two teeth are vibrating in perfect time with each other. If the combs are close together, then the sounding of one tooth can cause the other to vibrate in sympathy. Should the tooth to be tuned be known to be the same note as the tooth next to it on the same comb, then this can be put to good use by tuning until first the pulse and then the good clear sound emerges. Provided one is certain of the perfect pitch of the next tooth, it is always better to tune to that, rather than to tune to another comb.

It is not a good thing to take a note to 'near enough'; it is always best to tune to what you consider perfect before going on to the next tooth. When all the weights are on, and you are sure that the comb is tuned to the best of your ability, go over it once more, carefully, just to make sure. When this is done, do not replace the comb on the movement, but leave it for a few hours and then go over it again. It is easy for the ear to fool one, and it is surprising how much one can be out with tuning after listening intently for a long time. If by chance you have taken too much metal from the new weight, or it is found to be too small for some reason, it is much better to take off completely the offending lead and replace it with a larger piece.

REPLACING LEAD TUNING WEIGHTS

Tuning a weighted tooth from a scale

If you have no knowledge of music then it is far better to make every effort to obtain a comb with which to tune the one on which you are working. Should you be in the position of having no knowledge and no comb, then someone who does know music is essential. Hopefully, you will have the notes for tuning, and the best use of these, once you have made certain the pitch is the same as for your comb, is to tune in octaves from the leadless part of the comb. This is simply to take, say, the lowest 'C' on the still tuned teeth of the comb, and tune the tooth next down which is designated 'C' on the scale, and so on through all the 'C's. Take the next still tuned tooth and do the same, and continue until the whole comb is tuned to itself.

Before octave tuning, it is well to check the teeth from which you are tuning are themselves in tune.

Final tuning checks

When the tuning of the newly-leaded comb is felt to be as good as it will ever be, then that is the time to make certain with one or two final checks. Replace both the tuning comb and the tuned comb on their movements, and place them as near together as possible. You now have the comb in the position in which it will be playing (for resetting the comb, see the chapter on 'Cleaning a Disc Musical Movement'). The obvious thing to do would be to put a disc on the movement, and play it while you sit back and listen to the wonderful change your work has wrought. The chances are, however, that although one major job has been done, there is much more to do to the rest of the movement before the benefit of your efforts can be heard. If the rest of the movement is not ready, simply pluck each note with its star wheel, using the edge of a screwdriver or a similar tool, and match once more—this time on the movement—the notes of the combs.

Matching a pair of releaded combs

Should you have been working on a pair of opposed combs from a duplex movement, then a good way to find if they are in tune with each other is to bolt them securely through two of the fixing screw holes, back-to-back on to a stout metal plate with the teeth pointing upwards.

REPLACING LEAD TUNING WEIGHTS

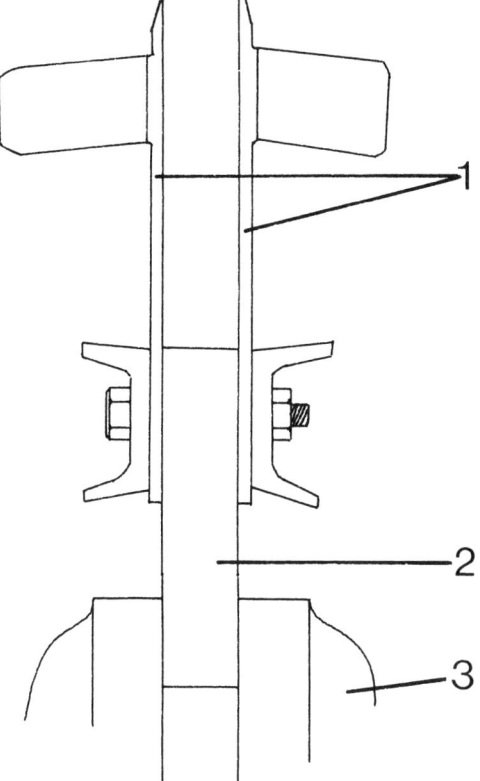

Dwg. 36. A pair of combs ready to be matched
1. combs   2. metal plate   3. vice

The metal plate should have enough spare beneath the combs to allow it to be fixed firmly in the vice. With each of the matching teeth close to each other, it is possible, when sounding one, to see the other vibrate in sympathy. Apart from the by now familiar beat or warble, if the notes are out with each other the vibrations will clearly be seen to differ in speed. When the teeth are in exact pitch with each other they will vibrate at exactly the same speed, and go up and down together.

RUST AFFECTED BED-PLATE ASSEMBLY

A large number of disc musical boxes are found that have suffered, not so much from the wear of their hundred year life, but from bad storage conditions. While, in the main, cylinder boxes are small enough to have been tucked away somewhere in the house, larger disc machines have often been consigned to an outhouse, where both case and movement have suffered badly.

Often, the drive mechanism, protected both by a motor cover or a fully enclosed box, and the oil it has accumulated during its active years, is hardly affected, while the bed-plate assembly, or at least its ferrous parts, is attacked, to a greater or lesser degree, by rust.

This chapter is intended to show how, with the aid of some of the new parts and materials now available, particularly for Polyphon, a seemingly too badly rusted assembly may be rescued.

Rust affected star wheels

It sometimes happens that an instrument is found with its star wheels literally a lump of rust. With new star wheels obtainable for at least the Polyphon, the repair of such a piece is rather less of a problem than repinning a cylinder musical box. In fact the rusted star wheels are treated in the same way as the pins of a cylinder, eaten out with acid.

The whole of the work from start to finish, is described below. Before starting, though, it is well to consider whether to undertake the whole of the work yourself.

It is possible to do all of it except, say, the actual work of decaying the star wheels with the acid, giving only this part to someone who is repinning all the time, and can just slot your job in with the cylinders.

Another possibility is obtaining a new gantry along with the new star

RUST AFFECTED BED-PLATE ASSEMBLY

wheels and other parts. This, though, is likely to be expensive! From a conservation point of view, of course, it is always best to keep the instrument as original as possible.

First it is necessary to obtain sufficient star wheels and height wheels, and a star wheel rod of the correct size. The exact location of the gantry being highly critical, it is sensible to fit locating pins before it is removed. It is then removed, the wheels eaten out, together with the centre bar, new wheels and bar set in place, and the reconditioned gantry returned to its exact position.

Because acid is to be used, a place of work, out of all possible danger, is essential.

N.B. Some very few gantries of early models were made of cast iron. It is obviously not possible to use the method on these.

Here is a list of tools and equipment required. An asterisk means that an explanation is appended.

Star wheels* ⎱ do not start until these are actually in your posses-
Height wheels ⎰ sion and known to be correct
Ground silver steel rod*
Acid container*
Polythene bowl*
Polythene jug
Thermostatic heater*
Sulphuric acid*
Clock cleaner*
Polythene box (large enough to take the gantry in clock cleaner)
Length of brass wire
Drill and bits
Small metal saw
Good small files
Glass or plastic rod
Washing-up liquid
Oil
Rubber apron and gloves
Wood blocks to support bed-plate
Penetrating oil
Clockmaker's taper-pins

Small piece of 1mm. gauge plate
Junior hacksaw and blades

*Star and height wheels

These are available for Polyphons, one size, in fact, fitting most sizes. An exception is some 15½-inch models, where the new wheel will be found to be some 6 thou. thinner than required. Even in this case the wheels can be used with spacers made up from shim stock brass. These are discussed later. Remember, all must actually be in your possession before starting.

*Ground silver steel rod [stainless steel]

Obtainable from good metal merchants in (to my knowledge) lengths of 33.3 cm (approx 13 inches) and 200 cm (approx 6 foot 6 inches). The 13 inch length will normally serve for the star wheel rod. At the same time a length of about 1mm. silver steel rod can be obtained to make the dowel or positioning pins to fix the gantry's position before it is removed.

*Acid container

If the work of repinning a cylinder has already been carried out, or if it is intended to do such work at a later date, the container for the acid can be the same. For cylinders, professionals use a 2 litre laboratory measuring cylinder, since this will contain a cylinder up to 22 inches long and 2½ inches diameter. The easy alternative is a glass spaghetti sauce jar, or any glass container that will take the whole gantry. There need only be enough room to cover the gantry with acid. In fact almost any container large enough will do—horizontal or vertical.

*Polythene bowl

The bowl is used as a 'catch tank', partially filled with water kept at a constant temperature by the thermostatic heater, in which the acid container is stood. In case of accident the acid solution will fall into the bowl of water, rather than cascade over the table or bench. At the same time the heated water will keep the solution at or near the optimum temperature to allow it to work properly.

RUST AFFECTED BED-PLATE ASSEMBLY

*Thermostatic heater

The acid solution works best in warm conditions. Since the place used is, necessarily for safety's sake, out of the way, it is probably unheated. In really cold conditions the acid will hardly work at all! For this reason the container for the solution is stood in heated water.

A heater used for a tropical fish aquarium will produce about 30°C (86°F), and this temperature, though it could be a little higher, will do the job. In general, the higher the temperature, the faster the process. Too much heat, however, is dangerous!!

*Sulphuric acid

The acid required is pharmaceutical (in Britain BPC) rather than commercial. This can be obtained in concentrate form (about 95%) from large chemists or pharmacies. It is highly dangerous if used improperly, and requires great care in handling, whether dilute or concentrated.

For decaying cylinder pins the recommended solution is 7 parts water to 1 of acid. Here, since much more iron is to be decayed, a ratio of 5 parts of water to 1 of acid is better.

This, together, with the recommended temperature, will usually give the required result in about 1 to 2 days.

> N.B. Never add water to acid!! Always add acid to water— SLOWLY, even then, heat will be generated. When handling acid, always wear a protective apron and gloves, and keep a solution of sodium bicarbonate handy to apply to the skin in case of accident.

The solution may be used more than once, but if you keep it, remember to store it properly!

*Clock cleaner

A chemical clock cleaner is excellent for cleaning brass. In Britain 'Horolene' is recommended. It has the added advantage of neutralising sulphuric acid. It is necessary that the cleaner be of the water-based ammonia type.

*Drill and bits

A 1mm drill is required to drill through the bed-plate, into the 'meat' of the gantry at either end, so that dowel or positioning pins can be placed.

RUST AFFECTED BED-PLATE ASSEMBLY

This, together with carefully remembering exactly where the washers between gantry and bed-plate come from, will enable the gantry to be returned to its proper position. The position is highly critical! Other drill bits are required. See where as you read through.

It is now assumed that all the essentials to the work have been obtained.

Preparing the movement

If the bed-plate assembly is from an ordinary upright Polyphon, detach from it any pieces that might interfere with the work, such as the star wheel guard if there is one—though if the star wheels are rusty enough for this method it is doubtful if it has survived—and the pressure arm and bracket. Remove the combs, and remove the dampers and brakes, making sure you remember where washers or packing will return.

Should the movement be of the table or horizontal type, remove also the complete motor assembly, to leave the bed-plate accessible from both sides.

Attempt to get penetrating oil to the area of the holding screws in the tiny space between gantry and bed-plate.

Fixing the gantry position

In fixing the current position of the gantry, we must assume that it has not been moved in the past. The reason for fixing its position is that it is highly critical. To be able to return it to its exact line and height will save many hours of work, not to mention the possibility that even then the whole thing may need to go to an expert to be set up. At least if we fix it with our own dowel pins, only to find it is wrongly set, all we lose is a little time and work.

Make sure the screws holding the gantry to the bed-plate from below are tight, and check to see whether they hold any clue as to whether they have been moved since put in at the factory. If the screws have been moved, continue with the dowelling anyway, the gantry may still be in the correct position, just note the fact for future reference.

Star wheel gantries of Polyphons are normally held to the bed-plate by 3 screws, though there are exceptions: the 6½ inch movement normally has only two; more important is that early 24½ inch movements

RUST AFFECTED BED-PLATE ASSEMBLY

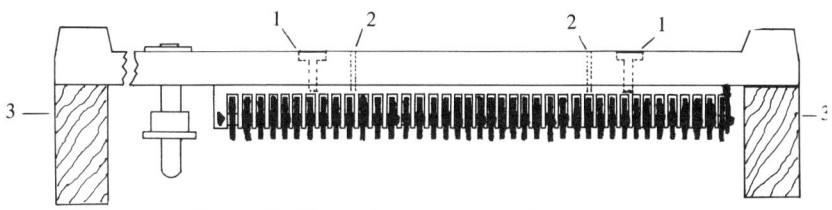

Dwg. 37. Fixing the position of the gantry
1. fixing screws   2. new dowel pins   3. wood block supports

used a 19⅝ inch gantry (3 screws) and an added, smaller gantry (2 screws). In the latter case, 4 dowel pins will be required, 2 for each gantry, but in normal cases 2 will suffice.

Place the bed-plate, gantry down, firmly on wood blocks, making sure the blocks are high enough to hold it from contact with the surface of the bench or table, and wide enough to give a firm seat.

Choose a spot some ⅛ inch inside the first of the outside screws and, using the 1mm drill, carefully make a hole that finishes about 3⁄16 inch into the solid metal of the brass gantry. The feeling of drilling into cast iron is much different to that of brass, and before the gantry is reached by the drill head there is a space, caused by the height washers, between it and the bed-plate that will also be felt—if enough care is taken.

When both positioning holes have been drilled, round off the tip of the silver steel and cut it to length with a good file. Repeat the operation and tap both pieces gently home.

Obviously the exact size of both pin and hole is not critical, but, equally obvious, they must match each other exactly.

Removing the gantry

Now remove the screws holding the gantry to the bed-plate, taking EXTREME CARE to note exactly where each washer or distance piece belongs. Remember that this is vital! Place all pieces belonging to each screw on or with that screw; mark the screw and its hole so that it will be returned to its right place after the job is done. It is usual to give each screw and hole area one, two or three pops with a punch before removing the screws. If, as is possible, the screws are rusted in, do not attempt to drill them out, but shear off the heads. The acid will eat out the rest of the screw and new ones can be fitted.

RUST AFFECTED BED-PLATE ASSEMBLY

Removing star wheels and rod

The steps taken now are the same as for eating out the pins of a cylinder musical box, except that it is not necessary to wait until all the ferrous metal is decayed.

The use of acid is always a potential danger. This operation should be carried out away from the domestic side of the house, and *well out of the way of anyone*, who may come upon it and cause an accident. Remember, too, the hydrogen gas given off during the work is highly flammable, and the fumes are corrosive.

Protect yourself with rubber gloves and apron, because the acid will destroy body tissue. If you are unfortunate enough to get an acid burn, wash the area immediately and soak in a solution of sodium bicarbonate (bicarbonate of soda).

Use the polythene jug to add the acid to the water. One part concentrate is added to the five parts of water by running the acid down a glass or plastic rod that is partly submerged in the water, *using great care*. *Never add water to acid*, or allow even a drop of water to drip into it. It will react violently. As it is, heat will be generated as the acid mixes with the water to form a solution.

Just as carefully, stir the solution with the rod, and, putting the rod down safely, pour it into the container. Wrap the brass wire round the gantry so that it can be pulled out easily, and lower it into the solution in the container so that it is fully submerged but at least an inch away from the bottom. Use some means of suspending the wire above the container to hold the gantry off the bottom, such as hooking it over a stick laid across the top.

When decaying the pins of a cylinder, all of the metal must be fully decayed. In the case of a gantry, it is only necessary to decay some of the metal, so the job is shorter, since in any case we are using a stronger solution, and rust is more readily decayed than clean metal. Using new acid, the process should take, roughly, about 24 hours to take the decaying to the point where all of the rust is dissolved and enough of the metal for the rod to drop down through the gantry to rest with its end on the bottom of the container. When this happens, the rod should fall out when the gantry is lifted from the container and the star wheels will be easy to remove once the acid is safely cleaned off. In fact they will probably fall free during this process.

If the rod fails to fall after 24 hours, there is no problem in leaving the

RUST AFFECTED BED-PLATE ASSEMBLY

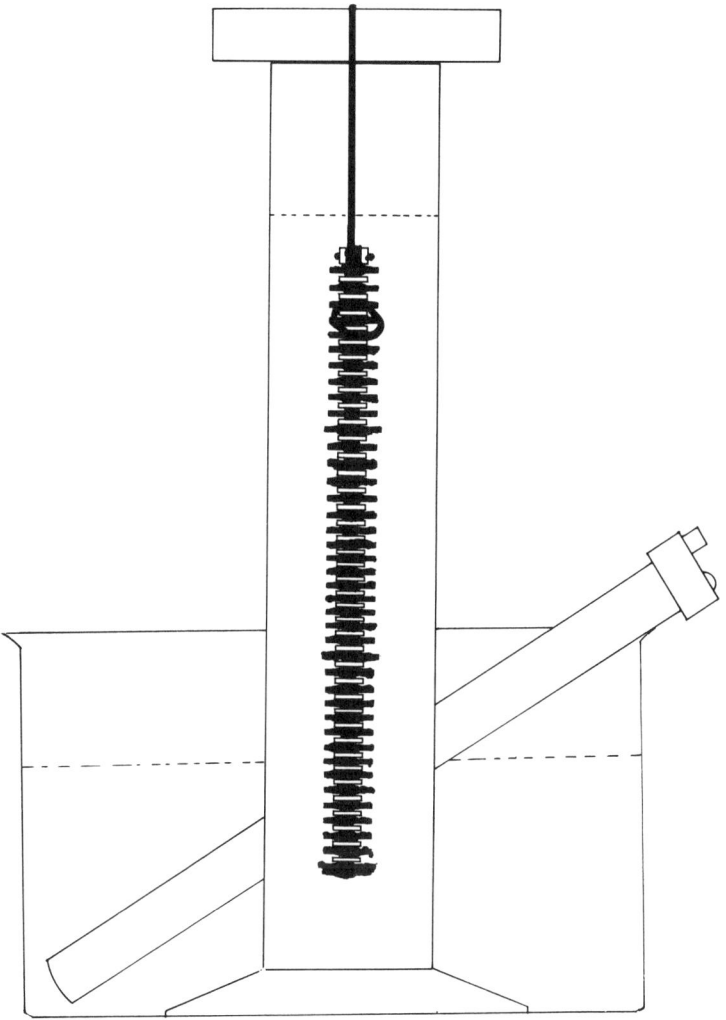

Dwg. 38. Set-up for removing star wheels etc.

acid to work for a further period, always remembering that as soon as all the iron is decayed the acid will attack the brass. Any serious damage to the actual gantry, however, would take at least several days. There is no harm, in fact, in leaving the gantry in the solution until the rod and star wheels have fully decayed.

RUST AFFECTED BED-PLATE ASSEMBLY

Cleaning and preparing the gantry

Using rubber gloves, rinse the gantry under running water to wash off most of the acid, and make sure all of the rod and star wheels are removed, to leave the gantry clear including the hole that holds a taper pin at one end, and the screw hole in the other, outer end, that holds the gantry end plate.

Place the cleaned gantry in a solution of clock cleaner, such as 'Horolene', or a solution of ammonia, to kill the remaining acid, leaving it overnight, or at least for several hours.

Rinse thoroughly, wash in hot water and detergent, scrubbing carefully, then rinse again in hot water, and dry in sawdust. To avoid the new parts starting to rust almost as soon as they are fitted, the gantry must be totally clean and dry, with no residue remaining.

Fitting the star wheels and rod

N.B. It is soul destroying to finish this job, only to find the star wheels round the wrong way. Make sure the strike/pluck sides of the teeth are facing the opposite way to disc rotation! Be sure, also, the height wheels go in their correct places.

The outer height wheel, that which goes next to the gantry end plate, will normally be found to be thicker than the others. One such should have been supplied with the new set.

The gantry end-plate will have been decayed with the rest of the steel, and one will need to be made. This can be done from a small piece of gauge plate steel, the thickness is not critical and can be from about 1 mm. or so.

The rod will need to be cut to length and drilled for the taper pin.

Carefully measure the length of the gantry from flush with the inner end (that with the taper pin hole), to about 3 mm. past the outer end (where the end plate goes). Cut the rod to length with a hacksaw and clean up both ends, putting a good chamfer to the edge of one. Oil the rod and its run, and begin to feed the rod into position, placing height wheels and star wheels as the rod progresses—in the correct way for the star wheels and the correct position for the height wheels. If you do not know where the height wheels should be, the comb(s) will show you when offered up. The rod should go in quite easily. If entry becomes difficult, *stop at once* because you are in danger of damaging the gan-

RUST AFFECTED BED-PLATE ASSEMBLY

try, and negating all the work done so far. Note where the obstruction or tightness seems to be, and sort it out. It may only be a piece of grit.

Making a new end plate

See the main drawings under the heading 'Star Wheel Assembly' for the shape and relative size of this piece.

When the last star wheel is in position, take the rod in a shade more until the outer end is flush with the first height wheel.

Take a small piece of gauge plate about 1 mm. thick and lay it flat on the bench. Place the outer end of the gantry on the plate and with a sharp tool mark out the bottom edge of the gantry and the width. Mark also where the top of the first wheel comes.

Now push the rod through just enough to release the first height wheel. Place the wheel with the top edge on the mark made for it, and etch a circle on the plate, without moving the wheel; etch also the outline of the centre hole onto the plate. Removing the wheel and replacing it, use a straight edge to etch two parallel lines up from the marks for the width of the gantry to the edge of the circle made with the wheel. You should now have a shape similar to a keyhole. Etch a line across the top of the circle to give it a straight top, as in the drawing, and measure and mark a centre for the holding screw hole. This is often found on the original as a horizontal slot, but an oversize hole will do to give room for maneuver.

Having now the shape of a keyhole with two potential holes, the top circle needs to be a shade smaller, say 1 mm. all round, or 2 mm. less in diameter. This is not essential, but it makes the piece more like the original. Find a washer of the right size, and mark an inner circle.

Drill the two holes first: the top one, to take the star wheel rod, more or less exact, and the lower one oversize, but not so oversize the screw head will not cover it.

With the hacksaw, rough-cut the outer shape in the vice, finish it with a good file, and clean up the whole with fine garnet paper.

Before the final fixing, make sure, once more, that the star wheels are facing the correct way.

Final fixing of rod

A screw will be needed to fix the end-plate. The original was a non-standard metric size. In the United States it will probably be found that a

RUST AFFECTED BED-PLATE ASSEMBLY

Unified National will fit. If it is not possible to find a correct screw, the hole will need to be retapped for an available thread.

Hang the plate by its hole from the end of the star wheel rod, and make sure it locates. Fix the plate to the end of the gantry.

At the other end of the gantry, make sure the rod is flush with the end. Use the holes already in the gantry as a guide to drill through the rod for the taper-pin, and fit a suitable size pin. Make sure you go in from the wider end of the hole.

Refixing the gantry

What we should have now is a fine, clean gantry, full of star wheels and height wheels that turn easily. Before returning it to the bed-plate, clean the bed-plate thoroughly, wire brush it to remove any loose flakes of paint, and give it two coats of new paint. Be most careful that no paint goes onto the area that holds the gantry, since, as we have discovered, the setting is most critical.

Clean the holding screws most carefully, removing every scrap of rust, and oil the threads to inhibit further rust. When doing this, handle the screws one at a time, so as not to mix up the spacers or washers, which must now be placed in position as the gantry is refixed to the bed-plate. Remember to set the gantry on to the locating pins properly.

When all is fixed, apply one drop of light oil, perhaps using a hypodermic needle, to the star wheel rod in each gap between the star wheels.

Star wheels too thin

In some cases, particularly with the 15½-inch Polyphon, the star wheels available are found to be narrower than the width required for the space they are to occupy in the gantry slots. It may well be that, by the time you are reading this, new star wheels of the correct width are now available. If not, a simple remedy, if a little makeshift, is possible.

On the 15½-inch Polyphon mentioned, the extra width required is about 6 thou. Brass shim stock of this thickness can be rough-cut slightly oversize to the meat of the star wheel, and drilled with a centre the right size for the star wheel rod. This last is done by clamping them all together for drilling. The pieces, one for each star wheel and height wheel, are then threaded on a bolt, the nut tightened on them, and the whole rounded up to size in a lathe. It is possible to obtain the shims ready made.

The shim must go onto the opposite side of the star wheel to the damper/brake. This is necessary so that the side of the star wheel is in correct position relative to the damper/brake.

RUST AFFECTED COMBS

Before starting on a review of what can be done to remedy a comb that has attracted considerable rust, it must be understood that such a comb can rarely be made to sound as good as one in perfect condition. This having been said, though, a great deal can be done to bring what appears to be a dead comb back to life.

Cleaning a comb

The comb to be cleaned is placed in a chemical clock cleaner such as 'Horolene', made up in solution as directed on the tin. A polythene box with an air-tight lid is used to hold solution and comb. Leave the comb in its bath for about 24 hours, then take it out and rinse it to see that it is free of dirt and oil. When fully satisfied that all that remains on the comb is the rust, wash it thoroughly in hot water and detergent (washing-up liquid will do), rinse it equally carefully in hot water, and dry in sawdust.

Removing the rust

Before any diagnosis can be made, the rust—all of it—must be removed.

Using a chemical rust remover such as 'Rust Eater', a formula made by the makers of 'Turtlewax', remove the rust. The instructions usually tell us to brush the chemical on to the article and leave it for a specific time. It is better to brush it on liberally, then continue to agitate the surfaces with the brush. Do this for about 15 minutes, then rinse the comb and examine it. The remover converts the rust to a grey powder and most of the rust—hopefully—will have been removed. Repeat the operation until *all* of the rust has gone, every scrap, so that only the good metal of the comb is left, damaged and etched as it may be. Again wash the comb, rinse, and dry as above.

RUST AFFECTED BED-PLATE ASSEMBLY

Examining the comb

Rust attacks at random. Some teeth will have escaped damage almost entirely, while others may have been badly hit. In ninety-nine out of a hundred cases, the pitch of the whole comb will have been generally lowered. Normally, this will have had relatively little effect on bass teeth, but the difference will be plain towards the treble end of the comb. This is further complicated by the more vicious attack on some teeth than on others, even when side by side, particularly if the flexing area of the tooth has been affected. Though all teeth should ring now that they are free of rust, some may sound muted. If the damage has been really severe, some teeth may be so badly affected that they need to be replaced, because the difference will be heard in places in the tune where perhaps a mandolin run is set.

Examining for volume

The first examination takes no account of the actual note the tooth will now play. At this stage we must see whether all of the teeth are in relatively good condition, i.e. if they all have sufficient metal left to ring at more or less the same volume. Disregarding the bass teeth for the moment, pluck each tooth of, say, the treble third of the comb, and decide whether this is so. In the case of a pair of combs, test them both in this way, particularly if one shows more damage than the other. If some teeth sound softer than others, you must decide whether these teeth should be broken out and replaced so as to even out the volume. This decision may only be possible when the whole comb(s) are tuned again, or it may be one that does not need to be made because a large section needs to be replaced. This possibility is discussed later.

Examining for tuning

Provided the general tone and volume of the comb(s) is good (if they were not we assume they are now), the next step is to see what can be done for the tuning.

It has already been stated that, in general, rusting has the effect of lowering the pitch of the comb. This being so, it may not be possible to take the pitch up to where it was originally. Remember, too, that where two combs are concerned, both must be at the same pitch! It is quite

RUST AFFECTED BED-PLATE ASSEMBLY

likely, though, that the comb(s) can be tuned to a lower pitch, say one, or even two semi-tones down from the original.

For the moment we can again disregard the bass teeth with tuning weights, because these are relatively easy to bring up by reducing the lead weight. A scale is required, of course, and hopefully one for your machine is to be found among those in the back of this book. Tuning is discussed under the heading 'Replacing Broken Teeth'.

Cosmetic cleaning

Before attempting to tune the comb, dress the top of it with *fine* garnet paper, taking the paper gently over the surface the way of the teeth. This will lose the grey colour left on the metal by the rust remover, and restore the surface to a semi-polished finish. Be careful not to remove any more metal than necessary. Do not attempt, for instance, to remove the pitting and etching caused by the rust.

Tuning

From the top (say) third of the comb(s), take the most badly affected teeth and attempt to bring them up to original pitch. If this is successful, then continue through the comb(s) to bring all the teeth into line. If it is not possible to bring these poor teeth right up to pitch, see how far down you will have to go to get the whole comb(s) tuned to itself. If this is no more than the one or two semi-tones mentioned above, there will be no problem. If not, all is not lost! We have already discussed the possible need to replace a whole section of teeth, and the possibility may have become a reality.

Sections of teeth

As stated, the effect of rust is far more important on the treble teeth than on bass, or heavier teeth. If the damage to the treble end of the comb is so bad that it is necessary, for one reason or another, to replace them, sections of teeth are available for the purpose.

It is not recommended that an attempt be made to make a section of teeth, since it takes more work and practice than the amateur could normally undertake.

Sections of teeth, made to include the whole of the comb section, are available off the shelf for 19⅝ and 24½-inch Polyphons, and this, of course, includes the 22-inch Polyphon with bells. The reason these sizes are readily available is that, apart from the fact that the 19⅝-inch at least is fairly common, the spacing of the gaps between the teeth is ⅛-inch (125 thou.) and this coincides exactly with the automatic spacing on a milling machine. Sections up to 7 inches long and for other sizes and makes are also available, either off the shelf if the supplier has had need to make some, or by order, which will cost more. A section for a Stella, for instance, is difficult to get and expensive, because of the extra hand-filing required for the spade-shaped tooth tips.

It is also possible to obtain new, a completely leaded and tuned pair of combs for the above size Polyphons, ready to place on the machine, but this is a very expensive way of solving your problem. Considerably cheaper would be to buy the combs only, unleaded and not yet tuned, to place on your own comb bases, which will still be in good condition, and follow the instructions in the relevant chapters to complete the job yourself. When this is the case, be sure the combs are hardened and tempered before you get them. Replacing the whole comb is only necessary when the whole comb is virtually destroyed, which, fortunately, is rarely the case.

Replacing a section of teeth

The method of replacing what is, in fact, a section of comb rather than teeth, is virtually the same as that discussed under the heading 'Extreme bass tooth' in the chapter 'Replacing Broken Teeth'. That these are treble teeth is not relevant in this instance, since part of the comb is being replaced.

Because the work is with two metals, some distortion may be caused when the comb is fixed to its base. If the distortion is not more than, say, 1/16 inch, it will tend to correct itself when the comb is set on the bed-plate.

The shaping and setting of the comb piece is, of course, critical, but if a mistake is made nothing is lost but time, and the job can be undone and redone fairly easily. Remember that a good full join is essential for the comb to sound properly.

When the comb is complete again, with everything in order and with the teeth ringing well, the tips of the new teeth must be honed to *exactly* match those of the original comb, before tuning commences (see 'Honing teeth' in the chapter 'Minor Adjustments and Repairs'). Use a straight-edge to make sure all of the tooth tips are exactly level.

Tuning a section

It is important to remember that the section is now part of the whole comb. The tuning is best done in octaves, each tooth of the same note being tuned throughout the comb before going on to the next. If a pair of combs is involved it is obvious they must also be in tune with each other. Equally, all work to be done must be finished on both combs before tuning commences.

Combating distortion

Where a whole comb, or a large section, is soldered to a base, there is often a problem of distortion caused by the joining of two different metals.

Distortion normally has what is known as a 'banana' effect, where the centre of the comb and base is lifted above the ends. As already discussed, if the distortion is not more than about $\frac{1}{16}$ inch, there is little problem. More than this, however, means the fault must be rectified before the comb is set on the bed-plate. The remedy appears to be a little amateur, but it is simple, and it works!

A good solid bench is required, a pair of wood blocks, and a G clamp (C clamp). Place the comb, right side up, with its ends supported by the two blocks of wood, close to the front edge of the bench, with its teeth pointing away from you. Place a piece of padding at the centre of the back of the comb, and set the G clamp so that its screw is below the bench top and the top end of the G on the padding. Gently tighten the clamp, making sure that it is set only on the back of the comb and definitely not touching any part of the teeth. Take the screw up until it is just tight, and inspect the job once more to make sure all is well. Now apply the screw, a little at a time, until the comb and base appear straight, and loosen the screw to see whether the process has taken permanently. If necessary repeat the process, perhaps taking the screw up until the comb is just over the straight, very slightly bowed the other way. Continue, gently and bit by bit, to straighten and test, until the piece conforms to a straight-edge.

DISC MUSICAL BOX DAMPERS

When we talk of dampers in a disc musical box we must naturally include the brakes. Although seldom mentioned, brakes are an integral and necessary part of the machine, and are often fixed together with the dampers on the actual damper rail.

The damper rail

The damper rail is a long, thin piece of metal, usually brass, which runs parallel to the star wheel gantry, sometimes above and sometimes below the bed-plate. Into the rail are set strips of spring metal which extend up between each star wheel on the gantry. The star wheel acts on these, by various methods according to the make and model of machine, to cause them to damp off any tooth immediately before the tooth is plucked. By this method a tooth still vibrating from a previous note is made ready to be plucked again cleanly, and with no metallic sound to mar the note.

The dampers

There are many types of dampers, almost as many as there are different machines, but most of these fall into two main categories. The most

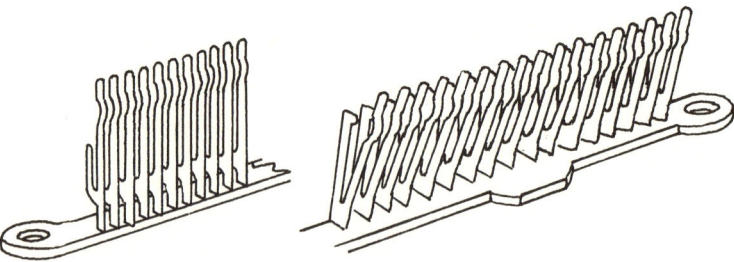

Dwg. 39. Damper rails for a 19⅝-inch Polyphon (*left*) lower rail (*right*) upper rail

DISC MUSICAL BOX DAMPERS

common type, which includes those used in most Polyphons and Symphonions, are those lifted by the star wheel from the tooth as the note is plucked, and allowed to push themselves back on to the tooth by the spring of the metal just before the note is plucked again. Another type, which includes dampers used in most Reginas are those which work with the star wheels both ways. The star wheel pushes the damper away from the tooth when the note is plucked, and when the time comes to damp the note, pulls the damper on as it prepares to pluck the tooth again.

The brakes

Brakes are strips or wires of spring metal which lie against the side of each star wheel under slight tension. The simple purpose of the brake is to arrest the star wheel after the disc projection has pushed it round. The reason for the necessity of braking is that the projection on the disc leaves the star wheel in exactly the right position to engage the following projection. If the star wheel is out of position and if for instance the point of a star wheel tooth was hit head on by the projection, apart from the noise during the tune, damage could easily be caused.

Brakes on many machines are on a rail of their own, and may need separate treatment when adjusting or repairing dampers.

ADJUSTMENT—REPAIR—REPLACEMENT

Damper adjustment

Most disc movements have dampers the tips of which are easily seen rising between the teeth. It is possible to ascertain whether in fact all the dampers are in position; if they are all in position but the machine is playing with the groaning and squeaking noise associated with maladjusted dampers then it may be—if the machine is otherwise in good order—that the dampers can be adjusted with the combs in position. Advice on the adjustment of otherwise good dampers is given at length later in this chapter under the heading 'Individual damper adjustment'. If, when adjustment is attempted, the dampers are not responding, it may well be that adjustment of the complete damper set is required. This is discussed at length under the heading 'Fitting new dampers'.

Since dampers are most difficult to fit properly, it would be advisable not to remove them unless one is sure that this is necessary. The chances are that, if the movement shows every sign that it has not been worked on for many years, the dampers were originally set properly as to height. It is possible that the rail may have slipped back a shade under the tension of the dampers; it is more likely that the dampers themselves have lost their tension.

Renewal of damper tension

If the dampers appear not to be returning fully to the tooth, so that many of them are not working, it may well be that by loosening the screws and pushing the whole damper rail along so that the dampers move a little more on to the teeth, sufficient pressure may be obtained to make the action right again. If, however, there is not room for this maneuver, it might be necessary to remove the damper assembly completely, and alter the rake of the dampers to make them press more firmly on the teeth. If for any reason the dampers *are* removed, remember always to note the washers under the damper rail so that they can be replaced in *exactly* the same positions to keep the height as originally set. If the angle of rake of the dampers has been altered, full instructions for resetting the damper rail are to be found later in this chapter under the heading 'Inserting the dampers'.

Worn dampers

It may be that when malfunctioning dampers are examined, they are found to be worn where the dampers should touch the teeth. Since the shape of the dampers is all important these dampers must be replaced. If more than, say, fifteen dampers on any rail show signs of wear, it would be best to replace them all if possible.

Replacing single dampers

When one or more of the dampers of a disc machine are missing, or so badly damaged as to be useless, it is necessary to replace them. If the machine is a Polyphon, replacement dampers can be obtained.

Making replacement dampers

If your machine is of the type for which a Polyphon damper cannot be used (as it is, or with simple adaptation), it will be necessary to make

DISC MUSICAL BOX DAMPERS

some dampers for yourself, or get someone to make them for you. It will depend on your personal skill whether it is advisable to attempt to make one or more complex dampers and place them in the damper rail. Even a simple damper is not easy to make so that it works. More difficult types will take a good deal of patience and skill. Where only two or three dampers are in need of replacement, it may be possible to take them from the extreme treble-end of the rail and place them in the position needed, without detriment to the sound. This, of course, cannot be done on any damper set containing brakes, unless it is possible to make brakes more easily than dampers, so as to replace those taken from the treble end. *No star wheel should be left without a brake!*

Making a few dampers

Broken or missing dampers numbering up to about six may be made almost freehand. A list of tools required for this purpose is given here. Should a considerable number of dampers be needed, a process for making in quantity is described later in this chapter, together with the tools required.

> Sharp tool for marking metal
> Pair of metal shears
> Several small files
> Very fine emery paper
> Fine round-nosed pliers
> Hand vice (or small vice)
> Junior hacksaw (prepared)
> Two perfect dampers of the type to be copied
> Anvil or similar
> Small hammer
> Some fully hard 30-70 brass (spring brass) or metal more suitable

To prepare the hacksaw for use, file both ends of the teeth of the blade from each side leaving only a fine cutting edge down the centre.

The damper to be copied must be clean and in perfect condition. Tap out any crimpling or bending from *one* of the dampers with the small hammer on the anvil so that you have a flat piece of shaped metal. Do not tap so hard as to spread the metal. Use this to mark the shape required for one damper on to the new metal. Cut the new damper roughly to shape with the shears; if any slots are to be made, leave them at this time. Place the cut-out metal in the hand vice and, using the jaws of the vice as a guide if possible, obtain the exact shape required by using the files. When the shape is accurate and the edges are smooth and clean, use the prepared hacksaw blade to cut any slits necessary. The final silhouette having been obtained, the new damper may be cleaned and smoothed by gently stroking all its sides against the *fine* emery paper held on a flat surface.

All that remains in the actual making is to crimp or bend the new damper into the exact form required by using the second damper as a pattern. Most bends can be faithfully copied with a pair of fine round-nosed pliers. When shaping, try not to kink the damper in any places where it is not required. If a damper is spoiled, it is better by far to make another than to attempt to use a piece which is not perfect. The setting of single dampers into the damper rail is dealt with later.

Making a set of dampers

Making a large number of dampers is made easier by using a more sophisticated method, on the lines of mass production. This involves the use of two templates or patterns of gauge plate. The metal for the dampers is cut roughly to size with shears, and several—up to about fifteen—are placed between the previously made templates and shaped to pattern while they are held together in this way.

Here is a list of tools and materials needed:

Sharp tool for marking metal
Pair of metal shears
Several small files
Very fine emery paper
Fine round-nosed pliers
Hand vice
Small smooth-jawed vice
Junior hacksaw (filed as before)
Two perfect dampers of the type to be copied
Anvil or similar
Small hammer
16-gauge steel plate (.062 inch)
Suitable metal for the dampers (spring brass?)

The templates

Dwg. 40. A template

Obviously, to make perfect dampers the shaping of the templates is all important. Every effort must be made to be exact. The templates can be made in much the same way as single dampers although of course the work will be more difficult owing to the hardness of the metal and the greater thickness involved. An important point to remember is to keep all edges at right angles to the surfaces since if a thin edge is made on the metal by filing on the slant it will not present enough surface to the file when filing the dampers within the two templates. When the templates are exact and perfect the dampers can be rough-cut to size.

Using the templates

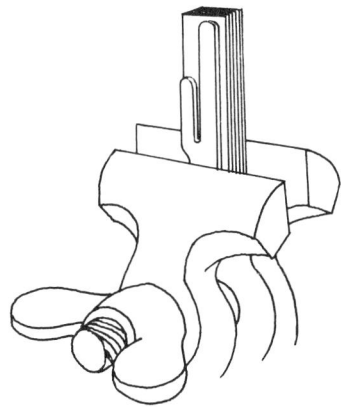

Dwg. 41. Templates and embryo dampers in hand vice

DISC MUSICAL BOX DAMPERS

Set the rough-cut dampers, in between the two carefully-made templates, in the hand vice in such a way as to make it possible to reach three quarters of the sides to be shaped before the set-up has to be moved in the vice. Once the vice is tightened and work has started, all the pieces must, of course, be kept in exact position. Place the whole in the jaws of the hand vice so that one complete side is free on top and the two ends free on each side. If the jaws of the vice are true they can be lined up with the top sides of the templates to give an even better guide. This will also ensure that the templates are in the correct position. For this the jaws *must* be true; if they are not, the templates can be lined up with the eye by looking along the jaws of the vice from one side. Make quite sure before finally tightening the hand vice that there is enough metal proud all round on all the dampers. The hand vice can be placed in turn in the table vice to make the shaping easier. The three sides of the new dampers must be shaped exactly before the position is changed to allow the fourth side to be filed. When changing, it is essential to make sure that the sides already shaped are in perfect alignment. When the shaping has been done to your complete satisfaction, the dampers can be separated and cleaned up individually on the emery paper. Lastly, the bends or kinks can be put in with the round-nosed pliers. A little practice on a spare slip of metal will ensure that you put the kink where you want it.

Dwg. 42. Damper shaped   Damper crimped

Fixing the new damper into the rail

Having secured a new damper, or having made a close copy of the type of damper required, place the damper rail in the vice as shown in the drawing, with the dampers (or brakes) resting on the back jaw of the vice with their tops pointing to the back. The slot for the new damper should be in the centre of the vice and care must be taken to ensure that the rail is positioned so that the dampers are supported by the jaw of the vice. In this way, should more heat than is necessary be used when cleaning out the slot, the dampers will be prevented from moving out of position. When the rail is secured in the vice, remove any part of the old damper from the slot. If a good part of the old damper is still in place it

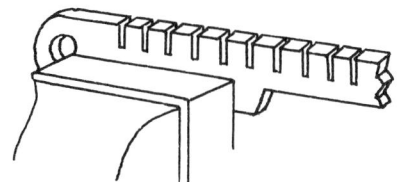

Dwg. 43. Damper rail in vice ready for new dampers

may be possible to lever it out in one piece with the fingers or a pair of long-nosed pliers. If only the base of the damper is left then apply a soldering-iron until the piece can be pushed out with a small tool. To clean out damper slots in a rail, a good tool to make is a tiny saw blade, using a piece of shim stock or feeler blade jagged along one edge with a grinding-wheel or such. The rough edge of the saw can be used to clear the slot of old solder. Make sure that the slot is really clean and flux it. Flux and tin the base of the new damper and push the damper home into the slot; the new piece should be a good push-fit. Be certain that the new damper is of the correct size and that it matches the rest of the assembly in shape and angle. Make especially certain that the 'crimp' of the new damper is exactly in line with the others. Apply the soldering iron until the tinning moves, and the job is complete. After removing the rail from the vice, check once more the position of the new damper, and make sure that none of the other dampers has been put out in line during the work.

NEW DAMPER SETS

Where there are no dampers at all on the machine, and even the rails are missing, then if the machine is a 15½-inch, 19⅝-inch or 24½-inch Polyphon it is possible to obtain complete new sets of dampers. These damper sets can be fitted at home, with patience. Unfortunately the demand for dampers for other sizes and makes of machine is so small that they are not yet produced.

DISC MUSICAL BOX DAMPERS

The new damper sets which are made will not fit all machines of these two sizes, since some 15½-inch and 19⅝-inch machines have separate wire brakes. In such a case it would be better to order dampers and rail separately, because the brake needs to be removed, and the damper placed where the brake would normally be. When fitting the dampers make sure that these separate brakes are in good condition and working properly. The wire which may be required to replace any faulty brakes is normally easy enough to match up and position. Remember, too, there are differences in the 15½-inch comb set-up, and so different sets of dampers are required.

Fitting new dampers

To fit the new damper sets very few tools are needed; what is needed is a good deal of patience and perseverance. Here is a list of the tools required:

Various sizes of shim stock
A drill
A medium screwdriver
A pair of tweezers
Two large darning-needles or jeweller's screwdrivers
Some cheesehead set screws with washers and nuts to fit, or metric screws of the right size.

Preparing the movement

If the machine is of the upright type, first take the bed-plate assembly from the case and place it on a bench or table so that the work can be done in comfort and in sufficient light. Remember to place a platform under the end of the bed-plate nearest the bass teeth so that the tuning weights do not touch the surface of the table and force the teeth upwards. Remove the pressure arm by taking out the two screws which attach it. Take off the star wheel guard, a strip of metal which is made to spring into place when the disc is removed. This strip is pushed on to the centre rod of the gantry at each end and has a spring at the top end, near the dome on which the disc rotates. Take out the screw holding the spring, and then gently lever the guard off the centre rod with a screwdriver; the guard can then be lifted away complete. Take care not to lose

DISC MUSICAL BOX DAMPERS

the screws since they may be awkward to replace. We have now only to remove the combs and we are ready to start work. When the combs are removed, it can be seen there are two holes on each side of the star wheel gantry, one at the bass end and the other some two inches from the treble end. These are the holes used to attach the original dampers.

Preparing the job

Since there is a slight variation in the fitting of the sizes of damper rails we will first assume that the ones to be fitted are for a 19⅝-inch Polyphon; the 24½-inch size will be dealt with afterwards. If metric screws of the right type have been obtained, that's fine. If not, it is necessary to make it possible to use other screws to hold the damper rails in position. If it is easy for you to retap the holes, then the 4ba screws can be used without the nuts. Should you favour the simplest way, then the drill should be used to make the existing holes larger to take the 4ba screws. The screws may then be used as bolts with the nuts on the underside of the bed-plate. If it has been decided to bolt the damper rails, use the drill with the appropriate size of bit to ream out the holes to the right size. When doing this take care to keep clear of the mechanism. When the holes are ready, the next step is to adjust all the star wheels so that they are in the 'ready to play' position, which is with the top tooth pointing slightly 'over the hill' of the gantry. The positioning can be done with any small, straight edge, a matchbox being ideal. One edge is used to jockey the star wheels to the point required. The positioning of the wheels in this way will help when attempting to get the dampers between.

Inserting the dampers

On all machines where double combs face one another, there are an upper and a lower comb. The side on which we set the first damper rail is the upper side. The two damper rails are different on the Polyphon in that the rail for the upper comb also contains the brakes. Although we usually talk only of dampers, the brakes which go with them are of equal importance since they are placed at the side of each star wheel, held against it by the spring in the metal, to prevent the wheel turning freely. If there were no brake the wheel would be carried on by the momentum given by the disc projection, and would then be out of position when the next projection was presented.

The rail for the upper comb contains the brakes for *all* star wheels, and the dampers for only those star wheels (every other one) which operate the upper comb. The brakes are nearest the centre of the gantry when in position, and are perpendicular from the side view of the damper rail. The dampers are behind the brakes and lean outwards from the side view. Both rails and dampers are raked over to press against the star wheel on the side.

The upper comb

Take the damper rail in both hands and, holding it by the rail, lean the rail away from the body. Attempt to engage the treble end first and with a combing motion—most gently—(making sure all brakes and dampers are in their right gaps), ease the assembly down between the star wheels until the base of the rail is flat against the bed-plate. The first brake and damper will be held together in the gap between the first star wheel and the end depth wheel. After that there will be a brake in every gap, and a damper in every other gap. No attempt should be made to do any more than get the brakes and dampers well home at this stage. When all are nicely in position and the rail flat down, the rail can gently be pushed towards the bass end until the screw holes coincide with the holes in the bed-plate. Insert the screws and top washers but do not tighten, although the nuts may be threaded on and the one at the bass end made *almost* hand tight.

Adjusting for depth

First ensure that all brakes and dampers are well slotted in and then push the rail against the slant of the dampers until they are *almost* upright. If the dampers are not upright enough, the lower part of the damper will be caught by the star wheel behind it. Tighten the end screws fully to hold the rail in that position. Do not worry about the height of the dampers at this stage.

We now have to check whether the dampers are at the correct depth into the star wheel assembly. Using any small tool which comes to hand, turn the first star wheel at the treble end gently. The ideal is that when the star wheel is turned, the damper will be seen to move first out and then in again as the tooth of the wheel pushes against the D-shape of the damper. If the damper is too far in, there will be little or no action and the assembly will need moving out slightly. Should the star wheel catch the damper so that it pushes it on to the wrong side, then more depth is needed. When satisfied that the treble end is correct, tighten up the screw and, loosening the bass-end screw, do the same to this part until the whole damper assembly is working well. We can now be fairly sure that the notes will be damped when the comb is replaced. We must now decide *when* the note will be damped.

At this stage the largest possible lateral movement of the dampers should have been obtained.

Adjusting for height

The height of the damper assembly is as critical as the depth. There is little likelihood that when the rail is flat on the bed-plate the assembly is too *high*, since the new dampers are made a little lower to cover this possibility. It is normally necessary to add a little height and this is done by placing shim washers on the screws between the rail and the bed-plate of the machine.

The D-shape towards the top of the damper should be nicely nestled in the gap between two teeth in the star wheel when the star wheel is in the position it would have had immediately before plucking the tooth. The damping action on the tooth would, in fact, be operating at that instant. If in doubt as to the position of the star wheels, it might be well to fit a disc to the machine and run it round by hand, making sure of normal contact between the projections and the star wheels, until the gap between the beginning and end of the tune is reached on the disc. Most of the star wheels should then be in the right position, and any that are not can be lined up.

Should the dampers appear to have the right height, then leave them, with just a final tighten up of the screws. If this is not the case, it is necessary to make some thin washers from the shim. The best way to do this is first to drill a hole of the right size in the shim, and then cut round the hole to make a small ring. If the shim is thin enough it can be cut with scissors. Loosen the screws and, taking great care not to upset the depth setting of the dampers, lever up the rail gently. Take out one screw at a time, slip the right amount of shim between the rail and the bed-plate and in line with the screw holes, and tighten the assembly down again. Try to do this right the first time, and then check the damper action once more; if they are not all moving well and freely with the star wheels the adjustment is wrong, and it is no good going any further until the fault is remedied.

Testing with the comb

Only when you are sure the dampers are working really well should the next step be taken. If all is as it should be, then put the comb in position carefully, and secure it with every other screw. Now test the treble notes by pushing the star wheels round gently and slowly. When the note is plucked and it sounds clear, continue the movement of the star wheel until the note is about to be plucked again. The damper should come into play and cut the notes cleanly before the star wheel plucks the tooth. If instead of being cut cleanly the note ends in a buzz, the damper is either not coming on at all or coming on too late. This may well be caused by the dampers being set too high, so that less shim may be required. Test for the length of the comb to see if this fault is the same all over, and if so take off the comb and adjust the height. If, when tested, the note does not sound at all, or very little, the dampers may be too low and need more shim, or it may be that the rail has not been pushed along enough when first secured.

Continue the adjustment and the testing until a good 95 per cent of the dampers are working well— now it is time to start adjusting individual dampers.

Individual damper adjustment

To adjust individual dampers it is necessary to bend the top part of the damper one way or the other. To do this, the damper must be supported so that only the top is bent without affecting the whole length of the metal. There is very little distance between the teeth to allow much room for tools, so that two pieces of thin metal are required. One of the best methods is the use of two jeweller's screwdrivers.

First test each damper by turning the star wheel and sounding the note. Watch carefully the action of the damper and listen to the note of the tooth at the same time. Where you are certain that the damper is acting *perfectly*, place the star wheel in a different position to the others or, if you prefer, mark the tooth in some way. When the whole length has been tested in this way, concentrate on the first damper in the line which is not working properly. Having ascertained whether the top of the damper requires moving nearer to the tooth or further away, take a screwdriver in each hand. Place one against the damper a little below the D-shape and on the side towards which the damper is to be bent. The other is now used to bend the damper into what is thought to be the right position. Always remember to err on the side of caution when adjusting. Continually test the action with the star wheel until the damper is *perfect* in performance. When you are satisfied, mark the tooth and carry on to the next one needing setting.

When at last all the dampers appear to be working correctly and a final check of all the star wheels has been made, it is best to set the movement up so that a disc can be played. Although at this point we only have one comb in position, we are not listening to the tune but to the individual teeth. If the movement is out of the case (as of course it will be) it is possible to see under the disc and, with the aid of a torch, view the star wheels as they turn. If the job has been well done up to now, there will be only a few dampers still not correctly set. By watching the star wheels and listening to the notes as the disc revolves, these dampers can be pinpointed so that, when the tune is finished and the disc removed, these few can be adjusted.

The lower comb

Only after the top set of dampers has been adjusted *exactly*, should work commence on the setting up of the dampers for the lower comb. It will be noticed that not only are the brakes missing for this damper rail, but that also the dampers are of a different shape. The top part of the damper has a prong coming off it from behind, which is the part that actually damps the tooth; the main stem is the part actuated by the star wheel. The fitting of the bottom damper rail is very similar to the one already done, except that it fits into a trough to make it lower since the comb upon which its dampers act is lower. All the steps in tackling the lower rail are the same as with the upper rail, except that it is necessary when placing the shim beneath the rail to adjust for height, to use half discs of shim only, and a rod of some kind to push them along the trough from the end to their position under the screws.

When setting the lower damper rail take extra care not to bring the dampers too far upright. If this is done, and two adjacent star wheels are rotated together, the damper for the wheel on the right may be flicked back so far that it interferes with the left-hand star wheel. The damper

DISC MUSICAL BOX DAMPERS

concerned would be buckled at once. This is particularly important on machines which have closely-set teeth such as the 'duplex' 15½-inch Polyphon table model.

Individual damper adjustments

Once more, when the setting of the whole rail is as correct as possible, the individual adjustment is made with the screwdrivers. In the case of the lower comb, the rearmost prong of the damper is the one which damps the tooth. It is this piece only which must be adjusted, leaving the main stem untouched. It sometimes happens that on the lower comb the very low bass teeth are too heavy for the damper to cause a complete stop on the tooth before it is struck again. When this occurs it may be possible to twist the damper slightly so that both the finger *and* the side of the damper can apply more friction to the vibrating tooth and so stop it more quickly. This method is only recommended on those notes with large weights, and is not to be used for any teeth but these, and then only where all else fails.

Adjustment after use

New dampers, whether bought or made at home, may have some rough edges which will wear as the machine is run in. It is quite possible that after some use the dampers will require readjustment. Should damper noise be heard on one or two teeth after a short while, it might be better to wait until the machine has had more playing time before adjusting. It will save considerable effort if all the dampers which are likely to give trouble are treated at the same time.

24½-inch Polyphon dampers

Where it is found necessary to replace the damper rails on a 24½-inch Polyphon, the same method may be used almost exactly. The main difference is that the new rails supplied may be in two lengths for each side. In some cases this may be the same as the original rails, but mostly it will be found that in manufacture one rail only was used, as in the 19⅝-inch Polyphon. The preparation for replacing the 24½-inch rails will be complicated a little by the necessity of drilling two extra holes on each side of the gantry to take the extra fixing screws. Take care

DISC MUSICAL BOX DAMPERS

when marking the holes to make sure that they are in the exact position needed. In some cases, on both sizes, the new rail may be found to extend too far back so that there is either some obstruction to its lying flat or perhaps it is fouling the lead weights. When this occurs it is possible to file the rail to the thickness required.

Other types of dampers

Although types of damper differ with each make of machine, many will be found similar enough to those described to make the hints given worth while. Even if they are entirely different, reading this chapter may help at least to give a general impression of repairing or adjusting dampers on most disc machines.

A LIST OF DISC MUSICAL BOXES

Here is given, in alphabetical order, a list of disc musical boxes. That the list is incomplete is beyond doubt; it is only during the last few years that serious research has been done at all in the field of mechanical music. However the list has been considerably augmented for this edition, thanks mainly to the efforts of various researchers who are mentioned in the acknowledgements.

Of some machines little more than a discovered advertisement in a forgotten magazine is known; they are included in the hope that the name alone may mean something to someone.

The sizes given for discs are apt to differ from those given at other times or by other authors. This is caused by the fact that individual discs do vary in size by as much as ¼ inch or more, particularly those using centre drive, since small variations of size are not so important in this type. We are also prone to using an approximate size where it has been generally accepted. For instance the Polyphon disc known universally as the 15½-inch is, in fact, 15⅝ inches to 15¾ inches in diameter. On Polyphon catalogues and similar material the same disc is referred to as '15¾ inches'. The smaller Regina sizes of discs differ a little from those of the Polyphon but are, in fact, interchangeable.

When using this list, for further information on the manufacture of a particular machine see the 'List of Manufacturers and Agents'. There may also be mention of a particular model in the chapter 'Rare Types of Disc Musical Box'.

Adler. Made by Adler Musikwerke (German-American Musical Boxes), Gohlis, Leipzig, Germany. The company was set up in 1896, the trademark, an eagle in flight before a sunrise, was continued by Zimmermann who took over the firm in 1900, changing the name of the range to Fortuna. Many models were made in both upright and table designs, including a double disc machine (introduced

A LIST OF DISC MUSICAL BOXES

September 1897). Disc sizes range from 7¼-inches to 26-inches, the size used for the Fortuna Marvel model playing tuned steel combs accompanied by a 14 note reed organ, drum and triangle. This machine was made by Adler in 1900, shortly before Julius Heinrich Zimmermann took over the firm. The Fortuna name was then given to all machines of the range. In 1902, a double-disc version of this instrument was made by Zimmermann, but none are known to exist today, in fact though many Adler and Fortuna instruments were made few still exist. Of these, small models tend to be Fortuna, and larger, Adler. Some instruments, including the organ model, use a disc having diagonally cut slotted drive holes, a refinement patented in Britain in 1895 and the United States in 1898 by Ernst Malke, one of the original Adler partners, the other being F. H. Oberlander.

Baskánion. (Bascanion). A lever-plucking card disc-playing instrument. The machine is believed by the author to have been the first disc musical box to follow the Symphonion into commercial production. Made by Fabrik Leipziger Musikwerke (formerly Paul Ehrlich), the Baskánion was first advertised on 11 May, 1889, and still in production at Easter, 1891, when it was exhibited in the Leipzig Easter Fair.

40. The card disc of the Baskánion, bearing the only reference to the maker of the machine, Ehrlich. (Grace Thompson collection).

The machine is believed by the author to be a 'lever-plucker', similar to one that passed through his hands some years ago. If so, it corresponds to patents accorded to Ehrlich in 1886 and 1888. The only mark of identification on the machine seen was the name 'Ehrlich' on the card disc. Though Baskánion advertisements have been seen before, it was, until now, erroneously considered to be just another card disc organette, while the one example known was termed the 'Ehrlich'. It plays a disc of 11¼ inches.

The two advertised models were finished in black polish, one with a lid, one without. This last, looking so much like an organette, caused the confusion.

Britannia (see also Imperial). Made by B.H. Abrahams (B.H.A.) of Ste-Croix, Switzerland, founded 1857, who also made cylinder boxes. The Britannia has a loud, bell-like tone similar to some late cylinder boxes. It was made in many models, both upright and horizontal, but rarely with coin operation. Perhaps the most popular model today is the 'Smokers Cabinet' which is a small upright machine playing a 9-inch or 11¾-inch steel discs with periphery drive

41. A 9-inch 'Britannia' upright machine, commonly known as a Smokers' Cabinet from the shape of the case. The case is often found with a small clock surmount. (Late F. Greenacre Collection).

A LIST OF DISC MUSICAL BOXES

holes in rectangular form. Other disc sizes are: 5-inch, 17¼-inch, 19⅝-inch (with same scale intervals as Polyphon) and 25-inch. A peculiarity of the Britannia is that no composer's name appears on the discs with the tune title. The larger upright models, where they are not free standing, generally use a matching table as a base rather than the more conventional disc bin.

Upright cases are generally in walnut veneer, sometimes with transfer decoration; table model cases tend to be 'blinded' and transferred on the lid overall with 'crossbanding and veneer' as with late cylinder boxes by this and other makers.

Capital. Made by F.G. Otto, Jersey City, New Jersey. The Capital was not truly a disc musical box since it used a 'cuff', so called because of its open-ended cone shape, similar to the take-off cuffs used by many clerks of the period. Fitting over an open frame mandrel, the cuff revolved to cause its projections to turn star wheels to pluck the comb(s), as with normal disc machines.

Three sizes of cuff were used for eight models, their lengths 4¼-inch, 5½-inch, and 7¾-inch. Styles A to E used single combs, while style F used double opposed duplex combs. There is great similarity between the comb set-up of these machines and equivalent Reginas, comb scales being the same intervals except for the addition of several notes. For instance, where the Regina 15½-inch comb has 76 teeth, that of the 7¾-inch Capital comb has 81, 5 of which double up on some treble notes of the otherwise identical scale (for full scales see that chapter). This size of cuff, and comb, was used on Styles C, D and E, doubled up on Style F.

All of these instruments were table models, Styles D and G being coin-operated versions of C and B. Style O was the economy version.

This peculiar design of note carrier, certainly used to circumvent the patents of Regina, whose Gustave Brachhausen lived across the road from the Ottos, was in production by early 1895, and continued to be made until about the end of 1897. In 1896 the Company's first true disc box, the Criterion, was in production.

Celesta. Introduced by Pietschmann & Sohn, Berlin, in February, 1895. These machines were made in both upright and horizontal (table) models, and were distinguished by most colourfully decorated discs. The name 'Celesta' is found on the discs in the form of a scroll across

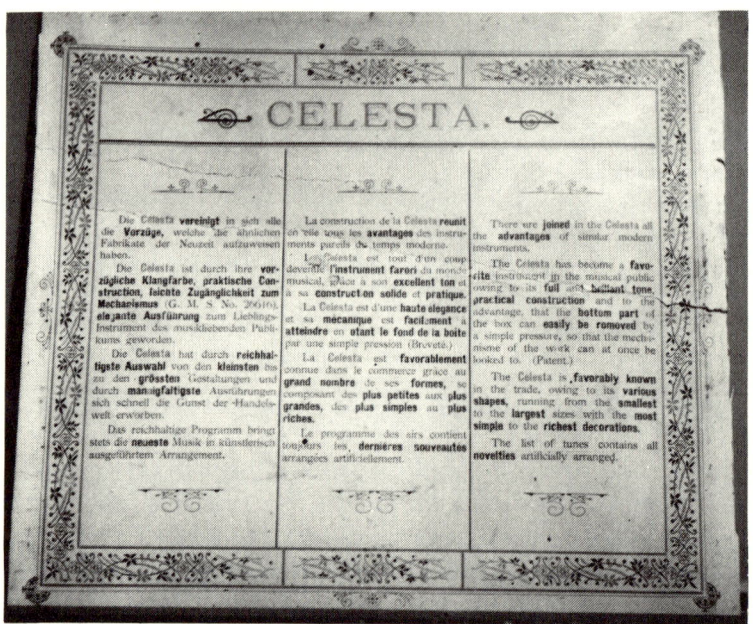

42. The 'blurb', in three languages, from the interior of the lid of a small Celesta disc box. (Graham Webb).

a bed of flowers. Inside the lid of some horizontal models is the picture of a young lady. Upright models, some of which have the motor at the back of the bed-plate rather than below, tend to have a picture in the door of the cabinet rather than plain glass. The several sizes of disc used included 8¼-inch, 11⅜-inch, 15½-inch and 19⅝-inch, these latter said to be interchangeable with the same size of Polyphon disc.

It may be that the 19⅝-inch size is the only disc to have been physically compared to a Polyphon so far. Both 11⅜-inch and 15½-inch Celesta combs have the same number of teeth as the equivalent Polyphon movements, so that, should the need arise, it may be found that the scales for these also match. This, however, is speculation.

Celeste. At the time of writing, a mystery machine. It was marketed about the turn-of-the-century by Heinrich Hermann of Bernau, Berlin; bore on the discs the trademark of Pietschmann & Sohn of Berlin (maker of the Celesta above), and the two sizes of disc 'known' are

A LIST OF DISC MUSICAL BOXES

11-inch and 19⅝-inch, these, according to Ord-Hume (*Musical Box*) 'apparently interchangeable' with Polyphon. To add to the mystery, it has been suggested that the instrument was made by Otto Helbig & Co.

Criterion. Made by F.G. Otto & Sons, U.S.A., makers of first the 'Capital' music box, then the 'Criterion' and finally the 'Olympia'.

The 'Criterion' range was the first true disc box from this company and was made in the disc sizes 11⅝-inch, 15¾-inch and 20½-inch. The first two sizes were made only in horizontal models but some uprights were made in the 20¾-inch size. The discs were made of zinc, or, in the smaller sizes, of mild steel. The range eventually included an auto-change in the 20½-inch size using a selection of 15 discs.

Because of the many similarities between the Criterion and Regina, a patent infringement suit was brought against the main agent, Alfred E. Paillard, of M.J. Paillard, New York, in December 1896. The case dragged on for two and a half years, and by this time the Criterion had been replaced by the Olympia. See also Euphonia and Sterling.

Edelweiss. Made by Hermann Thorens of Ste-Croix, Switzerland. There are two distinct types of disc machine found both under this name, and the other house name, Helvetia.

43. A 4½-inch disc Edelweiss by Thorens, Ste-Croix. The company still makes an instrument using the same size of disc.

A LIST OF DISC MUSICAL BOXES

The first model used a 'lever-plucker' mechanism, patented in 1897 by Louis Hössly. Discs were projectionless, and with lozenge-shaped peripheral drive holes. They have been found in the sizes 12-inch, 15½-inch, 20-inch, and 22¼-inch; the first two sizes are table-model machines, the last two upright machines (for another 'lever-plucker' disc movement see 'Baskánion').

The other model has been found only in smaller, table-model sizes, though the smallest—using the 4½-inch disc—was used for many articles, including photograph albums, miniature 'barrel pianos', etc. This size is still produced by Melodies S.A., the modern firm of Thorens, bearing the name of Thorens. Other sizes were 7¹¹⁄₁₆-inch, a two-bell version with 8¹⁄₁₆-inch discs, and 11-inch. Again, this last size is made today by the same firm, but still bearing the original name of Edelweiss.

Ehrlich. See Baskánion.

Empress. Made by Mermod Frères, Ste-Croix, Switzerland. This machine is identical to the 'Mira' and was made with the name 'Empress' expressly for Lyon & Healy of Chicago, Illinois, under an agreement, presumably to be represented as of their own manufacture.

Euphonia. A name used for a later version of the Criterion disc box, made by F.G. Otto & Sons. See also Sterling.

Euphonion. At least sold by Euphonion-Musikwerke, Vienna. Some of these instruments used Polyphon discs, but not all. So far, 11-inch, 15½-inch, and 19⅝-inch disc sizes are known, all said to be interchangeable with Polyphon.

Euterpephon. First introduced in 1893 by A. W. Neumann in Gohlis, Leipzig. By 7th. December, 1894, he was bankrupt. Production recommenced at the same address in September, 1895, by Otto Helbig and Polikeit. Though these two brought out at least two patents for disc musical boxes, the Euterpephon was not heard of again. Only two examples of this machine have been found, one of these incomplete. Interestingly, Dr. Coulson Conn has examined several discs, and found that, in a batch having notage for 56-note comb, some are

11¾-inch discs, while others are 12¼-inch. Both sizes are apparently for the same comb set-up. He also states that, contrary to what has been stated elsewhere, the discs do not match up to the comb set-up of an 11-inch Polyphon or Regina.

The centre-drive discs bear a central trademark of a lyre with a banner bearing the word 'Euterpephon'. The lid interior contains a picture of the muse Euterpe with trumpets.

44. Part of the interior of a table model Fortuna with bells. (Late F. Greenacre Collection).

Fortuna. Made by Julius H. Zimmermann, Leipzig, Germany. The Fortuna range is virtually the same as that using the name 'Adler' including the machine with organ reeds, drum and triangle, which was made by the Adler Musikwerke in early 1900, the same year in which Zimmermann took over the company. The machine was a success and Zimmermann took the name of this particular machine, Fortuna, and used it as his trademark for the whole range.

A LIST OF DISC MUSICAL BOXES

Gloria (1). Made by *Société Anonyme des Fabriques Reunies de Boîte à Musique, Anciennes Maisons Rivenc, Langdorff et Billon*, Geneva, Switzerland, a long title for a company formed under the names of three cylinder musical box makers. The Gloria range of this company was made in both upright and table models. The bed-plate assembly differs from the norm in having the comb set-up at an angle on the bed-plate. Two disc sizes are known, 11¾-inch and 18¼-inch. Later the firm made the Polymnia disc box.

Gloria (2). Made by Leipziger Musikwerke (Paul Ehrlich & Co.). Leipzig, Germany. The name given to a twin-disc musical box by these makers, playing from two 26½-inch discs (see 'Rare Types of Disc Musical Box', Multiple-disc machines). Makers of the 'Monopol' range of instruments.

45. The bed-plate assembly of a Harmonia projectionless disc musical box. (Michael Gilbert Collection).

Harmonia. Made by Harmonia S.A. of L'Auderson, Ste-Croix, Switzerland. One of the first machines to use projectionless discs and sprung star wheels, a system made popular in the Mermod Frères' 'Stella'. Chapuis (*Histoire de la Boite à Musique*) tells us that André Junod brought the idea to L'Auberson.

No upright machines are known to date, and only three sizes of disc: 8-inch, 9⅞-inch, and 16-inch.

Helvetia. Made by Hermann Thorens, Ste-Croix, Switzerland. See Edelweiss.

Imperator. Introduced in March, 1900, by Friedrich Adolf Richter & Co., Rudolstadt, Germany. Though a range of Imperator disc boxes were made (disc sizes 4½-inch, 5½-inch, 10¼-inch, and 21-inch are known), the only model of this machine actually seen by the author was of the 21-inch disc upright type, style 49, and had the case for the movement and the disc bin built as one unit including the door. The comb arrangement was interesting in that two sets of combs were used, a double set below the centre dome of the bed-plate and another above the dome. The movement had the accompaniment of 12 bells. The trademark of the range is a flaming torch. The Richter company is known for another rare machine, the 'Libellion', using folded card music in place of a disc to play the tuned steel combs by means of a 'lever-plucker' mechanism (see also 'New Century').

Imperial. The same machine in every respect but name as the 'Britannia'.

46. An extremely rare Imperial Symphonion triple disc machine by Symphonion Manufacturing Co., New Jersey. (Jon D. Wenzel Collection).

A LIST OF DISC MUSICAL BOXES

Imperial Symphonion. Made by Symphonion Manufacturing Co., Bradley Beach, near Asbury Park, New Jersey, branch of the German *Symphonionfabrik* parent company. As with Polyphon and Regina, the parent company, at least at first, supplied mechanisms which were placed in American cases. Perhaps the best known Imperial Symphonion is the triple disc machine which, unlike the better known Eroica, plays its 17½-inch discs in a horizontal line. The American company also made a similar machine to the German 27½-inch upright Symphonion Orchestrion with a 12 bell accompaniment to the tuned steel combs. Though many styles and types of Symphonion were sold by Symphonion Manufacturing Co., many of them were either made completely in Germany or used a mechanism made there, in an American case. Relatively few of the company's sales were of true 'Imperial Symphonion' machines.

Junghans. Many musical clocks using a 4½-inch disc are known to be by this maker, Junghanssche Uhrenfabrik of Schramberg, Wurttemberg, Germany, later the Vereingte Uhrenfabriken Gebr. Junghans and Th. Haller of Schwenningen. Since the actual disc and movement are remarkably like those of Symphonion, except that the discs bear the Junghans trademark of a 'J' within a star, it is generally assumed that these were obtained from Symphonion to fit in the clocks. What is most interesting, however, is that a machine using an 11⁵⁄₁₆-inch disc with the Junghans trademark has recently come to light (John Cowderoy). This size of disc does not appear in Symphonion's large range of disc sizes normally used! There is no doubt, however, that there was a connection between the two companies, since Symphonion used clocks with some of their own trademark instruments that were at least from the Junghans area of manufacture.

Kalliope. Made by Kalliope Musikwerke, Leipzig, Germany. This company entered the field in 1895 and their machines quickly became popular with the very pleasant musical sound of even their smallest box, many using bell accompaniment. Smaller models are wound through the centre spindle. Kalliope movements were used in a number of novelties including gambling machines, automata and Christmas tree stands. Especially sought are the 'Panorama' models featuring moving race-horses which race as the music plays. Sizes of disc include: 5¾-inch, 7-inch, 9¼-inch, 10-inch, 13½-inch, 14⅛-inch,

A LIST OF DISC MUSICAL BOXES

47. A good example of a 13¼-inch disc Kalliope with 10 bells. (Werner Baus Collection).

18-inch, 21-inch, 23-inch, 24-inch, 25¾-inch, 28½-inch and 29½-inch. The 'Kalliophon' was a disc box/gramophone.

Kalliope used various comb set-ups. This can be seen in the chapter on scales, where the two 18-inch disc models shown use the same 80 notes, one on a single comb, the other on no less than four combs, two of which are plucked simultaneously (2 × 23 notes), and two are plucked alternately (29 and 28 notes) to make the same total.

Komet. Introduced by Franz Louis Bauer in the summer of 1894. From the beginning the instrument used projectionless discs, though later some models used the more common discs with projections. It is probable that this machine was the first *metal* disc musical box to use the types of disc normally associated with makers such as Harmonia S.A., and Mermod Frères, of Stella fame. Many patents were granted to Franz Louis Bauer, including several for plucking a tooth from a projectionless disc, the first of these as early as 16th. May, 1888,

A LIST OF DISC MUSICAL BOXES

(German patent number 47924). There was also a patent for a dimple projection (German patent 25th. December, 1888, number 48377); and one for a disc-shifting system (German patent 17th. October, 1899, number 111970).

The firm was incorporated on 1st. July, 1895 to become 'Firma Komet Musikwerke, Pollnitz & Bauer. Bauer was eventually sacked at the beginning of 1899, and the firm continued until 1902.

Known disc sizes are 10¼-inch, 13-inch, 17-inch, 20½-inch, 21⅝-inch, 24½-inch, 25¼-inch, and a massive 33⅜-inch, this last being for an upright machine with bell accompaniment.

Libellion. See Imperator.

Lipsia. A rough translation from an article on the Easter Fair of 1897, by the editor of '*Zeitschrift*', states: . . . at the stand of Holzweissig was a small *automat* (called) 'Lipsia', exhibited from an anonymous firm. The pressed-tin frontpiece did not give evidence of good taste, and the music offered nothing new'.

The name was to be found on an upright model in the *Mekanisk Musik Museum*, Copenhagen (now disbanded), the instrument played by a 17¾ in. disc. The name is on a decorative panel on the door, together with the trademark of a female figure holding a shield-shaped plaque with the initials W & R. At the time of writing, this is the only instrument of this name known.

Lochmann Original. Made by Paul Lochmann, Zeulenroda, Germany. The discs of all machines made in this range had lipped edges. The range included both upright and horizontal models, many with bells. The bells used were tubular and this type of bell was even used in horizontal models. The cases of the machines of both styles tend to be plain with rounded corners and are often without a name. The discs are marked Lochmann-Original, and are also quite plain. A disc orchestrion was made by this company, which played strings, tuned tubular bells, drum and triangle. It was weight driven and named 'Original Konzert Piano'. Paul Lochmann started the Original Musikwerke in 1901, at about the same time that his Symphonion Musikwerke was taken over by Hupfeld.

Known disc sizes are: 5⅛-inch, 7-inch, 8¼-inch, 11-inch, 15⅜-inch, 17-inch (with 8 tubular bells), 21½-inch, 24½-inch (with

A LIST OF DISC MUSICAL BOXES

48. A Lochmann 'Original 60' table model disc box. (Grace Thompson Collection).

12 tubular bells) (the same size being used for the 'disc orchestrion' with piano strings and tubular bells. In this case the disc was projectionless), 29-inch (with 12 tubular bells, bass and snare drum and cymbal). A 32-inch disc was also used for a piano-orchestrion, for which a gramophone attachment was a 'recommended extra'.

Lyraphon. Introduced by Bruno Rückert, Leipzig, Germany, in 1891. The firm is well known for its manufacture of the Orphenion. The date of 1891 makes the Lyraphon one of the early commercial disc musical boxes, arriving soon after Polyphon. It is thought that the instrument gave way to the Orphenion in 1893.

Only two examples of the Lyraphon are known, noted by Ord-Hume. They are both hand-cranked and use 6½-inch discs.

Mira. Made by Mermod Frères, Ste-Croix, Switzerland, manufacturer also of the 'Stella' disc machine and a range of cylinder boxes. The

A LIST OF DISC MUSICAL BOXES

Mira range is believed to have contained no upright machines, although this is not certain, but some were housed in console style cases, sometimes with inlay in the 'Art Nouveau' style. The Mira is of a more orthodox design than the Stella, since it uses projections and the normal type of star wheel assembly. They have a good sweet tone, and the smaller sizes in particular play much better music than one would expect. The Mira machine was also marketed by Lyon & Healy, Chicago, Illinois, under the name 'Empress'. This did not prevent the box being sold there under its own or other names. The Mira was also produced as a combination disc box/gramophone under the name Miraphone.

Known disc sizes are: 4½-inch, 7-inch, 8-inch, 9½-inch, 12-inch, 15½-inch, and 18½-inch.

Monarch. Made by the American Music Box Company, Hoboken, New Jersey. A 15½-inch disc model of this machine has been recorded with discs that would play on a Regina of this size except for a difference in drive systems (Hughes Ryder). See 'Triumph'.

Monopol. Made by Fabrik Leipziger Musikwerke (Paul Ehrlich & Co.), Leipzig, Germany. The Monopol range of boxes is very similar in some disc sizes to the 'Symphonion'. The discs of these machines are interchangeable, the set-up of one comb at one end of the bed-plate and one at the other (diametral) common to both. The main difference between these sizes of machine is that the Monopol tends to be more decorative in their bed-plates, which are cast in a rather florid style. There is virtually no difference in the sound or set-up. The discs of Monopol again reflect a more garish mood, being finished in many different colours from royal blue to chocolate brown and lavishly decorated with gold designs. The larger upright instruments do not retain the likeness to the Symphonion: the bed-plate takes on an even more unusual shape, the sizes of discs differ entirely and so does the motor assembly. The large rachet wheel which is also one end of the spring housing is at the top of the movement, the governor assembly is to the left and the stop/start arm is governed by a time wheel which is of unusual design and is placed on top of the movement. Monopol is also known for the large variety of novelties into which their movements were placed. These included a child's dog cart, a toy motor bus and motor car, and a clever coin-operated automaton gnome who

49. A 13⅝-inch disc table model Monopol. Note the use of the diametral comb set-up, shared with Symphonion. (Graham Webb).

would shake his head if the wrong coin was inserted and only play a tune for the right coin.

Monopol disc machines first appeared at the Leipzig Easter Fair in April 1893. Ehrlich had entered the disc box market earlier with his 'Baskánion', but this was his first commercial metal disc machine. An early advertisement shows a 20-note, hand turned instrument, a small 40-note upright machine, and a larger upright model, coin-operated, and with integral disc bin. This last carried a plate bearing the legend: 'Monopol/Ehrlich's Musik Automat'. The advertisement is headed: *'PATENT-RESONATOR-SPIELDOSE/MONOPOL'*, a reference to a 'resonator' connected to the comb for better tone. A further refinement, shown at the same Fair, was an easily dismantled 'under-lid' (base of the case?), by which access to the motor was possible. A similar feature was also used for the Celesta. Fabrik Leipziger Musikwerke (formerly Paul Ehrlich) went into liquidation in April, 1904. Production of the Monopol, and the Ariston, was rec-

A LIST OF DISC MUSICAL BOXES

ommenced in October of the same year by G.A. Buff-Hedinger, mainly producing the 'Premier' and other automatic pianos. He died in July, 1906, and his widow continued to produce a diminishing amount of Monopols until about January, 1909, when the line finally finished.

Known disc sizes are: 5¾-inch (used in hand-turned boxes and toys), 7½-inch, 8½-inch, 9⅜-inch, 11⅞-inch, 13⅝-inch, 14⅛-inch, 17⅛-inch, 19⅛-inch, 20½-inch, 21¾-inch, 26⅜-inch, and 32-inch.

The 26⅜-inch disc was used for the twin-disc Gloria. Some sizes were used on the diametral comb Symphonion type set-up, though there were differences in motor design and comb set-up on some.

New Century. Under this name are found several different types of movement. The mechanisms of the 'shifting disc' and other types are thought to have been made by Mermod Frères (Bowers, *Encyclopedia*). It was this company's practice to supply movements only, the agents making the cases. The types produced were the shifting disc mentioned, an orthodox movement, and a movement of 2 sets of double combs one each side of the centre dome. The only known size of disc is 18½-inches. This size is arranged to play all three types of movement. See also Imperator and Sirion.

Olympia. Made by F.G. Otto & Sons, Jersey City, New Jersey, who also manufactured the 'Capital' and the 'Criterion' machines. The Olympia is of exceptional quality in both tone and design. In many ways it is similar to the Regina in style. The disc sizes were 8¾-inch, 11⅝-inch, 15¾-inch, the last being made both as upright and horizontal models, 20½-inch, and 27-inch. The machines are naturally very rare in Europe and quite rare in America. Named after Admiral Dewey's flagship 'Olympia' of Spanish-American War fame, the ship now anchored in Philadelphia, Pa.

Orphenion. Introduced by Bruno Rückert, Leipzig, Germany, in 1893. This machine was manufactured in upright and table models. The discs bear an ornate lyre with foliage and the word 'Orphenion' above. They are peripheral drive with oval drive holes and the projections are formed like those of a cheese grater. The dampers are in the shape of a Y. Some models have an extra set of teeth forming a piccolo comb, which are extremely fine, as are the star wheels of this

A LIST OF DISC MUSICAL BOXES

50. A 16¼-inch disc table model Orphenion. This example uses 4 combs, 3 visible, one below the bed-plate. (Werner Baus collection).

section. A common decoration for the cases of the Orphenion is a lyre and two crossed horns; the motif is incised into the wood. The movement of the table models is in full view, and is unusual in that the drive wheel is part of the gearing of the motor. The range was sold by Hupfeld until c. 1900 when they ceased to advertise them. In 1898 the premises were taken over by the Adler company, production of the Orphenion having finished in April of that year.

Known disc sizes are: 5¼-inch (manivelle), 8¼-inch, 10¾-inch, 13½-inch, 16⅛-inch, and 26-inch.

Orpheus. Made by Ludwig & Co., Leipzig, Germany. The few instruments seen indicate a range of both horizontal and upright machines. In table (horizontal) models the motor is to the right of the bed-plate assembly. Upright machines display an ornately etched glass front and a distinctive bed-plate, the top of which continues to a mushroom shaped terminal. Known disc sizes are: 12-inch, and 22⅝-inch.

A LIST OF DISC MUSICAL BOXES

Perfection. Made by the Perfection Music Box Company, Jersey City, New Jersey, and later Newark, New Jersey. The Perfection disc box was produced from 1898 to 1901. It differs from all other disc musical boxes in the design of the dampers. Perfection used a star wheel made from two thin metal walls enclosing a centre piece of felt. The felt was intended to damp the tooth before it was plucked. It did this very well until it was worn out, the problem then was to replace the star wheels. The discs bear the name 'The Perfection' in a scroll and have peripheral drive holes which are square. It would appear that only two models were made, both horizontal, with disc sizes 10⅝-inch and 15½-inch.

Phänomenal. The name given to a 'disc' musical box using helicoidal tune sheets for the playing of longer tunes. Introduced in March, 1901 by the firm of A.C.F. Staffelstein & H.F.F. Kluge, whose British patent 4469 dates from 8th. March, 1900, the machine was short lived. No examples are known.

Polyhymnia (1) Advertised by K. Heilbrunn Söhne, Berlin, and exhibited by them at Leipzig Easter Fair of 1895. The advertisement showed a large upright, coin-operated machine with 'Polyhymnia' written on the glass centre panel. The instrument was described as 'Sublime Harmonie-Piccolo', with 100 teeth.

The 13⅝-inch disc of Symphonion plays on Sublime Harmonie and Sublime Harmonie Piccolo comb arrangements using 100 teeth. Heilbrunn K. Söhne were agents for Symphonion, among others.

Polyhymnia (2). Introduced by Metall-Industrie Schönebeck, Leipzig, Germany, in April, 1900. Originally four different sizes were made, one of them, noted at the time, used 19⅝-inch discs interchangeable with Polyphon. The machine lasted until early 1903.

Only one Polyhymnia is known to exist today. Noted by Bowers (*Encyclopedia*), it plays a disc of 7⅝-inches. This model may belong to the heading 'Polyhymnia'(1), since this, too, is a Symphonion size.

Polymnia. Made by *Société Anonyme des Fabriques Reunies de Boîte à Musique, Anciennes Maison Rivenc, Langdorff et Billon*, Geneva, Switzerland. This mouthful of a title represents a company formed

A LIST OF DISC MUSICAL BOXES

under the names of three well known firms in the making of cylinder musical boxes. Manufacture of the 'Gloria' range of disc boxes began in 1902, and this was followed by the 'Polymnia'. This machine has an off-set gantry so as to remove the line of play from the point of drive. Among several innovations is a continuous tune set-up on the dimple projection discs, with no gap between the beginning and end of the tune, to allow the music to be used for dancing (Horngacher). As can be imagined the motor parts owe much in design to those of a cylinder musical box, though a weight type centrifugal governor is used rather than an air-brake. Few machines were made and by 1904 the firm was in liquidation. Not to be confused with the 'Polyhymnia'.

Polyphon. Made by Polyphon Musikwerke, Leipzig, Germany. First examples made by this company used a card disc to dictate the melody. Such an instrument was shown at the Michaelmas Fair in Leipzig in October, 1890, but was quickly withdrawn. It is assumed that either Lochmann, maker of 'Symphonion', or Ehrlich, maker of the 'Baskánion', warned the company off because of existing patents.

An arrangement must have been made because on 21st. November little more than a month later, the same instrument was being advertised by Hugo Hennig, an agent. The advertisement ran until 1st. June, 1891, the machine having been exhibited in the 1891 Easter Fair.

Exactly a year to the day after the first advertisement, a Polyphon was advertised that used a metal disc, the illustration shown had the appearance of a 15½-inch disc model, and was with opposed combs (2×78 teeth). No examples of the card disc instrument are known to exist. The Polyphon is by far the most common disc musical box we have with us today. For this reason extra discs and parts are that much easier to obtain. Polyphons were made in varied cases in both upright and horizontal models. The discs are peripheral drive on those of 14⅛-inches in diameter and above, and centre drive on the smaller sizes, though there are exceptions. All of the machines are marked 'Polyphon' and the trademark of the company is a woman in flowing dress crowned with a laurel wreath. In her left hand she holds a small harp and in her right, which is out-stretched, another laurel wreath. Above her head is a star which is shooting toward the upheld wreath and in the tail of the star is the word 'Polyphon'. The trademark ap-

A LIST OF DISC MUSICAL BOXES

51. A classic single comb, 15½-inch disc, table model Polyphon. A double comb model uses a more ornate case. (Drs. L. Goldhoorn collection).

pears on the discs and often in a round medal on the casework. Sizes of discs are 6½-inch, 8½-inch, 9⅝-inch, 11-inch, 11⅛-inch, 14⅛-inch, 15½-inch, 17¾-inch, 19⅝-inch, 22-inch, and 24½-inch. Besides these discs three more sizes were used for the disc piano orchestrion named the 'Concerto', the sizes being 25¼-inch, 28-inch and 32-inch. The sizes 11-inch, 14⅛-inch, and 22-inch belong to movements which play bells as well as the normal comb(s). The 11¼-inch size discs and larger were used on both upright and horizontal models, although it is very rare to see a 19⅝-inch, 22-inch or 24½-inch horizontal model. The cases for these were of the type with a double lid which hinged back to make supports for the discs, though occasionally a 19⅝-inch horizontal model is to be found in a larger version of the 15½-inch double comb type case.

Since there are more 15½-inch disc machines extant, it would appear that these were made in greater quantity and for a longer period

A LIST OF DISC MUSICAL BOXES

than any other size. This size used various types of comb. In the horizontal models three main designs are seen; a single comb, double combs of the opposed type, and a 'comb and a half' which has an extra piece of bass comb. In the upright models double opposed combs are generally used but, in this case, the teeth of the combs are plucked by alternate star wheels, unlike double-comb horizontal models in which each star wheel plucks two teeth at once, one on each comb. Many Polyphon clocks were made, in a variety of styles; the most common of these are those of about 7 feet high which use an 11¼-inch disc movement and those of about 9 feet high which use a 15½-inch movement. The clock cases are generally in walnut and the clock has a round dial and a strike mechanism which also trips the musical movement, which is wound separately at the side of the case. Some of these clocks also have coin slots. The 15½-inch, 19⅝-inch, 22-inch, and 24½-inch disc movements were also used in automatic disc-changing machines. Some models were made in combination with a gramophone.

Regina. Made by Regina Music Box Co., Rahway, New Jersey. The Regina range of disc musical boxes is recognized by most as having a tone superior to any other disc machine. This was effected by the use of sound posts from the movement to the case and generally using the case as a sounding board. The machines are of excellent design. The story of Regina can be found in the chapter 'The Principal Manufacturers'. The Regina comes in a large variety of designs of casework, and both upright and horizontal models were made. The casework is generally plain and of good quality. The fittings are particularly well finished. Sizes of discs used were 8½-inch, 11-inch, 12¼-inch, 15½-inch, 20¾-inch, 27-inch, and 32-inch in the Concerto, a disc piano orchestrion. A machine of the horizontal type was made which used a 15½-inch disc to play bells as well as the normal comb. These machines are extremely rare since they did not prove very popular. The discs do not play on an orthodox movement using a 15½-inch disc. The 12¼-inch disc is a peripheral drive version of the 11-inch disc, which is centre drive. All disc sizes were used in both upright and horizontal models, the smaller sizes, when in upright cases, being usually some sort of small vending machine or savings bank. The 20¾-inch and 27-inch sizes, when in horizontal cases, used a double flap similar to the large horizontal Polyphon cases. All Reginas have

A LIST OF DISC MUSICAL BOXES

52. A most interesting and rare Regina 'Savings Bank'. The instrument is played by an 8¼-inch centre drive disc. (Graham Webb).

the name on the bed-plate of the machines, on the discs and often on the cases. The trademark is the ubiquitous lyre, this time with 'Regina' on a banner across the lyre and the words 'Trade Mark' underneath, on a scroll, the whole on a branch of what appears to be honeysuckle. Many long case clocks were made containing Regina movements, mostly using a 15½-inch disc, including an autochange model placed in the base of a long case clock. Automatic disc-changing machines were made in quantity, using the 15½-inch, 20¾-inch, and 27-inch size discs. The Reginaphone, a combination of disc machine and gramophone, was made in a variety of case designs and using 12¼-inch, 15½-inch, 20¾-inch, and 27-inch disc sizes, together with a turntable, sound arm and (sometimes) horn for the 'talking machines', supplied by Columbia.

Saxonia. Introduced by *Phönix Musikwerke* (Schmidt & Co), Leipzig, Germany in September, 1895. Almost unknown, the Saxonia was ad-

A LIST OF DISC MUSICAL BOXES

vertised as "The Cheapest and nevertheless good toned automaton in existence" (1895). Its makers were far better known for their range of Phönix (Phoenix) Organettes. The Saxonia disappeared after being shown at the Leipzig Easter Fair in 1896.

Silvanigra. Marketed by Junghans, Schramberg, Germany. A series of small musical boxes made about the turn-of-the-century, as was another, termed the 'Coronation'.

Sirion (1). A shifting-disc instrument first introduced in September 1894, by Jentzsoh. An advertisement for October, 1895, shows a table model with a sun-burst trademark on the disc. A rough translation of part of the text is: 'Sirion is the newest self-playing musical box. Without changing the disc serveral tunes may be played'. In February, 1896, the firm applied for an official moratorium.

Sirion (2). Introduced in January, 1896, by G. Bortmann & A. Keller. Whether this was by arrangement with the previous firm is not known. A patent was granted to Bortmann and Keller for a shifting-disc mechanism, the British version of which, number 7443, is dated 8th. April, 1896. The instrument was exhibited at the Leipzig Easter Fair for 1896 for the one and only time.

Sirion (3). Introduced in September, 1899, by Seidel & Maumann. The instrument was seen for the last time at the Leipzig Easter Fair for 1901.

The foregoing is made even more of a mystery by the belief held by Bowers (*Encyclopedia*) that the instrument itself, without the case, was made by Mermod Frères of Ste-Croix, Switzerland, though these last may well be simply later users of the Bortmann and Keller patent. This is born out by two U.S. patents granted to Alfred Keller, described as a German residing in Ste-Croix. The patents, number 752683, dated 23rd. February, 1904, and number 788265, dated 25th. April, 1905, were both assigned to Mermod Frères. They related to a type of governor fan, and a clutch winding system, both of which are used on known examples of Sirion. Also mysterious is that all known discs for these machines bear the legend: 'Made in Dresden!'

Two sizes of instrument are known: a table model, played by a 19¼-inch disc on two sets of opposed combs, one either side of the

A LIST OF DISC MUSICAL BOXES

centre dome, and a model played by a 22¼-inch disc on three sets of opposed combs. On each model some of the teeth are plucked alternately, and some simultaneously. See Tannhauser and New Century.

Stella. Made by Mermod Frères, Ste-Croix, Switzerland. The Stella uses a projectionless disc in which slots allow the star wheel teeth to spring up, the rear edge of the slot pushing the tooth of the star wheel forward so that the comb tooth is plucked. The disc sizes of the Stella are 9½-inch, 14-inch, 15½-inch, 17¼-inch, and 26-inch. Only the last size is used in an upright machine. Because of the practice of selling movements to wholesalers for them to house in cases of various designs there is no classic design of case, though the beautiful

53. View of the open case of a 17¼-inch Stella, by Mermod Frères, Ste-Croix. Note the disc compartment, which stores a surprising number of the projectionless discs. (Grace Thompson collection).

A LIST OF DISC MUSICAL BOXES

'Art Nouveau' is best known. The trademark of the company, which appears on the machine, is a cross upon a letter S in a five-pointed star with the word 'Swiss' beneath. The Stella is quite rare and consequently extra discs are hard to find. The movement is particularly easy to identify because of the design of the pressure arm, which runs the complete length of the bed-plate and has metal disc rollers rather than the classic wooden rollers of most machines. The star wheel assembly is hidden, as is the second comb, which is directly *under* the star wheel assembly with its teeth at right angles to those of the other comb.

A point of interest (Jim Weir) is that some models, though having a bed-plate for a double comb assembly, were sold as single comb machines. This has led to the uninitiated thinking that one of the combs has been removed at some time. A single comb is made possible by the more usual double combs being 'simultaneous pluck' i.e. tuned the same, or an octave away from each other using the same scale.

Sterling. The name under which a later style of the Criterion was marketed. It would seem that both this model and the Euphonia were brought out after the problems of the makers F.G. Otto and Sons, with Regina, over similarities between the Criterion and Regina. Both Sterling and Euphonia models bore a list of 8 patents on the case and one of these, plus another, on the discs. Since all of the big three manufacturers were owners of one or more of some of these patents, it would seem a license had been granted to use them, though many appear not to apply to any part of either machine. (Sterling information by Steve Boehck, *MBSI Journal*, Autumn 1979).

Sun. Made by Schramli & Tschudin (Sun Musical Box Manufacturing Co.,) Geneva, Switzerland. None are known to exist.

Symphonion. Made by Paul Lochmann, Leipzig, Germany. The first practical disc musical box made. The trademark is a lyre with 'Symphonion' written on a banner across the front. Symphonion, in common with Monopol, set their combs in a manner different from the classic, in that each comb was set either side of the centre dome on a separate star wheel assembly, though there were some exceptions to this style which used a conventional, opposed-comb setting and, of course, those machines using a single comb. Sizes of discs

54. An excellent upright coin-operated 11⅞-inch disc Symphonion with clock. (Graham Webb).

were many. Among them were: 4½-inch, 5¾-inch, 7⅝-inch, 9½-inch, 10⅛-inch, 10⅝-inch, 11⅞-inch, 13⅛-inch, 13⅝-inch, 13⅞-inch, 14⅞-inch, 17¾-inch, 19⅛-inch, 21½-inch, 25-inch, and 27-inch. The 21½-inch and 27-inch sizes were used for machines playing bells as well as the normal combs. The discs up to, and including, 17¾-inches were centre driven, with the exception of the 13⅛-inch size, which was in *some* cases periphery drive; again *some* of this size had a normal hole in the periphery and some a dimple. It is difficult to generalize with this make since one is constantly coming across odd disc sizes; for instance the 17¾-inch size centre-drive disc plays on exactly the same comb set-up as does the periphery-drive 19⅛-inch size disc. The Symphonion is found in a great many different styles of case in both upright and horizontal models. Many of the smaller discs were used in upright cabinets, clocks and other designs of case. Several of the rarer Symphonion machines are discussed in the chapter 'Rare Types of Disc Musical Box'. See also 'Monopol'.

Tannhauser. Introduced in July 1898, by Caspar & Plessing of Lindenthal, Leipzig, Germany. The Tannhauser is one of the small breed of shifting-disc boxes that allows the disc to move, after playing a tune, to present a further set of projections to the teeth to play another tune. At first only one model was obtainable, the disc shifted by manual movement of a lever, which could be supplied, with or without a motor, to be operated manually or mechanically. The disc-shifting mechanism was the subject of a patent the German version of which, number 99899, dates from 21st. May, 1897, granted to T. Alwin Plessing.

A review of the Leipzig Autumn Fair for 1898 described the machine as very good, but thought the case of poor design. The music was considered beautiful and melodious. Three new models were introduced at the Michaelmas Fair for 1899, two using 58 teeth, and

55. A fine 11¾-inch disc, table model Troubadour. (Werner Baus collection).

A LIST OF DISC MUSICAL BOXES

one with 42 teeth. By the next Leipzig Fair in 1900, the range included two models with automatic shifting of the disc, one a large upright machine with 118 teeth, probably a double comb version of the 58 tooth model, which was the other machine to be shown with automatic shift. These were well received, but already there was trouble in the Company. Traugott Alwin Plessing had resigned in February, 1899, and by April, 1900, the Tannhauser was finished. Only 3 examples are known to still exist. See Sirion and New Century.

Triumph. Made by the American Music Box Co., Hoboken, New Jersey. There appears to have been only one size of Triumph made, using a 15½-inch disc (See Monarch).

Troubadour. Made by Troubadour Musikwerke, B. Grosz & Co., Leipzig, Germany. A machine rarely seen, the Troubadour was made in both upright and horizontal models. Known disc sizes are: 7-inch, 8⅞-inch, 11¾-inch, and 20½-inch.

TUNING SCALES FOR COMBS

The following pages are devoted to various scales in which the combs of different models and makes of disc musical box were tuned. The information is not complete, but a large number of instruments are represented, including most of those we are likely to encounter.

That these scales are available is due to the co-operation of many collectors, dealers, and repairers, most of them good friends of the author, from many parts of the Western world. They are mentioned individually in the acknowledgements, but once more I tender my grateful thanks.

Perhaps the most important thing to remember when using a scale for the tuning of a particular comb, is that although the scale is shown in definite intervals, this is not always strictly in accordance with the actual original tuning. The comb will be in tune with itself, but often the original tuner, as with a good piano tuner, will have 'stretched' the scale. For an example of this, see the table below, which shows fairly typical tuning, taken from original combs.

Also to be taken into account are the restrictions involved in simply putting a name — or number — to a particular note. Apart from the 'stretching' mentioned above, often made harder to follow by wear, a note may be 'out' from the written note by any degree to a shade below or above where the note written would be required to be changed for the next semi-tone.

Wear itself is also a problem. While the tuning of the treble teeth can be raised considerably by very little wear, the bass teeth need considerably more wear to be put badly out of tune. At the same time we need to remember that, because of their weight, bass teeth *do* get somewhat more wear. The table will show, though, that in general, the bass notes are tuned lower than the 'actual' scales.

For instance: if you require to tune a replacement tooth, you look up the scale for the comb on which you are working, and see that it is, say A#. It is not enough for the tooth to be tuned exactly to that note, simply because the comb as a whole may be out *an average* of as much as 35 or more hundredths—or cents—from the exact notes. Your tuning must be sympathetic to the rest, or it will be wrong, however closely you cling to the '*correct*' scale.

Because the scales shown are taken from particular instruments, they are in a key that may not necessarily correspond to that of other combs for the same types of instrument. For this reason, below the notes of each scale are numbers to represent the notes of the scale and make it unnecessary to transpose, since, of course, the intervals are the same, whatever the key. Use of a prime (1) with some numbers indicates a sharp of that number.

Throughout these scales sharps are used for accidentals rather than flats, firstly because it is simple to use only one rather than both, secondly because most electronic tuners are calibrated in sharps, and finally because original tuners of musical boxes in general appear to have used only sharps in their notation.

All of the foregoing will show that the scales should be used only as a guide to the tuning. However 'true' the written scale may be, no two combs are tuned exactly the same. It is highly important that the present tuner is true to the original tuner of the comb. His work may appear wrong, but it is far more likely that he was trying to get just that little bit extra from the music.

N.B. A good ear, or the skillful use of some form of electronic tuner is essential!

A TABLE TO SHOW THE PERCENTAGE 'OUT' FROM THE GIVEN SCALE* OF THE 3 RIGHT-HAND COMB-SETS OF AN *UNRESTORED* 13 ⅝-INCH 3-DISC SYMPHONION

The table is taken from a 3-disc Symphonion because this machine, playing as it does three differently arranged discs, gives a truer picture than, say, three 15½-inch Polyphon combs. The loss of metal from wear should be more random. Obviously however, treble notes, being lighter, have their tuning much more affected by wear than bass notes.

If we draw a graph containing a record of the amount the tuning varies from the norm on each of the three comb-sets, we see that the variation of the lowest and highest teeth is out of line with the others. In

*Scale taken by Ralph Heintz

A LIST OF DISC MUSICAL BOXES

	1	2	3	4	5	6	7	8	9	10
TOP RIGHT COMB-SET	−39	−19	−18	−16	−33	−25	−17	−24	−25	−17
MIDDLE RIGHT COMB-SET	−36	−19	−6	−4	−20	−23	−4	+2	±0	+2
BOTTOM RIGHT COMB-SET	−55	−21	±0	−11	−19	−8	−5	−6	−9	−2

	11	12	13	14	15	16	17	18	19	20
TOP RIGHT COMB-SET	−13	−12	−14	−14	−11	−8	−10	−22	−7	+5
MIDDLE RIGHT COMB-SET	+3	−11	−12	−10	−4	−13	−7	−13	−5	+2
BOTTOM RIGHT COMB-SET	−4	−12	−9	−5	−10	−7	−5	−8	+6	+13

	21	22	23	24	25	26	27	28	29	30
TOP-RIGHT COMB-SET	−3	−2	−2	+6	−1	−3	+10	+5	+3	+10
MIDDLE RIGHT COMB-SET	+8	+1	+3	+7	+3	+12	+7	+10	+11	+15
BOTTOM RIGHT COMB-SET	+8	+5	+5	+12	+4	±0	+5	+4	+4	+8

	31	32	33	34	35	36	37	38	39	40
TOP RIGHT COMB-SET	+10	+20	+15	+20	+47	+45	+47	+49	+35	+37
MIDDLE RIGHT COMB-SET	+15	+32	+12	+40	+30	+26	+15	+23	+23	+34
BOTTOM RIGHT COMB-SET	+16	+25	+13	+20	+32	+37	+41	+37	+45	+36

	41	42	43	44	45	46	47	48	49	50
TOP RIGHT COMB-SET	+37	+38	+43	+56	+57	+75	+75	+76	+85	+40
MIDDLE RIGHT COMB-SET	+38	+42	+42	+54	+59	+70	+71	+68	+75	+14
BOTTOM RIGHT COMB-SET	+26	+24	+27	+38	+39	+71	+56	+59	+68	+25

the highest note, this could be from less wear, since it is played less often. In the lowest note the anomaly could only have been created by the original tuner.

If we postulate a curve from the graph, leaving out the first and last notes, together with other anomalies, we find that the three sets of figures, averaged, give a curve that runs from about—20 cents, dissecting the line representing the exact given scale at notes 24/25—almost precisely half way on the comb-sets—to about + 68 cents.

A large amount of the variation of the higher teeth can be attributed to wear, but not all. With those teeth varying *below* the given scale—just about half—wear should, if anything, have brought them nearer to the given scale.

Though the well known, seemingly exotic, method of tuning used by Symphonion must be taken into account, above all else the table shows how careful one must be when dealing with comb scales.

TUNING SCALES FOR COMBS

11-Inch ADLER and FORTUNA Scale

1	2	3	4	5	6	7	8	9	10	11	12	13	14	15	16	17	18	19	20	21	22	23	24	25	26	27	28	29	30	31
B	C#	F#	F#	G#	A#	B	B	C#	D#	D#	E	F#	G#	A#	B	B	C#	D#	E	F	F#	G#	F#	G#	A	G#	A#	A#	B	B
1	2	5	5	6	7	1	'1	2	3	3	4	5	6	7	1	1	2	3	4	4'	5	6	5	6	6'	7	7	7	1	1

11-Inch ADLER 50 TEETH Also FORTUNA

32	33	34	35	36	37	38	39	40	41	42	43	44	45	46	47	48	49	50
B	C	C#	C#	D#	D#	E	E	F	F#	F#	G	G#	G#	A#	B	B	B	C#
1	1'	2	2	3	3	4	4'	5	5	5'	6	6	6	7	1	1	1	2

TUNING SCALES FOR COMBS

CAPITAL 'CUFF' BOX SCALES

All would seem to have same intervals as Polyphon and Regina, but with extra notes added.

Style 'O' Style 'A' CAPITAL 'CUFF' BOX 44 TEETH Cuff 4¼-Inch

1	2	3	4	5	6	7	8	9	10	11	12	13	14	15	16	17	18	19	20	21	22	23	24	25	26	27	28	29	30	31
C	D	G	C	C	D	E	E	F	G	G	A	B	C	C	D	E	F	F#	G	G	A	A	B	B	C	C	D	D	E	E
1	2	5	1	1	2	3	3	4	5	5	6	7	1	1	2	3	4	4'	5	5	6	6	7	7	1	1	2	2	3	3
		mid mid					*			*			*																	

32	33	34	35	36	37	38	39	40	41	42	43	44
F	F	F#	G	G	G	A	A	B	C	C	D	D
4	4	4'	5	5	5	6	6	7	1	1	2	2

*Extra Notes - Otherwise Scale Has Same Intervals as 8¼-inch Polyphon/Regina (40 Teeth)

Style 'B' Style 'G' CAPITAL 'CUFF' BOX 58 TEETH - Cuff 5½-Inch

No scale available at present but it would seem sensible to assume that this comb would have the same intervals as the 11-Inch Polyphon, with four extra notes.

See other 'Cuff' Box Scales, also 11⅜ criterion (57 Teeth)

250

TUNING SCALES FOR COMBS

Styles C, D & E Style F (Duplex) CAPITAL 'CUFF' BOX 81 TEETH - Cuff 7¾-Inch (or 2 × 81 if Duplex Style F)

1	2	3	4	5	6	7	8	9	10	11	12	13	14	15	16	17	18	19	20	21	22	23	24	25	26	27	28	29	30	31
E	E	A	A	A	B	C#	D	E	E	F#	G#	A	A	B	C#	C#	D	E	E	F#	G#	A	A	B	C#	C#	D	D#	E	E
5	5	1	1	2	3	4	5	5	6	7	1	1	2	3	4	4'	5	5	6	7	1	1	2	3	4	4'	5	5		

32	33	34	35	36	37	38	39	40	41	42	43	44	45	46	47	48	49	50	51	52	53	54	55	56	57	58	59	60	61	62
E	F#	G#	A	A	A	A	A#	B	B	C	C#	D	D	C#	D	D#	E	E	F	F#	F#	G	G#	G#	A	A	A	A	B	C#
5	6	6	7	7	1	1	1'	2	2	2'	3	3	4	4'	5	5	5'	6	6	6'	7	7	1	1	1	2	2	2	3	

Extra notes at positions 40 (A#) and 50.

63	64	65	66	67	68	69	70	71	72	73	74	75	76	77	78	79	80	81
C#	D	D	D#	E	E	E	E	E	F#	F#	F#	G#	A	A	A	A	B	C#
3	4	4	4'	5	5	5	5	5	6	6	6	7	1	1	1	2	2	3

*Extra Notes - Otherwise scale has same intervals as 15½-Inch Polyphon & Regina, & 14⅞-Inch Symphonion (76 Teeth) and Criterion and Olympia

TUNING SCALES FOR COMBS

CRITERION AND OLYMPIA SCALES

For 15½-Inch See 15½-Inch Polyphon or Regina

11⅝-Inch CRITERION 57 TEETH Key of D Also for 11⅝-Inch OLYMPIA

#	Note	Scale
1	A	5
2	D	1
3	D	1
4	E	2
5	F#	3
6	A	5
7	A	5
8	B	6
9	C#	7
10	D	1
11	D	1
12	E	2
13	F#	3
14	F#	3
15	G	4
16	A	5
17	A	5
18	B	6
19	C#	7
20	D	1
21	D	1
22	E	2
23	F#	3
24	G	4
25	G#	4'
26	A	5
27	A	5
28	B	6
29	B	6
30	C	6'
31	C#	7
32	C#	7
33	D	1
34	D	1
35	D#	1'
36	E	2
37	E	2
38	F#	3
39	F#	3
40	G	3
41	G	4
42	G#	4
43	G	4
44	G	4
45	A	4'
46	A	5
47	A	5 *
48	A	5
49	B	6 †
50	B	6
51	C#	7
52	C#	7
53	D	1
54	D	1
55	E	2
56	E	2
57	F#	3

*Extra Notes - Otherwise scale has same intervals (with † exceptions) as 11-Inch Polyphon & 12¼-Inch Regina (54 Teeth)
†2 Exceptions To Above - Note 49=6 (=47=5'), 51=7 (=49=6) - Brackets contain equivalent teeth on Polyphon/Regina Scale

18-Inch OLYMPIA 2 × 92 TEETH

TUNING SCALES FOR COMBS

1	2	3	4	5	6	7	8	9	10	11	12	13	14	15	16	17	18	19	20	21	22	23	24	25	26	27	28	29	30	31
C	C	F	F	F	G	A	A#	C	C	D	E	F	F	G	G	A	A	A#	A#	C	C	D	D	E	E	F	F	F#	G	G
5	5	1	1	1	2	3	4	5	5	6	7	1	1	2	2	3	3	4	4	5	5	6	6	7	7	1	1	1'	2	2

32	33	34	35	36	37	38	39	40	41	42	43	44	45	46	47	48	49	50	51	52	53	54	55	56	57	58	59	60	61	62
G#	A	A#	A#	B	C	C	C	C#	D	D	D#	E	E	F	F	F	F#	G	G	G	G#	A	A	A	A#	A#	B	B	C	C
2'	3	4	4	4'	5	5	5	5'	6	6	6'	7	7	1	1	1	1'	2	2	2	2'	3	3	3	4	4	4'	4'	5	5

63	64	65	66	67	68	69	70	71	72	73	74	75	76	77	78	79	80	81	82	83	84	85	86	87	88	89	90	91	92
C	C#	D	D	D#	E	E	F	F	F#	G	G	G#	A	A	A#	A#	B	C	C	C	C#	D	D	D	E	F	F	G	A
5	5'	6	6	6	6'	7	7	1	1	1'	2	2'	2	3	3	4	4'	4	5	5	5	6	6	6	7	1	1	2	3

EDELWEISS SCALES

TUNING SCALES FOR COMBS

4½-in. = Modern Thorens
11½-in. = Edelweiss II (modern Thorens)

4½-Inch EDELWEISS 30 TEETH Also NEW THORENS

1	2	3	4	5	6	7	8	9	10	11	12	13	14	15	16	17	18	19	20	21	22	23	24	25	26	27	28	29	30
F	C	F	G	A	C	C	D	E	F	G	A#	C	D	E	F	F	G	G	A	A	A#	B	C	C	D	D	E	E	F
1	5	1	2	3	5	5	6	7	1	2	4	5	6	7	1	1	2	2	3	3	4	4	4'	5	5	6	6	7	1

11-Inch EDELWEISS II (Modern Thorens) 41 TEETH

1	2	3	4	5	6	7	8	9	10	11	12	13	14	15	16	17	18	19	20	21	22	23	24	25	26	27	28	29	30	31
C	D	G	C	C	D	E	E	F	G	G	A	B	C	D	E	F	G	G	A	A	B	B	C	C	D	D	E	E	F	F
1	2	5	1	1	2	3	3	4	5	5	6	7	1	2	3	4	5	5	6	6	7	7	1	1	2	2	3	3	4	4

32	33	34	35	36	37	38	39	40	41	42	43
F#	G	G	A	A	B	C	D	G		*	*
4'	5	5	6	6	7	1	2	5			

*Star wheel - but no tooth intended

TUNING SCALES FOR COMBS

9⅞-INCH HARMONIA SCALE

9⅞-Inch HARMONIA 40 TEETH

1	2	3	4	5	6	7	8	9	10	11	12	13	14	15	16	17	18	19	20	21	22	23	24	25	26	27	28	29	30	31
F#	G	G#	A	A#	B	C	C#	D	D#	E	F	F#	G	G#	A	A#	B	C	C#	D	D#	E	F	F#	G	G#	A	A#	B	C

32	33	34	35	36	37	38	39	40
C#	D	D#	E	F	F#	G	G#	A

NOTE: Scale is sequential, and this *may* apply to other sizes

KALLIOPE SCALES

TUNING SCALES FOR COMBS

9½-in. = New 'Symphonion'.

7-Inch KALLIOPE 36 TEETH

1	2	3	4	5	6	7	8	9	10	11	12	13	14	15	16	17	18	19	20	21	22	23	24	25	26	27	28	29	30	31
D#	A#	A#	D#	F	G	G#	A#	A#	C	C	D	D#	F	G	A#	A#	C	C	D	D#	D#	F	F	G	G	G#	G#	A	A#	A#
1	5	5	1	2	3	4	5	5	6	6	7	1	2	3	5	5	6	6	7	1	1	2	2	3	3	4	4	4'	5	5

		*			
32	33	34	35	36	37
C	D	D#	F	G	
6	7	1	2	3	

*Extra tooth - not used

Tuning the same where Bells are used

9½-Inch KALLIOPE/New SYMPHONION 48 TEETH

	*			*		*	*	*																						
1	2	3	4	5	6	7	8	9	10	11	12	13	14	15	16	17	18	19	20	21	22	23	24	25	26	27	28	29	30	31
A#	D#	D#	F	A#	C	D#	A#	C	D#	D#	F	G	G	G#	A#	C	D	D#	D#	F	G	G#	A	A#	C	C	C#	D	D	D#
5	1	1	2	5	5	6	1	2	3	3	4	5	5	6	7	1	2	3	3	4'	5	5	6	6	6	6'	7	7	7	1

TUNING SCALES FOR COMBS

32	33	34	35	36	37	38	39	40	41	42	43	44	45	46	47	48
E	F	F	F#	G	G	G#	A	A#	A#	B	C	D	D#	F	G	
1'	2	2'	3	4	4	4'	5	5	5'	6	7	1	2	3		

*Tuning for Bells where used

13¼-Inch KALLIOPE 60 TEETH

1	2	3	4	5	6	7	8	9	10	11	12	13	14	15	16	17	18	19	20	21	22	23	24	25	26	27	28	29	30	31
G#	G#	C#	C	D#	F	F#	G#	G#	A#	C	C#	C#	D#	F	F#	F#	G	G#	G#	A#	C	C#	C#	D#	F	F	F#	G	G#	G#
5	5	1	1	2	3	4	5	6	7	1	1	2	3	4	4'	5	5	5	6	7	1	1	2	3	3	4	4'	5	5	*

32	33	34	35	36	37	38	39	40	41	42	43	44	45	46	47	48	49	50	51	52	53	54	55	56	57	58	59	60	61
A#	B	C	C	C#	C#	C#	D	D#	D#	E	F	F	F	F#	F#	G	G#	G#	A	A#	A#	C	C	C#	C#	D#	F		
6	6'	7	7	1	1	1'	2	2	2'	3	4	4	4	4'	5	5	5	5'	6	6	7	7	1	1	2	3			

*Extra Tooth - not used

TUNING SCALES FOR COMBS

18-Inch KALLIOPE 80 TEETH - Single Comb

Tooth	Note	Octave
1	G	5
2	G	5
3	C	1
4	C	1
5	D	2
6	E	3
7	F	4
8	F	4
9	F#	4'
10	G	5
11	G	5
12	A	6
13	B	7
14	C	1
15	C	1
16	D	2
17	E	3
18	E	3
19	F	4
20	F	4
21	G	5
22	G	5
23	A	6
24	B	7
25	C	1
26	C	1
27	D	2
28	E	3
29	E	3
30	F	4
31	F#	4'
32	G	5
33	G	5
34	A	6
35	A#	6'
36	A#	6'
37	B	7
38	B	7
39	C	1
40	C	1
41	C	1
42	C#	1'
43	D	2
44	D	2
45	D#	2'
46	E	3
47	E	3
48	F	4
49	F	4
50	F#	4'
51	G	5
52	G	5
53	G	5
54	G#	5'
55	A	6
56	A	6
57	A#	6'
58	B	7
59	B	7
60	C	1
61	C	1
62	D	2
63	D	2
64	D#	2'
65	E	3
66	E	3
67	F	4
68	F	4
69	F#	4'
70	G	5
71	G	5
72	A	6
73	A	6
74	A	6
75	B	7
76	C	1
77	C	1
78	D	2
79	D	2
80	E	3

18-Inch KALLIOPE 1 × 29, 1 × 28, 2 × 23, TEETH (4 Combs)

Upper Comb (1)-Nearer Centre Dome-29 Teeth-Alternate Pluck with (2)

1	2	3	4	5	6	7	8	9	10	11	12	13	14	15	16	17	18	19	20	21	22	23	24	25	26	27	28	29
G	C	D	F	F#	G	B	C	E	F	G	A	C	D	E	F#	G	A	A#	B	C	C#	D	E	F	F#	G	G#	A
5	1	2	4	4'	5	7	1	3	4	5	6	1	2	3	4'	5	6	6'	7	1	1'	2	3	4	4'	5	5'	6

Lower Comb (2)-Nearer Centre Dome-28 Teeth-Alternate Pluck With (1)

1	2	3	4	5	6	7	8	9	10	11	12	13	14	15	16	17	18	19	20	21	22	23	24	25	26	27	28
G	C	E	F	G	A	C	D	E	G	A	B	C	E	F	G	A	B	C	C	D#	E	F	G	G	A	A#
5	1	3	4	5	6	1	2	3	5	6	7	1	3	4	5	6	7	1	1	2	2'	3	4	5	5	6	6'

Upper and Lower Combs (3) & (4) 2 × 23 Teeth-Simultaneous Pluck

1	2	3	4	5	6	7	8	9	10	11	12	13	14	15	16	17	18	19	20	21	22	23
B	B	C	C	D	D#	E	E	F	F	F#	G	G	G	A	A	A	B	C	C	C	D	E
7	7	1	1	2	2	2'	3	3	4	4'	5	5	5	6	6	6	7	1	1	2	3

TUNING SCALES FOR COMBS

23-Inch KALLIOPE 1 × 48, 2 × 22, 1×51 TEETH = 143 TEETH - Alternate Pluck Where Combs Opposed

Comb 1. - To Left Above Centre Dome-Plucked Upward-22 Teeth

1	2	3	4	5	6	7	8	9	10	11	12	13	14	15	16	17	18	19	20	21	22*
A	E	E	F#	A	A	A	B	C#	D	E	E	F#	G	G#	A	B	C	C#	D	D#	E
1	5	5	6	1	1	1	2	3	4	5	5	6	6'	7	1	2	2'	3	4	4'	5

Comb 2. - Upper Right Nearest Centre Dome-51 Teeth

1	2	3	4	5	6	7	8	9	10	11	12	13	14	15	16	17	18	19	20	21	22*	23	24	25	26	27	28	29	30	31
A	E	E	G#	A	A	B	C#	D	D#	E	E	F#	G#	A	A	B	C#	D	D#	E	E	F	F#	F#	G	G#	A	A	A	A
1	5	5	7	1	1	2	3	4	4'	5	5	6	7	1	1	2	3	4	4'	5	5	5'	6	6	6'	7	1	1	1	1

32	33	34	35	36	37	38	39	40	41	42	43	44	45	46	47	48, 49	50, 51
A#	B	B	C	C#	C#	D	D#	D	D#	E	E	E	F	F#	F#	G	G#
1'	2	2	2'	3	3	4	4'	4	4'	5	5	5	5'	6	6	6'	7

*Notes Have Same Value

Comb 3. - Lower Right Near Pressure-Bar Bracket-22 Teeth

1	2	3	4	5	6	7	8	9	10	11	12	13	14	15	16	17	18	19	20	21	22
A	A	A	A♯	B	B	B	C	C♯	C♯	C♯	C♯	D	D	D	D	D♯	E	E	E	E	F♯
1	1	1	1′	2	2	2	2′	3	3	3	3	4	4	4	4	4′	5	5	5	5	6

Comb 4. - To Left Below Centre Dome-48 Teeth

1	2	3	4	5	6	7	8	9	10	11	12	13	14	15	16	17	18	19	20	21	22	23	24
F♯	F♯	F♯	F♯	F♯	F♯	G	G♯	G♯	G♯	G♯	A	A	A	A	A	A♯	B	B	B	B	C	C♯	C♯
6	6	6	6	6	6	6′	7	7	7	7	1	1	1	1	1	1′	2	2	2	2	2′	3	3
25	26	27	28	29	30	31	32	33	34	35	36	37	38	39	40	41	42	43	44	45	46	47	48
C♯	C♯	D	D	D	D♯	E	E	E	E	E	F♯	F♯	F♯	F♯	G♯	G♯	G♯	A	A	A	B	B	C♯
3	3	4	4	4	4′	5	5	5	5	5	6	6	6	6	7	7	7	1	1	1	2	2	3

Scale is continuous from Combs 2-3 and 3-4 (half tone intervals between treble and bass)
Comb 4 Duplicates some comb 3 bass notes and fills in some half tone gaps in bass tuning

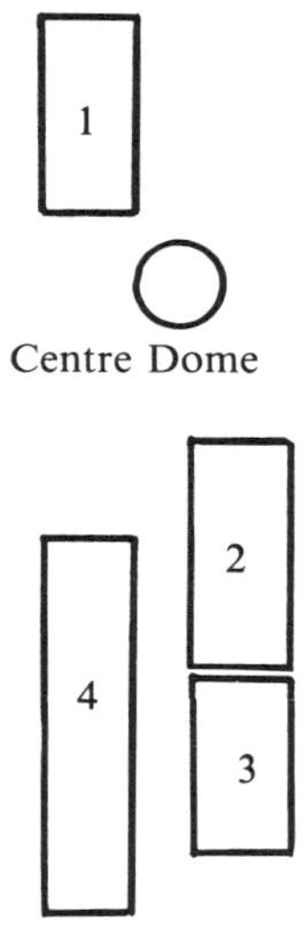

Position of Combs

Not in Scale

TUNING SCALES FOR COMBS

KOMET SCALES

8¼-Inch KOMET 40 TEETH

1	2	3	4	5	6	7	8	9	10	11	12	13	14	15	16	17	18	19	20	21	22	23	24	25	26	27	28	29	30	31
G	mid C	mid C	D	E	F	G	G	A	B	C	C	D	E	F	F#	G?*	A	A	B	B	C	C	D	D	D	E	E	F	F	F#
5	1	1	2	3	4	5	5	6	7	1	1	2	3	4	4'	5	5?	6	6	7	7	1	1	2	2	3	3	4	4	4'

32	33	34	35	36	37	38	39	40
G	G	G	A	A	B	C	D	E
5	5	5	6	6	7	1	2	3

*Unknown-Probably G

10¼-Inch KOMET 48 TEETH

1	2	3	4	5	6	7	8	9	10	11	12	13	14	15	16	17	18	19	20	21	22	23	24	25	26	27	28	29	30	31
A	C#	D	F	A#	A#	D	D#	D	F	F#	F	G	A	A	B	C#	D	D	E	F#	G	G#	A	A	B	B	C	C#	C#	D
1	3	4	5'	1'	1'	4	4'	4	5'	6	6	6'	1	1	2	3	4	4	5	6	6'	7	1	1	2	2'	3	3	3	4

32 33 34 35 36 37 38 39 40 41 42 43 44 45 46 47 48
D D# E E F# F# G G G# A A A# B C# D E F#
4 4' 5 5 6 6 6' 7 1 1 1' 2 3 4 5 6

TUNING SCALES FOR COMBS

25-INCH LOCHMANN ORIGINAL SCALE

25-Inch LOCHMANN ORIGINAL with 12 Bells 2 × 80 TEETH-Simultaneous Pluck

1 2 3 4 5 6 7 8 9 10 11 12 13 14 15 16 17 18 19 20 21 22 23 24 25 26 27 28 29 30 31
C C G G A B C C# D D E F# G G A A B B C D D E E F# F# G G A B B C
4 4 1 2 3 4 5 5 6 6 7 1 1 2 2 3 3 4 5 5 6 6 7 7 1 1 2 3 3 4

32 33 34 35 36 37 38 39 40 41 42 43 44 45 46 47 48 49 50 51 52 53 54 55 56 57 58 59 60 61 62
C# D D# E E F F# F# G G G# A A A# B B C C C C# D D D# E E F F# F# G G G#
4' 5 5' 6 6 6' 7 7 1 1 1' 2 2 2' 3 3 4 4 4 4' 5 5 5' 6 6 6' 7 7 1 1 1'

63 64 65 66 67 68 69 70 71 72 73 74 75 76 77 78 79 80
A A A# B B C C C# D D D E E F# G G A B
2 2 2' 3 3 4 4 4' 5 5 5 6 6 7 1 1 2 3

Bells (Tubular)

1 2 3 4 5 6 7 8 9 10 11 12
F# G A B C C# D E F# G A B

TUNING SCALES FOR COMBS

MIRA SCALES

11-Inch MIRA 2 × 63 TEETH - Simultaneous Pluck Also EMPRESS

#	Note	Oct	#	Note	Oct	#	Note	Oct
1	C#	5	32	G	1'	63	F#	1
2	F#	1	33	G#	2			
3	F#	1	34	A	2'			
4	G#	2	35	A#	3			
5	A#	3	36	A#	3			
6	C#	5	37	B	4			
7	C#	5	38	B	4			
8	D#	6	39	C	4'			
9	F	7	40	C#	5			
10	F#	1	41	C#	5			
11	F#	1	42	D	5'			
12	G#	2	43	D#	6			
13	A#	3	44	D#	6			
14	B	4	45	E	6'			
15	C#	5	46	F	7			
16	C#	5	47	F	7			
17	D#	6	48	F	7			
18	F	7	49	F#	1			
19	F#	1	50	F#	1			
20	G#	2	51	G#	2			
21	G#	2	52	G#	2			
22	A#	3	53	G#	2			
23	A#	3	54	A#	3			
24	B	4	55	A#	3			
25	C#	5	56	B	4			
26	C#	5	57	B	4			
27	D#	6	58	C#	5			
28	F	6	59	C#	5			
29	F	7	60	D#	6			
30	F#	1	61	D#	6			
31	F#	1	62	F	7			

TUNING SCALES FOR COMBS

15½-Inch MIRA 76 TEETH Single Comb

1	2	3	4	5	6	7	8	9	10	11	12	13	14	15	16	17	18	19	20	21	22	23	24	25	26	27	28	29	30	31
C#	C#	F	F#	G#	A#	B	C#	C#	D#	F	F#	F#	G#	G#	A#	A#	B	C#	C#	D#	D#	F	F#	F#	G#	G#	A#	B	C	C#
5	5	7	1	2	3	4	5	5	6	7	1	1	2	2	3	3	4	5	5	6	6	7	1	1	2	3	3	4	4'	5

32	33	34	35	36	37	38	39	40	41	42	43	44	45	46	47	48	49	50	51	52	53	54	55	56	57	58	59	60	61	62
C#	D#	F	F	F	F#	F#	G	G#	G#	A	A#	A#	A#	B	B	C	C#	C#	C#	D	D#	D#	E	F	F	F#	F#	G	G#	G#
5	6	6	7	7	1	1	1'	2	2	2'	3	3	4	4	4'	5	5	5	5'	6	6	6'	7	7	7	1	1	1'	2	2

63	64	65	66	67	68	69	70	71	72	73	74	75	76
A#	B	B	C	C#	C#	D#	D#	F	F#	F#	G#	A#	
3	3	4	4'	5	5	6	6	7	1	1	2	3	

TUNING SCALES FOR COMBS

18½-Inch MIRA 2 x 81 TEETH—93 Notes
Part Alternate Pluck Double Opposed Combs

1	2	3	4	5	6	7	8	9	10	11	12	13	14	15	16	17	18	19	20	21	22	23	24	25	26	27	28	29	30	31
C	C	D	E	F	F	F	G	A	A#	C	C	D	D	E	F	F	G	G	A	A#	A#	B	C	C	D	D	E	E	F	F
5	5	6	7	1	1	1	2	3	4	5	5	6	6	7	1	1	2	3	4	4'	4	5	5	6	6	7	7	1	1	1

32	33	34	35	36	37	38	39	40	41	42	43	44	45	46	47	48	49	50	51	52	53	54	55	56	57	58	59	60	61	62
G	G	A	A	A#	A#	B	B	C	C	C	D	D	E	E	F	F	F#	F#	G	G	G	G#	A	A	A	A	A#	B	B	C
2	2	3	4	4	4	4'	5	5	5	5	6	6	7	7	1	1	1	1'	2	2	2	2'	3	3	3	4	4	4	4'	5

63	64	65	66	67	68	69	70	71	72	73	74	75	76	77	78	79	80	81	82	83	84	85	86	87	88	89	90	91	92	93
C	C#	D	D	D#	E	E	F	F	F	F#	G	G	A	A	A	A#	A#	B	C	C	C	D	D	D	E	E	F	F	G	A
5	5'	6	6	6'	7	7	1	1	1'	2	2	3	3	4	4	4	5	5	6	6	6	7	7	7	1	1	1	2	3

N.B. First 24 Notes Alternate = Upper Comb 1,3,5,7,9,11,13,15,17,19,21,23.
Lower Comb 2,4,6,8,10,12,14,16,18,20,22,24.
The rest are simultaneous pluck.

ORPHENION SCALES

8¼-Inch ORPHENION 35 TEETH

1	2	3	4	5	6	7	8	9	10	11	12	13	14	15	16	17	18	19	20	21	22	23	24	25	26	27	28	29	30	31
G#	A#	D#	G#	A#	C	C	C#	D#	D#	F	G	G#	A#	C	C#	D#	D#	F	F	G	G	G#	A#	C	C	C#	D	D#
				1	2	3	4	5	6	7	1	2	3	4	5	6	7	1	2	3	4	4'	5

32	33	34	35
D#	F	G	G#
5	6	7	1

N.B. Teeth tuned in pairs should have second tooth of pair tuned very slightly higher to give a slow beat between the two.

10¾-Inch ORPHENION 50 TEETH

1	2	3	4	5	6	7	8	9	10	11	12	13	14	15	16	17	18	19	20	21	22	23	24	25	26	27	28	29	30	31
G	A	D	D	E	F#	G	G	A	B	B	C	D	D	E	F#	G	G	A	B	C	C#	D	D	E	E	E#	F#	F#	G	G
1	2	5	6	7	1	1	2	3	4	5	5	6	7	1	1	2	3	4	4'	5	5	6	6	6'	7	7	1	1

32	33	34	35	36	37	38	39	40	41	42	43	44	45	46	47	48	49	50
G	G#	A	A	B	B	C	C	C#	D	D	D	D#	E	E	F#	G	G	A
1	1'	2	2	3	3	4	4	4'	5	5	5'	6	6	7	1	1	2

N.B. Teeth tuned in pairs should have second tooth of pair tuned very slightly higher to give a slow beat between the two.

TUNING SCALES FOR COMBS

13½-Inch ORPHENION 70 TEETH

1	2	3	4	5	6	7	8	9	10	11	12	13	14	15	16	17	18	19	20	21	22	23	24	25	26	27	28	29	30	31
G	C	C	D	E	F	G	G	A	B	C	C	D	E	F	G	G	A	B	C	C	D	E	F	F#	G	G	A
5	1	1	2	3	4	5	5	6	7	1	1	2	3	4	5	5	6	7	1	1	2	3	4	4′	5	5	6

32	33	34	35	36	37	38	39	40	41	42	43	44	45	46	47	48	49	50	51	52	53	54	55	56	57	58	59	60	61	62
A#	B	B	C	C	C#	D	D	E	E	F	F	F#	G	G	G#	A	A	A#	B	B	C	C	D	D	E	E	F	F	F#
6′	7	7	1	1	1′	2	2	3	3	4	4	4	5	5	5′	6	6	6′	7	7	1	1	2	2	3	3	4	4	4′

63	64	65	66	67	68	69	70
G	G	G	A	A	B	C	
5	5	5	6	6	6	7	1

N.B. Teeth tuned in pairs should have second tooth of pair tuned very slightly higher to give a slow beat between the two.

16-Inch ORPHENION 90 TEETH

Both Single Comb(s) and Part Alternate Pluck Double Opposed Combs—Lower Comb Mounted at 90° as Stella

1	2	3	4	5	6	7	8	9	10	11	12	13	14	15	16	17	18	19	20	21	22	23	24	25	26	27	28	29	30	31
E	E	A	A	B	C	D	E	F	G	A	B	C	C#	D	E	F#	G	A	B	C#	D	E	F#	G#	A	B	C#
5	5	1	1	2	3	4	5	5	6	7	1	1	2	3	4	5	6	6	7	1	1	2	2	3	3

TUNING SCALES FOR COMBS

No.	32	33	34	35	36	37	38	39	40	41	42	43	44	45	46	47	48	49	50	51	52	53	54	55	56	57	58	59	60	61	62
Note	D	D	D#	E	E	F	F#	F#	G	G#	G#	A	A	A#	B	B	C	C#	D	D	D#	E	E	F	F#	F#	G	G#	G#	G	A
Scale	4	4	4'	5	5	5'	6	6	6'	7	7	7'	1	1	1'	2	2	2'	3	3	3'	4	4	4'	5	5	5'	6	6	6'	1

No.	63	64	65	66	67	68	69	70	71	72	73	74	75	76	77	78	79	80	81	82	83	84	85	86	87	88	89	90
Note	A	A	A#	B	B	C	C#	C#	D	D	D#	E	E	D#	D	E	E	E	F	F#	F#	G#	G#	A	A	A	A#	B
Scale	1	1	1'	2	2	2'	3	3	3	4	4	4	4'	5	5	5	5'	5'	6	6	6	6'	7	7	1	1	1'	2

N.B. This machine is found in at least 2 formats:

1. Single Fine Comb and Ultra-Fine Piccolo Comb
2. 'Fortissimo' with upper and lower combs. Upper and lower have short bass combs of 8 broad teeth plucked alternately. The rest are simultaneous pluck.

   Upper Bass Comb = Nos. 1,3,5,7,9,11,13,15.
   Lower Bass Comb = Nos. 2,4,6,8,10,12,14,16.

Teeth tuned in pairs should have second tooth of pair tuned very slightly higher to give a slow beat between the two.

TUNING SCALES FOR COMBS

POLYPHON SCALES

11-in. = 14⅞-in. Polyphon with bells, and 12¼-in. Regina and Universal

15½-in. = 15½-in. Monarch, Triumph; Olympia; Criterion; Crown; Euphonion; Sterling; 14⅞-in. Symphonion; 17¼-in. Polyphon with bells, and 15½-in. Universal

19⅝-in. = 22-in. Polyphon with bells; 17¼-in. centre drive Polyphon, and 19⅝-in. Britannia

All sizes up to and including 15½-in. are compatible with Regina, except for 15½-in. Regina with bells.

6½-Inch POLYPHON 30 TEETH

1	2	3	4	5	6	7	8	9	10	11	12	13	14	15	16	17	18	19	20	21	22	23	24	25	26	27	28	29	30
F	F	A♯	A♯	C	C	D	D♯	F	G	A	A♯	C	F	F	G	A	A♯	A♯	C	C	D	D	D♯	E	E	F	F	G	A♯
1	4	4	4	5	6	6'	1	2	3	4	4	5	1	2	3	4	4	5	5	6	6	6'	6'	7	1	1	2	3	4

8¼-Inch POLYPHON 40 TEETH Also 8-Inch REGINA

1	2	3	4	5	6	7	8	9	10	11	12	13	14	15	16	17	18	19	20	21	22	23	24	25	26	27	28	29	30	31
F	G	C	F	F	G	A	A	A♯	C	C	D	E	F	F	G	A	A♯	B	C	C	C	D	D	E	E	F	F	G	G	A	A
1	2	5	1	2	3	4	5	5	6	7	1	2	3	4	4'	5	5	6	6	7	7	1	2	2	3	3

32	33	34	35	36	37	38	39	40
A♯	A♯	B	C	C	D	E	F	G
4	4	4'	5	5	6	7	1	2

TUNING SCALES FOR COMBS

9⅝-Inch POLYPHON 46 TEETH

```
 1   2   3  4  5  6  7   8   9  10 11 12  13 14 15 16 17  18 19 20  21 22 23 24 25 26 27 28  29  30  31
 F  A#   C  F  F  G A#  A#   C  D  D  D#   F  F  G  A A#   C  D D#   E  F  F  G  G  A  A A#  A#  A#   1
 5   1   1  2  5  5  6   1   1  2  3  4   5  5  6  7  1   1  2  3   4' 5  5  6  6  7  7  1   1

32 33 34 35 36 37 38 39 40 41 42 43 44 45 46
 B  C  C  D  D  D# D# E  F  F# G  A A#  C
 1' 2  2  3  4  4  4' 5  5' 6  7  1  2
```

11-Inch POLYPHON 54 TEETH (Or 108 if Double Comb with Simultaneous Pluck) Also 12¼-Inch REGINA

```
 1   2   3  4  5  6  7  8  9 10 11 12 13 14 15 16 17 18 19 20 21 22 23 24  25 26 27 28  29 30 31
 G   C   C  D  E  G  G  A  B  C  C  D  E  E  F  G  G  A  B  C  C  D  E  F  F# G  G  A  A#   B
 5   1   1  2  3  5  5  6  7  1  1  2  3  3  4  5  5  6  7  1  1  2  3  4   4' 5  5  6   6'  7

32 33 34 35 36 37 38 39 40 41 42 43 44 45 46 47 48 49 50 51 52 53 54
 B  C  C  C# D  D  E  E  F  F  G  G  G# A  A  B  C  C  D  E
 7  1  1  1' 2  2  3  3  4  4' 5  5  5' 6  6  7  1  1  2  3
```

271

TUNING SCALES FOR COMBS

15½-Inch POLYPHON 76 TEETH (Or 152 if Double Comb with Simultaneous Pluck) Key of C
Also for 15½-Inch REGINA; 14⅞-Inch SYMPHONION; 15½-Inch MONARCH; 15½-Inch TRIUMPH; 15½-Inch OLYMPIA; and 15½-Inch CRITERION

1	2	3	4	5	6	7	8	9	10	11	12	13	14	15	16	17	18	19	20	21	22	23	24	25	26	27	28	29	30	31
G	G	C	C	C	D	E	F	G	G	A	B	C	C	D	E	F	G	G	A	B	C	C	D	E	E	F	F	F#	G	G
5	5	1	1	1	2	3	4	5	5	6	7	1	1	2	3	4	5	5	6	7	1	1	2	3	3	4	4'	5	5

32	33	34	35	36	37	38	39	40	41	42	43	44	45	46	47	48	49	50	51	52	53	54	55	56	57	58	59	60	61	62
G	A	A	B	B	C	C	C	C#	D	D	D#	E	E	F	F	F#	G	G	G#	A	A	A#	B	B	C	C	D	D	E	E
5	6	6	7	7	1	1	1	1'	2	2	2'	3	3	4	4	4'	5	5	5'	6	6	6'	7	7	1	1	2	2	3	3

63	64	65	66	67	68	69	70	71	72	73	74	75	76
F	F	F#	G	G	G	A	A	A	B	C	C	D	E
4	4	4'	5	5	5	6	6	6	7	1	1	2	3

19⅝-Inch POLYPHON 1 × 60 TEETH 1 × 58 TEETH
Also 22-Inch POLYPHON PLUS BELLS (See Below) and 17¼-Inch Centre Drive POLYPHON

Upper Comb-60 Teeth

1	2	3	4	5	6	7	8	9	10	11	12	13	14	15	16	17	18	19	20	21	22	23	24	25	26	27	28	29	30	31
A#	F	G	A#	C	D	D#	E	F	G	G#	A	A#	C	C#	D	D#	E	F	G	G#	A	A#	B	C	C#	D	D#	E		
1	5	6	1	1	2	3'	4	5	6	6'	7	1	2	2'	3	3'	4	5	6	6'	7	1'	2	2'	3	3'	4			

272

TUNING SCALES FOR COMBS

32	33	34	35	36	37	38	39	40	41	42	43	44	45	46	47	48	49	50	51	52	53	54	55	56	57	58	59	60
F	F	F#	G	G	G#	A	A	A#	B	C	C	D	D	D#	E	F	F	F#	G	G	G#	A	A	A#	B	C	D	D#
5	5	5'	6	6	6'	7	7	7	1'	2	2	3	3	3'	4	5	5	5'	6	6	6'	7	7	7	1'	2	3	3'

Lower Comb-58 Teeth

1	2	3	4	5	6	7	8	9	10	11	12	13	14	15	16	17	18	19	20	21	22	23	24	25	26	27	28	29	30	31
A#	F	G	A#	A#	C	D	D#	E	F	G	G#	A	A#	C	C#	D	D#	E	F	G	G#	A	A#	B	C	C#	D	D#	D#	E
1	5	6	1	1	2	3	3'	4	5	6	6'	7	7	1'	2	2'	3	3'	4	5	6'	7	7	1'	2	2'	3	3'	3'	4

32	33	34	35	36	37	38	39	40	41	42	43	44	45	46	47	48	49	50	51	52	53	54	55	56	57	58
F	F	G	G	A	A	A#	C	C	C#	D	D	D#	D#	E	F	F	G	G	G#	A	A#	A#	C	C	C	D
5	5	6	6	7	7	1	2	2	2'	3	3'	3'	3'	4	5	5	6	6	6'	7	7	1	1	2	2	3

22-Inch POLYPHON

BELLS ONLY

(19⅞ Combs Plus 16 Tuned Metal Bars (Metalophone))

With Upper Comb

1	2	3	4	5	6	7	8
D	D#	E	F*	F*	G*	A*	A#*

TUNING SCALES FOR COMBS

With Lower Comb

1	2	3	4	5	6	7	8
F	G*	A	A#	A#	C	C	D

*Octave Higher

24½-Inch POLYPHON 1 × 60 TEETH-1 × 59 TEETH-2 × 20 TEETH

Large Upper Comb-60 Teeth

1	2	3	4	5	6	7	8	9	10	11	12	13	14	15	16	17	18	19	20	21	22	23	24	25	26	27	28	29	30	31
G	D	E	G	G	A#	B	C#	D	D	D	D#	E	F#	G	G	A	A	B	B	C	C	D	D	D#	E	E	F#	F#	G	G
1	5	6	1	1	2	2'	3	4'	5	5	5'	6	7	1	1	2	2	3	3	4	4	5	5	5'	6	6	7	7	1	1

32	33	34	35	36	37	38	39	40	41	42	43	44	45	46	47	48	49	50	51	52	53	54	55	56	57	58	59	60
A	A	B	B	C	C#	D	°D	D#	E	E	F#	F#	G	G	A	A	A#	B	B	C	C	C#	D	D	D	E	E	F#	G
2	2	3	3	4	4'	5	5	5'	6	6	7	7	1	1	2	2	2'	3	3	4	4	4'	5	5	6	6	7	1

Small Upper Comb-20 Teeth

1	2	3	4	5	6	7	8	9	10	11	12	13	14	15	16	17	18	19	20
D	E	F#	G	G#	A	A	B	B	C#	C#	D	D	D#	E	E	F#	G	G	A
5	6	7	1	1'	2	2	3	3	4	4	5	5	5'	6	6	7	1	1	2

TUNING SCALES FOR COMBS

Large Lower Comb-59 Teeth

1	2	3	4	5	6	7	8	9	10	11	12	13	14	15	16	17	18	19	20	21	22	23	24	25	26	27	28	29	30	31
G	D	D	F#	G	G	A	B	C	C#	D	D	E	F	F#	G	G	A#	B	B	C	C#	D	D	E	F	F#	G	G	G#
1	5	5	7	1	1	2	3	4	4'	5	5	6	6'	7	1	1	2	2'	3	3	4	4'	5	5	6	6'	7	1	1	1'

32	33	34	35	36	37	38	39	40	41	42	43	44	45	46	47	48	49	50	51	52	53	54	55	56	57	58	59
A	A#	B	C	C	C#	D	D	E	E	F	F#	G	G	G#	A	A	B	B	C	C	C#	D	D#	E	F	F#	G
2	2'	3	4	4	4'	5	5	6	6	6'	7	1	1	1'	2	2	3	3	4	4	4'	5	5'	6	6'	7	1

Small Lower Comb-20 Teeth

1	2	3	4	5	6	7	8	9	10	11	12	13	14	15	16	17	18	19	20
D#	F#	G	G	A	A	A#	B	B	C	C#	D	D	E	F	F#	F#	G	A	B
5'	7	1	1	2	2	2'	3	3	4	4'	5	5	6	6	7	7	1	2	3

REGINA SCALES

All sizes up to, and including, 15½-in. are compatible with Polyphon with the exception of the 15½-in. with bells.
12¼-in. = 11-in. Polyphon, 11-in. Regina, 11-in. Criterion, and 12¼-in. Universal
15½-in. = 15½-in. Monarch, Triumph, Olympia, Criterion, Crown, Euphorion, Sterling;
14⅞-in. Symphonion, 17¼-in. Polyphon with bells, and 15½-in. Universal.

8-Inch REGINA 40 TEETH Also 8¼-Inch POLYPHON

1	2	3	4	5	6	7	8	9	10	11	12	13	14	15	16	17	18	19	20	21	22	23	24	25	26	27	28	29	30	31
G	A	D	G	G	A	B	B	C	D	D	E	F#	G	G	A	B	C	C#	D	D	E	E	F	F#	G	G	A	A	B	B
1	2	5	1	2	3	3	4	5	6	7	1	2	3	4	5	6	6	7	1	1	2	2	3	3

32	33	34	35	36	37	38	39	40
C	C	C#	D	D	E	F#	G	A
4	4'	5	5	6	7	1	2	

12¼-Inch REGINA 54 TEETH Single Comb or 108 Double Comb-Simultaneous Pluck
Also for 11-Inch POLYPHON & CRITERION

1	2	3	4	5	6	7	8	9	10	11	12	13	14	15	16	17	18	19	20	21	22	23	24	25	26	27	28	29	30	31
A#	D#	D#	F	G	A#	A#	C	D	D#	F	G	G	G#	A#	A#	C	D	D#	C	D	D#	F	G	G#	A	A#	C	C	C#	D
5	1	1	2	3	5	5	6	7	1	1	2	3	4	5	5	6	7	1	1	2	3	4	4'	5	5	6	6	6'	7

32	33	34	35	36	37	38	39	40	41	42	43	44	45	46	47	48	49	50	51	52	53	54
D	D#	D#	E	F	F	G	G	G#	A	A#	A#	B	C	C	D#	F	G
7	1	1	1'	2	2	3	3	4	4	5	5	5'	6	6	7	1	1	2	3

TUNING SCALES FOR COMBS

15½-Inch REGINA Coin-Operated   2 × 76 TEETH Simultaneous Pluck
Same as Single Comb (1 × 76 TEETH) Also for 15½-Inch POLYPHON, 14⅞-Inch SYMPHONION
15½-Inch MONARCH, 15½-Inch TRIUMPH, 15½-Inch OLYMPIA, and 15½-Inch CRITERION

1	2	3	4	5	6	7	8	9	10	11	12	13	14	15	16	17	18	19	20	21	22	23	24	25	26	27	28	29	30	31
D#	D#	G#	G#	G#	A#	C	C#	D#	D#	F	G	G#	G#	A#	C	C	C#	D#	D#	F	G	G#	G#	A#	C	C	C#	D	D#	D#
5	5	1	1	1	2	3	4	5	5	6	7	1	1	2	3	4	5	5	5	6	7	1	1	2	3	3	4	4'	5	5

32	33	34	35	36	37	38	39	40	41	42	43	44	45	46	47	48	49	50	51	52	53	54	55	56	57	58	59	60	61	62
D#	F	F	G	G	G#	G#	A	A#	A#	B	C	C	C#	C#	D	D#	D#	E	F	F	F#	G	G	G#	G#	A#	C	C	C	
5	6	6	7	7	1	1	1	1'	2	2	2'	3	3	4	4'	5	5	5'	6	6	6'	7	7	1	1	2	2	2	3	

63	64	65	66	67	68	69	70	71	72	73	74	75	76
C#	C#	D	D#	D#	F	F	F	G	G#	G#	A#	C	
4	4	4'	5	5	6	6	6	7	1	1	2	3	

TUNING SCALES FOR COMBS

20¾-Inch REGINA 1 × 63 TEETH, 1 × 65 TEETH

Lower Comb—63 Teeth

1	2	3	4	5	6	7	8	9	10	11	12	13	14	15	16	17	18	19	20	21	22	23	24	25	26	27	28	29	30	31
A	A	F#	A	A	A	D	D	E	E	E	G	A	A	A	C	D	D	D#	F	F#	F#	F#	A	A	A	A	C	C#	C#	C#
4	4	2	4	4	4	4	6'	1	1	1	2'	4	4	4	5'	6'	6'	7	1'	2	2	2	4	4	4	4	5'	6	6	6

32	33	34	35	36	37	38	39	40	41	42	43	44	45	46	47	48	49	50	51	52	53	54	55	56	57	58	59	60	61	62
D#	D#	F	F#	F#	F#	G#	G#	G#	A#	C	C	C	D	D	D	D	D#	D#	F	F	F#	F#	F#	F#	A	A	A	A	C#	D
7	7	1'	2	2	2	3	3	3	4'	5'	5'	5'	6'	6'	6'	6'	7	7	1'	1'	2	2	2	2	4	4	4	4	6	6'

63
E
1

Upper Comb—65 Teeth

1	2	3	4	5	6	7	8	9	10	11	12	13	14	15	16	17	18	19	20	21	22	23	24	25	26	27	28	29	30	31
E	E	E	G#	B	B	C#	C#	D#	F	F#	F#	G#	G#	B	B	C#	C#	C#	E	E	E	E	G	G#	G#	G#	A#	B	B	B
1	1	1	3	5	5	6	6	7	1'	2	2	3	3	5	5	6	6	6	1	1	1	1	2'	3	3	3	4'	5	5	5

32	33	34	35	36	37	38	39	40	41	42	43	44	45	46	47	48	49	50	51	52	53	54	55	56	57	58	59	60	61	62
D	D	D	E	E	E	E	G	A	A	A	A	B	B	B	B	C#	C#	C#	C#	E	E	E	E	G	G	G#	G#	G#	A#	B
6'	6'	6'	1	1	1	1	2'	4	4	4	4	5	5	5	5	6	6	6	6	1	1	1	1	2'	2'	3	3	3	4'	5

TUNING SCALES FOR COMBS

27-Inch REGINA 1 × 86 TEETH, 1 × 84 TEETH Opposed Combs

Upper Comb—86 Teeth

Tooth	1	2	3	4	5	6	7	8	9	10	11	12	13	14	15	16	17	18	19	20	21 (mid)	22	23	24	25	26	27	28	29	30	31
Note	F#	D	D#	F#	G#	A	A#	B	C#	B	C#	D	E	F	G	G	A	A#	B	B	C	D	D	D#	E	F	F#	G	G	G	A
Octave	7	5'	7	7	1'	2	2'	3	4'	4'	5	6	6'	1	1	2	2'	3	3	4	5	5	5'	6	6'	7	1	1	1	2	2

Tooth	32	33	34	35	36	37	38	39	40	41	42	43	44	45	46	47	48	49	50	51	52	53	54	55	56	57	58	59	60	61*	62
Note	A	B	B	C	C	C#	D	D	D	E	E	F	F#	F#	G	G	G	G	G#	A	A	A#	B	B	B	C	C	C#	D	D	E
Octave	2	3	3	4	4'	5	5	6	6	6'	7	7	1	1	1'	2	2	2	2'	3	3	3	4	4'	5	5	5'	4'	5	5'	6

Tooth	63	64	65	66*	67	68	69	70	71	72	73	74	75	76	77	78	79	80	81	82	83	84	85	86
Note	F	F#	G	D#	F	F#	G	A	A	A#	B	B	C	C#	D	D	D#	E	E	F#	G	F#	A	A#
Octave	6'	7	1	5'	6'	7	1	2	2	2'	3	3	4	4'	5	5	5'	6	6	7	7	1	2	2'

*Teeth 61 & 66 tuned to same note

TUNING SCALES FOR COMBS

Lower Comb-84 Teeth

Tooth	1	2	3	4	5	6	7	8	9	10	11	12	13	14	15	16	17	18	19	20	21	22	23	24	25	26	27	28	29	30	31
Note	B	D	D#	F#	G	G	A	B	B	C	D	D	E	F	F#	G	G	A	B	B	C	C#	D	D	E	F	F#	F#	G	G#	A
	3	5'	7	1	1	2	3	3	4	5	5	6	6'	7	7	1	1	2	3	3	4	4'	5	5	6	6'	7	7	1	1'	2

mid

Tooth	32	33	34	35	36	37	38	39	40	41	42	43	44	45	46	47	48	49	50	51	52	53	54	55	56	57	58*	59*	60	61	62
Note	A#	B	B	C	C#	D	D	D#	E	E	F#	F#	G	G	G	G#	A	A	A	A#	A#	B	B	B	C	C	C#	D	D	E	E	F#
	2'	3	3	4	4'	5	5	5'	6	6	7	7	1	1	1	1'	2	2	2	2'	2'	3	3	4	4	4'	5	5	6	6	7

Tooth	63	64*	65	66	67	68	69	70	71	72	73	74	75	76	77	78	79	80	81	82	83	84
Note	G	D	E	F#	G	G#	A	A	B	B	C	C#	D	D	D	E	E	F	F#	G	A	A
	1	5	6	7	1	1'	2	2	3	3	4	4'	5	5	5	6	6	6'	7	1	2	2

*Teeth 58, 59 & 64 tuned to same note

STELLA SCALES

N.B. 12-in. and 14-in. scales show one comb tuned an octave 'out' from the other. This may not obtain in all cases!

12-Inch STELLA 2 × 40 TEETH

N.B.: Lower (vertical) comb tuned one octave higher than upper (horizontal) comb

1	2	3	4	5	6	7	8	9	10	11	12	13	14	15	16	17	18	19	20	21	22	23	24	25	26	27	28	29	30	31
G#	A#	D#	G#	A#	C	C	C#	D#	F	G	G#	A#	C	C#	C	D	D#	D#	F	F	G	G	G#	G#	A#	A#	C	C	C	C#
4	5	1	4	4	5	6	6	6'	1	1	2	3	4	5	6'	7	1	1	2	2	3	4	4	5	5	6	6	6	6	6'

32	33	34	35	36	37	38	39	40
C#	D	D#	D#	F	F	G	G#	
6'	7	1	1	1	2	3	4	

TUNING SCALES FOR COMBS

14-Inch STELLA 2 × 63 TEETH – Simultaneous Pluck
Upper comb tuned one octave below lower comb

1	2	3	4	5	6	7	8	9	10	11	12	13	14	15	16	17	18	19	20	21	22	23	24	25	26	27	28	29	30	31
G	G	A	B	B	C	D	D	E	F#	G	G	A	A	B	B	C	C#	D	D	E	E	F#	G	G	A	B	B	C	C#	D
1	1	2	3	4	4	5	5	6	7	1	1	2	2	3	3	4	4'	5	5	6	6	7	1	1	2	3	3	4	4'	5

32	33	34	35	36	37	38	39	40	41	42	43	44	45	46	47	48	49	50	51	52	53	54	55	56	57	58	59	60	61	62
D	D	E	E	F#	F#	G	G	G#	A	A	A	A#	B	B	B	C	C	C	C#	C#	D	D	D	D#	E	E	F	F#	F#	G
5	5	6	6	7	7	1	1	1'	2	2	2	2'	3	3	3	4	4	4	4'	4'	5	5	5	5'	6	6	6'	7	7	1'

63
G
1

15½-Inch STELLA 2 × 61 TEETH
Both upper and lower (vertical) combs

1	2	3	4	5	6	7	8	9	10	11	12	13	14	15	16	17	18	19	20	21	22	23	24	25	26	27	28	29	30	31
G	G	A	D	D	E	G	G	A	B	C	D	D	E	F#	G	G	A	B	C	C#	D	D	C#	D	E	E	F#	G	G	G#
1	1	2	5	5	6	1	1	2	3	4	5	5	6	7	1	1	2	3	4	4'	5	5	4'	5	6	6	7	1	1	1'

TUNING SCALES FOR COMBS

17¼-Inch STELLA 2 × 84 TEETH—Simultaneous Pluck Also Single Comb

Tooth	32	33	34	35	36	37	38	39	40	41	42	43	44	45	46	47	48	49	50	51	52	53	54	55	56	57	58	59	60	61
Note	A	A♯	B	B	C	C	C♯	D	D	D	D♯	E	E	F♯	F♯	G	G	A	B	B	C	C♯	D	D	D	D	E	E	F♯	G
Oct.	2	2	2′	3	3	4	4	4′	5	5	5	5′	6	6	7	7	1	1	2	3	3	3	4	4′	5	5	6	6	7	1

Tooth	*	†	1	2	3	4	5	6	7	8	9	10	11	12	13	14	15	16	17	18	19	20	21	22	23	24	25	26	27	28	29	30	31
Note			D	D	G	G	G	B	C	C♯	D	D	D	E	F♯	G	G	A	A	B	B	C	C♯	D	D	E	F♯	G	G	A	B	B	C
Oct.			5	5	1	1	3	4	4	4′	5	5	6	7	1	1	2	2	3	3	4	4′	5	5	6	6	7	1	1	2	3	3	4

Tooth	32	33	34	35	36	37	38	39	40	41	42	43	44	45	46	47	48	49	50	51	52	53	54	55	56	57	58	59	60	61	62
Note	C♯	D	D	D	E	E	F♯	F♯	G	G	G♯	A	A	A	A♯	B	B	B	C	C	C♯	C♯	D	D	D	D♯	E	E	F	F♯	
Oct.	4′	5	5	6	6	7	7	1	1	1′	2	2	2	2′	3	3	4	4	4′	5	5	5′	6	6	6′	7					

Tooth	63	64	65	66	67	68	69	70	71	72	73	74	75	76	77	78	79	80	81	82	83	84
Note	F♯	G	G♯	A	A	B	B	C	C	C♯	D	D	D	E	E	E	F♯	G	G	A	B
Oct.	7	1	1	1′	2	2	3	3	4	4′	5	5	6	6	6	7	1	1	2	3	

*Tooth No. 1 is tuned an octave higher on *upper* comb-Matching Nos. 9 & 10-On duplex model
†Tooth No. 2 is tuned an octave higher on *lower* comb-Matching Nos. 9 & 10-On duplex model
N.B. The above may not apply to all examples.

TUNING SCALES FOR COMBS

26-Inch STELLA 2 × 101 TEETH-Simultaneous Pluck

1	2	3	4	5	6	7	8	9	10	11	12	13	14	15	16	17	18	19	20	21	22	23	24	25	26	27	28	29	30	31
C#	C#	F#	F#	F#	G#	A#	B	C#	C#	D#	F	F#	F#	G#	A#	B	A#	B	C	C#	C#	D#	D#	E	F	F	F#	F#
5	5	1	1	1	2	2	3	4	5	5	6	7	1	1	2	2	3	3	4	4	5	5	6	6	6'	7	7	1

32	33	34	35	36	37	38	39	40	41	42	43	44	45	46	47	48	49	50	51	52	53	54	55	56	57	58	59	60	61	62
G	G#	A#	A#	B	B	C	C#	C#	D#	D#	E	F	F#	F#	G#	A#	F	F#	F#	G	G#	G#	A	A#	A#	B	B
1'	2	2	3	3	4	4	5	5	6	6	6	7	7	7	2	3	3	4	5	7	1	1	1	2	2	·2'	3	3	4	4

63	64	65	66	67	68	69	70	71	72	73	74	75	76	77	78	79	80	81	82	83	84	85	86	87	88	89	90	91	92	93
C	C	C#	·C#	D	D#	D#	E	F	F	F#	F#	F	G	G#	A	A#	A#	B	C	C	C#	C#	C#	D	D#
4'	5	5	5	5'	6	6	6'	7	7	1	1	1'	2	2	2'	3	3	3	4	4	4'	5	5	5	5'	6	6

94	95	96	97	98	99	100	101
D#	E	F	F	F#	F#	G#	A#
6	6'	7	7	1	1	2	3

SYMPHONION AND MONOPOL SCALES

For new 'Symphonion' scale see 9½-in. Kalliope

In smaller, centre drive, diametral comb machines, scales correspond to those of Monopol.

For 14⅞-in. see 15½-in. Polyphon or Regina

19⅛-in. = 17¼-in.

25-in. scales given for diametral combs and opposed combs

1	2	3	4	5	6	7	8	9	10	11	12	13	14	15	16	17	18	19	20	21	22	23	24	25	26	27	28	29	30	31
E	F#	B	E	E	F#	G#	A	B	B	C#	D#	E	E	F#	G#	A	A#	B	C#	C#	D#	D#	E	E	E	F#	F#	G#	G#	
1	2	5	1	1	2	3	4	5	6	7	1	1	2	3	4	4'	5	5	6	6	7	7	1	1	2	2	3	3		

5-Inch (?) MONOPOL MANIVELLE 40 TEETH

32	33	34	35	36	37	38	39	40	41
A	A	A#	B	B	C#	D#	E	F#	*
4	4	4'	5	5	6	7	1	2	

*Dummy tooth

N.B. Same scale (plus doubling of Note No. 3) as 7⅞-in. Symphonion

TUNING SCALES FOR COMBS

7⅞-Inch SYMPHONION 41 TEETH Single Comb

1	2	3	4	5	6	7	8	9	10	11	12	13	14	15	16	17	18	19	20	21	22	23	24	25	26	27	28	29	30	31
D	E	A	A	D	D	E	F#	G	A	A	B	C#	D	D	E	F#	G	G#	A	A	B	C#	D	D	C#	D	D	E	E	F#
1	2	5	5	1	1	2	3	4	5	5	6	7	1	1	2	3	4	4'	5	5	6	7	1	1	7	1	1	2	2	3

32	33	34	35	36	37	38	39	40	41
F#	G	G	G#	A	A	B	C#	D	E
3	4	4	4'	5	5	6	7	1	2

N.B. Same scale (plus two bass teeth) as Christmas Tree Holder movement shown
Same scale (less Note No. 4) as 5-in. Manivelle Monopol

7-Inch (?) Movement in Tree Stand–43 TEETH Single Comb
First few bass teeth wide and widely spaced

1	2	3	4	5	6	7	8	9	10	11	12	13	14	15	16	17	18	19	20	21	22	23	24	25	26	27	28	29	30	31
A	D	D	E	A	A	D	D	E	F#	G	A	A	B	C#	D	D	E	F#	G	G#	A	A	B	C#	D	D	C#	D	D	E
5	1	1	2	5	5	1	1	2	3	4	5	5	6	7	1	1	2	3	4	4'	5	5	6	7	1	1	7	1	1	2

TUNING SCALES FOR COMBS

32	33	34	35	36	37	38	39	40	41	42	43	44*
E	F#	F#	G	G	G#	A	A	B	C#	D	E	
2	3	3	4	4	4'	5	5	6	6	7	1	2

*Dummy tooth
N.B. Without the first two bass notes scale is as 7⅝-inch Symphonion

8¼-Inch SYMPHONION Diametral Combs-2 × 30 TEETH

Comb Nearer Pressure Bar *Hinge*-30 Teeth

1	2	3	4	5	6	7	8	9	10	11	12	13	14	15	16	17	18	19	20	21	22	23	24	25	26	27	28	29	30
A	D	E	G	A	B	C	C#	D	E	F#	F#	G	A	A	B	C	C#	D	D	E	F#	F#	G	G	G#	A	A
5	1	2	4	5	6	6'	7	1	2	3	3	4	5	5	6	6'	7	7	1	1	2	2	3	3	4	4'	5	5

Comb Nearer Pressure Bar *Clip*-30 Teeth. N.B. Bass Teeth at Periphery of Disc-Scale Reversed

1	2	3	4	5	6	7	8	9	10	11	12	13	14	15	16	17	18	19	20	21	22	23	24	25	26	27	28	29	30
E	D	C#	C	B	B	B	A#	A	A	A	G#	G	G	F#	F#	F#	E	E	E	D#	D	D	C#	C#	C	B	B	A#
2	1	7	6'	6	6	6	5'	5	5	5	4'	4	4	3	3	3	2	2	2	1'	1	1	7	7	6'	6	6	5'

TUNING SCALES FOR COMBS

10⅝-Inch SYMPHONION Diametral Combs - 2 × 42 TEETH

Bass Comb—42 Teeth

1	2	3	4	5	6	7	8	9	10	11	12	13	14	15	16	17	18	19	20	21	22	23	24	25	26	27	28	29	30	31
A	D	D	E	F#	G	G	G#	A	A	B	C	C#	D	D	E	E	F#	F#	G	G	G#	A	A	A	B	B	C	C#	C#	D
5	1	1	2	3	4	4	4'	5	5	6	6'	7	1	1	2	2	3	3	4	4	4'	5	5	5	6	6	6'	7	7	7

32	33	34	35	36	37	38	39	40	41	42
D	D	D#	E	E	F	F#	F#	G	G	G#
1	1	1'	2	2	2'	3	3	4	4	4'

Treble Comb—42 Teeth. N.B.: Bass Teeth at Periphery of Disc-Scale Reversed

1	2	3	4	5	6	7	8	9	10	11	12	13	14	15	16	17	18	19	20	21	22	23	24	25	26	27	28	29	30	31
G	F#	E	D	D	C#	C#	C	B	B	B	A#	A	A	A	G#	G#	G	F#	F#	F	F#	F#	F	F	E	E	E	D#	D	D
4	3	2	1	1	7	7	6'	6	6	6	5'	5	5	5	4'	4	4	3	3	3	2'	2	2	2	2	2	1'	1	1	1

32	33	34	35	36	37	38	39	40	41	42
C#	C#	C	C	B	B	B	A#	A	A	A
7	7	6'	6	6	6	6	5'	5	5	5

TUNING SCALES FOR COMBS

11⅞-Inch SYMPHONION 2 × 42 TEETH Diametral Combs

Comb Nearer Pressure-Bar Hinge

1	2	3	4	5	6	7	8	9	10	11	12	13	14	15	16	17	18	19	20	21	22	23	24	25	26	27	28	29	30	31
C♯	G♯	C♯	C♯	D♯	F	F♯	G♯	A♯	C	C♯	C♯	D♯	F	F	F♯	G	G♯	G♯	A♯	C	C♯	C♯	D♯	F	F	F♯	G♯	G♯	A	A♯
1	5	5	1	1	2	3	5	6	7	1	1	2	3	3	4	4′	5	5	6	7	1	1	2	3	3	4	5	5	5′	6

32	33	34	35	36	37	38	39	40	41	42
C	C♯	C♯	D	D♯	E	F	F♯	G♯	A♯	C
7	1	1′	2	2′	3	4	5	6	7

Comb Farther From Pressure-Bar Hinge

1	2	3	4	5	6	7	8	9	10	11	12	13	14	15	16	17	18	19	20	21	22	23	24	25	26	27	28	29	30	31
C♯	G♯	C♯	D♯	F	F♯	G♯	A♯	C	C♯	C♯	D♯	F	F	F♯	G	G♯	G♯	A♯	C	C♯	C♯	D♯	D♯	F	F	F♯	F♯	G	G♯
1	5	1	2	3	4	5	5	6	7	1	1	2	3	3	4	4′	5	5	6	7	1	1	2	2	3	3	4	4	4′	5

32	33	34	35	36	37	38	39	40	41	42
G♯	A	A♯	A♯	B	C	C♯	C♯	D♯	F	F♯
5	5′	6	6	6′	7	1	1	2	3	4

TUNING SCALES FOR COMBS

13-Inch SYMPHONION 60 TEETH
Discs with dimpled periphery drive

1	2	3	4	5	6	7	8	9	10	11	12	13	14	15	16	17	18	19	20	21	22	23	24	25	26	27	28	29	30	31
C#	G#	C#	D#	F	G#	A#	C	C#	D#	F	F	G#	A#	C	C#	D#	F	F#	G#	A#	C	C#	D#	F	F	F#	G	G#	A	A#
1	5	1	1	2	3	5	5	6	7	1	1	2	3	4	5	5	6	7	1	1	2	3	4	4'	5	5	5	5'	6

32	33	34	35	36	37	38	39	40	41	42	43	44	45	46	47	48	49	50	51	52	53	54	55	56	57	58	59	60
A#	B	C	C	C#	D	D#	D#	E	F	F#	F#	G	G#	G#	A	A#	A#	B	C	C#	C	C	C	C#	C#	D#	F	F#
6	6'	7	7	1	1'	2	2	2'	3	4	4	4'	5	5	5	5'	6	6	6	6	7	7	1	1	2	3	4

13⅝-Inch 'SUBLIME HARMONIE' SYMPHONION-Diametral Combs
2 × 34 TEETH, 2 × 16 TEETH Also for 'EROICA'
Large Comb Nearer Pressure-Bar Hinge-34 Teeth

1	2	3	4	5	6	7	8	9	10	11	12	13	14	15	16	17	18	19	20	21	22	23	24	25	26	27	28	29	30	31
G	D	G	A	B	C	D	E	F#	G	A	B	B	C	C#	D	D	D#	E	F	F#	G	G	G#	A	A	A#	B	B	C	C
1	5	1	2	3	4	5	6	7	1	2	3	3	4	4'	5	5	5'	6	6'	7	1	1'	2	2	2'	3	3	3	4

32	33	34
C#	D	E
4'	5	6

TUNING SCALES FOR COMBS

Small Comb-16 Teeth

1	2	3	4	5	6	7	8	9	10	11	12	13	14	15	16
D	D	D	D#	E	E	E	F	F#	F#	G	G	G	A	C
5	5	5'	6	6	6	6'	7	7	1	1	1	2	4

Large Comb Farther from Pressure-Bar Hinge-34 Teeth

1	2	3	4	5	6	7	8	9	10	11	12	13	14	15	16	17	18	19	20	21	22	23	24	25	26	27	28	29	30	31
G	D	D	G	G	A	B	C	D	E	F#	G	G	A	B	B	C	C#	D	D	D	E	F#	G	G	A	B	C	D	E	F#
1	5	5	1	1	2	3	4	5	6	7	1	1	2	3	3	4	4'	5	5	5	6	7	1	1	2	3	4	5	6	7

32	33	34
G	A	B
1	2	3

Small Comb-16 Teeth

1	2	3	4	5	6	7	8	9	10	11	12	13	14	15	16
D	D	E	F#	G	G	G	G#	A	A	B	B	B	C	C	C#
5	6	7	1	1	1	1'	2	2	3	3	3	4	4	4'

TUNING SCALES FOR COMBS

17⅞-Inch SYMPHONION 'SUBLIME HARMONIE' 2 × 53 TEETH

Comb Nearer Winder End of Bed-plate—53 Teeth

1	2	3	4	5	6	7	8	9	10	11	12	13	14	15	16	17	18	19	20	21	22	23	24	25	26	27	28	29	30	31
B	C#	E	F	F#	A	A#	B	C#	D	D#	E	F#	G	G#	A	A#	B	C	C#	D	D#	E	F	F#	F	F#	G	G#	A	A#
1	2		4	4'	5	6'	7	1	2	2'	3	4	5	5'	6	6'	7	1	1'	2	2'	3	4	4'	5	5'	6	6'	7	

32	33	34	35	36	37	38	39	40	41	42	43	44	45	46	47	48	49	50	51	52	53
B	C	C#	D	D#	E	F	F#	G	G#	A	A#	B	A	A#	B	C	C#	D#	E
1	1'	2	2'	3	3	4	4'	5	5'	6	6'	7	7	1	1	1'	2	3	4

Comb Further from Winder End—53 Teeth

1	2	3	4	5	6	7	8	9	10	11	12	13	14	15	16	17	18	19	20	21	22	23	24	25	26	27	28	29	30	31
B	F#	G#	A#	B	B	C#	D#	E	F#	F#	G#	A#	B	A#	B	C#	D#	D#	E	F	F#	F#	G#	A#	B	B	C#	C#	D#	D#
1	5	5	6	7	1	1	2	3	4	5	5	6	7	1	2	3	3	4	4'	5	5	6	7	1	1	2	2	3

32	33	34	35	36	37	38	39	40	41	42	43	44	45	46	47	48	49	50	51	52	53
E	E	F#	F#	G#	A#	A#	B	B	C#	D#	D#	E	F	G	G#	B	C#	F	F#	G	G#
4	4	5	5	6	6	7	7	1	1	2	2	3	3	4	4	5	5	5	6	6	6

TUNING SCALES FOR COMBS

19⅛-Inch SYMPHONION 2 × 53 TEETH Diametral Combs

Comb Nearer Drive Wheel

1	2	3	4	5	6	7	8	9	10	11	12	13	14	15	16	17	18	19	20	21	22	23	24	25	26	27	28	29	30	31
B	C#	E	F	F#	A	A#	B	C#	D	D#	E	F#	G	G#	A	A#	B	C	C#	D	D#	E	F	F#	F#	G	G#	A	A#	A#
4	5	6'	7	1	2'	3	4	5	6'	7	1	1'	2	2'	3	4	4'	5	5'	6	6'	7	7	1	1'	2	2'	3		

32	33	34	35	36	37	38	39	40	41	42	43	44	45	46	47	48	49	50	51	52	53
B	C	C#	D	D#	D#	E	F	F	F#	F#	G	G#	G#	A	A#	B	B	C	C#	D#	E
4	4'	5	5'	6	6	6'	7	7	7	1	1'	2	2	2'	3	3	4	4'	5	6	6'

Comb Further from Drive Wheel

1	2	3	4	5	6	7	8	9	10	11	12	13	14	15	16	17	18	19	20	21	22	23	24	25	26	27	28	29	30	31
B	F#	F#	G#	A#	B	B	C#	D#	E	F#	F#	G#	A#	B	B	C#	D	D#	E	F	F#	F#	G#	A#	B	B	C#	C#	D#	D#
4	1	1	2	3	4	4	5	6'	6	6'	7	1	2	3	4	5	6	6'	7	1	1	2	3	4	4	5	5	6	6	6

32	33	34	35	36	37	38	39	40	41	42	43	44	45	46	47	48	49	50	51	52	53
E	E	F#	F#	G#	A#	A#	B	B	B	C#	C#	D#	D#	E	E	E	F#	F#	F#	G#	G#
6'	6'	1	1	2	2	3	4	4	4	5	5	6	6	6'	6'	1	1	1	2	2	

TUNING SCALES FOR COMBS

21¼-Inch SYMPHONION with 10 Bells 1 × 60 TEETH, 1 × 58 TEETH Opposed Combs

Upper Comb

1	2	3*	4	5	6	7	8	9	10	11	12	13	14	15	16	17	18	19	20	21	22	23	24	25	26	27	28	29	30	31
F#	F#	A#/B	B	B	C#	D#	E	F#	F#	G#	A#	B	C#	D#	D#	D#	E	F#	F#	G	G#	A#	B	B	C#	C#	D#	D#	E	F
5	5	7/1	1	1	2	3	4	5	5	6	7	1	2	3	4	5	5'	6	7	1	1	2	2	3	3	4	4'

32	33	34	35	36	37	38	39	40	41	42	43	44	45	46	47	48	49	50	51	52	53	54	55	56	57	58	59	60
F#	F#	G	G#	A	A#	A#	B	B	C	C#	C#	D#	D#	E	E	F	F#	F#	G	G#	G#	A#	A#	B	C	C#	D#	E
5	5'	6	6'	7	7	1	1	1'	2	2	3	3	4	4'	5	5	5'	6	6	6'	7	7	1'	2	2	3	4

Lower Comb

1	2	3	4	5	6	7	8	9	10	11	12	13	14	15	16	17	18	19	20	21	22	23	24	25	26	27	28	29	30	31
B	F#	G#	B	B	C#	D#	E	F	F#	G#	A	A#	B	C#	D	D#	E	F	F#	G#	A	A#	B	C	C#	D	D#	E	E	F
1	5	6	1	1	2	3	4'	5	6	6'	7	1	2	2'	3	4	4'	5	6	6	6'	7	1	1'	2	2'	3	4	4'

32	33	34	35	36	37	38	39	40	41	42	43	44	45	46	47	48	49	50	51	52	53	54	55	56	57	58
F#	F#	G#	G#	A#	A#	B	B	C#	C#	D	D#	D#	E	E	F	F#	F#	G#	G#	A	A#	B	B	C#	C#	D#
5	5	6	6	7	7	1	1	2	2	2'	3	3	4	4'	5	5	6	6	6'	7	1	1	2	2	3

*Opinions differ

TUNING SCALES FOR COMBS

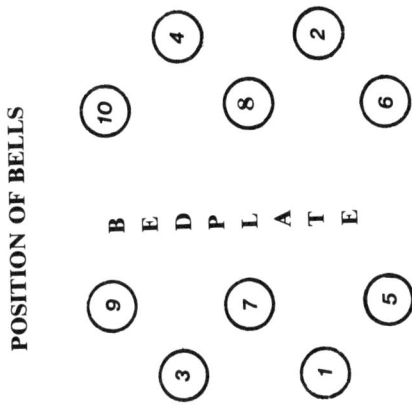

POSITION OF BELLS

Bells

1	2	3	4	5	6	7	8*	9*	10*
F#	G#	A#	B	C#	D#	E	F	F#	G#

*Tuned above highest comb note

TUNING SCALES FOR COMBS

25-Inch SYMPHONION 2 × 60 TEETH Opposed Combs

1	2	3	4	5	6	7	8	9	10	11	12	13	14	15	16	17	18	19	20	21	22	23	24	25	26	27	28	29	30	31
D#	D#	G	G	G	A	B	C	D	D	E	F	F	G#	G#	A	C	C	C#	D	D	C#	D#	F	F	F#	G	G	G	G#	A
1	1	3	3	4'	5'	6	7	7	1'	2	2'	4	4	4'	6	6	6	6'	1	1	2	1	2	2	2'	3	3	4	4	4'

32	33	34	35	36	37	38	39	40	41	42	43	44	45	46	47	48	49	50	51	52	53	54	55	56	57	58	59	60
A#	C	C	C#	C#	D	D	D#	D#	D#	E	F	F	F#	G	G	G#	G#	A	A#	A#	B	C	C	C	C#	C#	D
5	5	6	6	6'	6'	7	1	1	1'	2	2	2'	3	3	4	4	4	4'	5	5'	6	6	6	6	6'	6'	7

N.B. Not for diametral combs

25-Inch 'SUBLIME HARMONIE' SYMPHONION 2 × 53 TEETH, 2 × 27 TEETH Diametral Combs

Lower Large Comb (Nearest Drive Wheel)
*

1	2	3	4	5	6	7	8	9	10	11	12	13	14	15	16	17	18	19	20	21	22	23	24	25	26	27	28	29	30	31
F#	G	D#	F#	F#	G#	A	A#	B	C#	D#	B	C#	D	F	F#	F#	G#	G#	A#	A#	B	B	C#	D	D#	D#	F	F	F#	F#
1	5	6	1	1	2	2'	3	4	5	5'	6	7	1	1	2	2	3	3	4	4	5	5	5'	6	6	7	7	1	1

32	33	34	35	36	37	38	39	40	41	42	43	44	45	46	47	48	49	50	51	52	53
G#	G#	A#	A#	B	B	C#	C#	D#	D#	F	F	F#	F#	G#	G#	A#	A#	A#	A#	B	B
2	2	3	3	4	4	5	5	5'	6	6	7	7	1	1	2	2	2'	3	3	4	4

TUNING SCALES FOR COMBS

Lower Small Comb

1	2	3	4	5	6	7	8	9	10	11	12	13	14	15	16	17	18	19	20	21	22	23	24	25	26	27
C	C#	C#	D#	D#	F	F	F	F#	F#	G	G#	G#	A#	A#	B	B	C#	C#	D	D#	D#	F	F	F#	F#	G#
4'	5	5	6	6	6	7	7	1'	1	1	2	2	3	3	4	4	5	5	5'	6	6	6	7	1	1	2

*Lower than tooth No. 1

Upper Large Comb (Above Centre Dome)

*

1	2	3	4	5	6	7	8	9	10	11	12	13	14	15	16	17	18	19	20	21	22	23	24	25	26	27	28	29	30	31
F#	C#	C#	F	F#	G#	G#	A#	B	C	C#	C#	D#	E	F	F#	F#	G	A	A#	A#	B	C	C#	C#	D#	†	E	F	F#	F#
1	5	5	7	1	1	2	3	4	4'	5	5	6	6'	7	1	1	2	2'	3	3	4	4'	5	5	6	6†	7	7	1	1

32	33	34	35	36	37	38	39	40	41	42	43	44	45	46	47	48	49	50	51	52	53
G	G#	A	A#	B	B	C	C#	C#	D#	E	F	F#	F#	G	G#	G#	G#	G#	A#	B	B
1'	2	2'	3	4	4	4'	5	5	6	6	6'	7	1	1	1	1'	2	2	3	3	4

Upper Small Comb

1	2	3	4	5	6	7	8	9	10	11	12	13	14	15	16	17	18	19	20	21	22	23	24	25	26	27
C	C#	D	D	D#	E	F	F	F	F#	F#	G#	G#	A	A#	B	B	C	C#	C#	D#	D#	F	F	F#	G#	A#
4'	5	5'	6	6'	7	7	7	1	1	1	2	2	2'	3	3	4	4'	5	5	6	6	7	7	1	2	3

*Lower than tooth No. 1

TUNING SCALES FOR COMBS

27-Inch SYMPHONION With 12 Bells
1 × 44 TEETH, 1 × 42 TEETH, 2 × 16 TEETH Plus Bells Opposed Combs

Large Upper Comb-44 Teeth

*	†	*	*																												
1	2	3	4	5	6	7	8	9	10	11	12	13	14	15	16	17	18	19	20	21	22	23	24	25	26	27	28	29	30	31	
G	D	G	G	A	B	C	D	E	F#	G	G	A	B	C	D	D#	E	F	G	G#	A	A#	B	C	C#	D	D	E	E	F#	
1	5	1	1	2	3	4	5	6	7	1	1	2	3	4	5	5'	6	6'	1	1'	2	2'	3	4	4'	5	5	6	6	7	

32	33	34	35	36	37	38	39	40	41	42	43	44
F#	G	G#	A	A#	B	C	C	C#	D	D#	E	F
7	1	1'	2	2'	3	4	4	4'	5	5'	6	6'

Small Upper Comb-16 Teeth

1	2	3	4	5	6	7	8	9	10	11	12	13	14	15	16
F#	F#	G	G#	A	A	B	B	C	D	D	E	F#	G	G#	A
7	7	1	1'	2	2	3	3	4	5	5	6	7	1	1'	2

*Same Pitch
†Lower than Note 1 and in pitch with Note 2 on lower comb

Bells With Upper Combs

1	2	3	4	5	6
F#	A	C	D	F#	A*

*Octave higher

TUNING SCALES FOR COMBS

Large Lower Comb–42 Teeth

1	2	3	4	5	6	7	8	9	10	11	12	13	14	15	16	17	18	19	20	21	22	23	24	25	26	27	28	29	30	31
D	D	G	G	B	C	D	D	F	F#	G	A	B	C	C#	D	E	F	F#	G	A	B	B	C	C#	D	D#	E	F	F#	G
5	5	1	1	3	4	5	5	6'	7	1	2	3	4	4'	5	6	6'	7	1	2	3	3	4	4'	5	5'	6	6'	7	1

32	33	34	35	36	37	38	39	40	41	42
G	A	A	B	B	C	C#	D	D	E	E
1	2	2	3	3	4	4'	5	5	6	6

Small Lower Comb–16 Teeth

1	2	3	4	5	6	7	8	9	10	11	12	13	14	15	16
F	G	G	A	A#	B	C	C#	D	D#	E	F	F#	G	G#	A
6'	1	1	2	2'	3	4	4'	5	5'	6	6'	7	1	1'	2

*Octave below Note 2 and in pitch with upper comb Note 2

Bells With Lower Combs

1	2	3	4	5	6
G	B	C#	E	G*	B*

*Octave higher

TUNING SCALES FOR COMBS

14¼-INCH CHORDEPHON SCALE

14¼-Inch CHORDEPHON
(Disc-Playing Zither) - 44 Notes (Strings)

Bass						Octave							Octave																	
1	2	3	4	5	6	7	8	9	10	11	12	13	14	15	16	17	18	19	20	21	22	23	24	25	26	27	28	29	30	31
A	B	C	D	E	F	F#	G	A	A	B	B	C	C	C#	D	D	E	F#	G	D	E	F	F#	G	G	G#	A	A#	B	B

			Octave						Treble		
32	33	34	35	36	37	38	39	40	41	42	43	44
C	C#	C#	D	D	D#	E	F	F#	G	A	B	C

300

LIST OF MANUFACTURERS AND AGENTS

Abrahams, Barnett Henry, Ste-Croix, Switzerland. See B.H.A.

Adler Musikwerke (German American Musical Boxes) Gohlis, Leipzig. Makers of the Adler range of disc boxes, later to become Fortuna under J.H. Zimmermann. Several patents were granted to (F.) Ernst Malke and F.H. Oberlander, the two principals, the earliest in 1895. In 1898 the business moved to the premises where the Orphenion had been produced since 1893.

In 1900 the firm was taken over by Zimmermann, and the name of the range changed to Fortuna. The 'Fortuna Marvel', from which, presumably, the new name was taken, was a large disc musical box, introduced at the beginning of 1900, which played steel combs with the addition of a reed organ, drum, and triangle.

American Music Box Co., Hoboken, New Jersey. Makers of 'Monarch' and 'Triumph' disc musical boxes. Firm commenced about 1896 by Emile Cuendet (1858–1952), born in Ste-Croix, a member of a distinguished musical box family and a fine maker of cylinder boxes in his own right. A worker for Charles Henry Jacot, they both moved to the United States, where Cuendet became foreman of Jacot Music Box Co. in 1893. Though Cuendet's Company took out several patents, and advertised 'all types', the only machines seen under either name play 15½-inch discs. Peripheral drive holes and projections on the discs differ from the norm, but both machines use combs of the exact scale of the 15½-inch Regina, and have similar table model cases.

B.H.A., Ste-Croix, Switzerland. The initials of Barnett Henry Abrahams, founder of the company in 1857. Manufacturers first of cylinder musical boxes and later 'Britannia' and 'Imperial' disc boxes. The company had a warehouse at 128 Houndsditch, London.

LIST OF MANUFACTURERS AND AGENTS

Barnett, Samuel & Sons, London, founded 1832. Sole agents for the Orphenion disc musical box, and agents for the Britannia.

Bauer, Franz Louis, Leipzig, Germany. In summer, 1894, introduced the Komet disc musical box using projectionless metal discs with star wheels, probably the first to do so. Was granted many patents for this idea and others, including a shifting-disc mechanism (German patent number 111970, dated 17th. October, 1899). Firm became incorporated 1st. July, 1895, to become Firma Komet Musikwerke, Pollnitz & Bauer. Bauer was dismissed at beginning of 1899.

Bender, Karl & Co., Gilbert Street, London, D.C. Were the first London agents for Polyphon in 1890. They also sold other makes of disc boxes.

Benzing, Wilhelm, Leipzig, Germany. Main agent and member of *V.D.M-G*.

Berger & Wurker, Leipzig, Germany. Wholesale agent. Member of *V.D.M-G*.

Bernard, Frank J. Hoboken, New Jersey. Worked for American Music Box Co.

Beutner, Kühn & Co., London. Agent for Symphonion and others in 1889.

Billon-Haller, Jean. 1855–1935, Geneva, Switzerland. Son of Jean Billon, maker of 'blancs' and combs for cylinder boxes. Patented improvements to disc musical boxes (see Société Anonyme, late Maison Billon).

Bock, Christian H.R., Leipzig, Germany. Partner, then director, of Kalliope Musikwerke.

Bon, J.M., Leipzig, Germany. Main agent. Member of *V.D.M-G*.

Boom, Miguel, Port au Prince, Haiti. Patented in 1882 in U.S.A. the first idea of a disc musical box.

Bornand-Galaz, Auguste, L'Auberson. Director of Harmonia S.A.

Bortmann, G. & Keller, A., Leipzig, Germany. In January, 1896, took over production of the Sirion 'shifting-disc' musical box when Jentzsch ceased production. A patent covering the mechanism, the British version numbered 7443 and dated 8th. April, 1891, was granted to Bortmann and Keller. Exhibited by this firm at Leipzig Easter Fair for 1896. The one and only time. See also Seidel & Maumann and Mermod Frères.

Bortmann, G., Leipzig, Germany. Patented in 1896, together with A. Keller, a method of playing two tunes on one disc by shifting the

LIST OF MANUFACTURERS AND AGENTS

centre spindle to present a new set of projections to the star wheels. The 'Sirion' disc musical box uses this method. In 1897, together with R. Munkwitz, patented further improvements to disc musical boxes. See Jentzsch, and Seidel & Maumann, also Mermod Frères.

Brachhausen, Gustave Adolf, Leipzig, Germany and Rahway, New Jersey. 1861–1943. A most important figure in disc musical box history. A foreman at the Symphonion works, and there from the beginning of disc box manufacture, he left in 1890, and together with a fellow worker, Paul Riessner, started to manufacture the Polyphon. On 15th. September 1892, he left Germany and opened the Regina Company of Jersey City, N.J., later to move to Rahway, N.J. In this company he held equal shares with Riessner and a Leipzig banker, J. Korner (1894).

He had a hand in each of the three largest disc musical box companies (see 'The Principal Manufacturers'), and was responsible for many patents, including the auto-change disc machine.

Brachhausen, R., Rahway, New Jersey. Mentioned in the American *Music Trade Review*, 20th. July, 1901, as manager of Regina Music Box Co. It is possible that a printing error caused the wrong initial to be shown, but also possible that this was a relative of Gustave.

Breitkepf & Hartel, Leipzig, Germany. Main agent for Orpheus disc boxes.

Brewer, Camberwell, London. Was main agent for Polyphon and other machines up to about 1900.

British Polyphon Company, Newman Street, London. Successors to New Polyphon Supply Co. Became Dulcetto Polyphon Ltd. in 1927 (Gramophone). Terminated 1935.

Buff-Hedinger, G.A. Leipzig, Germany. In October, 1904 began to produce the Monopol disc musical box, together with the Ariston organette, after the liquidation, in April of the same year, of Fabrik Leipziger Musikwerke (formerly Paul Ehrlich). The firm mainly produced the Premier and other automatic pianos. After Buff-Hedinger's death in July, 1906, his widow continued until about January 1909, when Monopol production finished.

Campbell & Co., Glasgow, Scotland. Agent for the 'Celesta' disc musical box (Ch. F. Pietschmann & Sohn), and for Symphonion.

Caspar & Plessing, T.A., Lindenthal, Leipzig, Germany. In July, 1898 introduced the Tannhauser 'shifting-disc' musical box, subject of German patent 99899, dated 21st. May, 1897, granted to Traugott

LIST OF MANUFACTURERS AND AGENTS

Alwin Plessing. Production ceased by April, 1901, Plessing resigning from the firm in February, 1899.

Chaillet, Octave Félicien. A man of much talent, he was originally in education in Switzerland and became a tune arranger for cylinder musical boxes. He later joined Symphonion as arranger and composer. Later still he went to the U.S.A. to join Regina. Eventually his daughter married Gustave Brachhausen, co-founder of Polyphon and founder of Regina.

Cuendet, Emile L. 1858-1952. A Ste-Croix musical box worker for C.H. Jacot who went to America for the firm, eventually becoming foreman. He was president of the American Music Box Company.

Deurer & Kaufmann, Hamburg, Germany. Main agent and member of *V.D.M-G*.

Dienst, E. & Co., Leipzig, Germany. Wholesale agent. Member of *V.D.M-G*. Manufacturer of pianos and orchestrions.

Dietrich, Wilhelm, Leipzig, Germany. Wholesale agent. Member of *V.D.M-G*. Original shareholder in firm of *Kalliope Musikwerke* A.G.

Ehrlich, (Friederich Ernst) Paul. Gohlis, Leipzig, Germany. The author assumes that Friederich Ernst Paul Ehrlich and Paul Ehrlich are one and the same. Though patents were applied for under both names, we have the example of Oskar Paul Lochmann, who applied for patents under Oskar Paul, Paul, O.P., and P. Lochmann. Apart from the patents, there appears to be no evidence that there were two Ehrlichs.

Founded the firm of Paul Ehrlich & Co. A.G. about 1877, later (c.1886) to become Fabrik Leipziger Musikwerke, and began manufacture of the most successful Ariston disc organette, which used a slotted card disc to dictate the melody to a set of free reeds. A series of sprung levers were placed below the disc. When a slot in the disc corresponded to a lever, it was allowed to rise, opening a valve to allow a reed to sound.

A similar card disc was used for the company's first commercial venture into disc boxes, which was a 'lever-plucker' type, the Baskánion, again depending on a lever rising into a slot in the card. Better known is the Monopol range of disc boxes, in many ways similar to Symphonion. See 'Baskánion' and 'Monopol' in the list of disc musical boxes, also 'Development'.

Ernst, H.L., Leipzig, Germany. Main agent. Member of *V.D.M-G*.

Espenhain, Gustave Max, Leipzig, Germany. A merchant who became partner (1895) then director (1897) of Kalliope Musikwerke. He was

LIST OF MANUFACTURERS AND AGENTS

a member of the committee of the Association of German Musical Instrument Manufacturers (*Verein Deutscher Musikwerke-Fabrikanten*) formed in 1897. c.1900 formed the Apollo Musikwerke to make pianos and organs.

Fabrik Leipziger Musikwerke. See Ehrlich.

Gautschi, Henry. Philadelphia, Pennsylvania and Ste-Croix, Switzerland. A maker (?) and agent of musical boxes who, in 1903 in America, patented the first phonograph (gramophone) attachment for a disc musical box.

Geater, Alfred, 105., St. John's Street, London E.C. First agent for the Stella disc box by Mermod Frères until 1898.

Gerecke, William, 8 and 9, Goring Street, Houndsditch, London. Agent for Komet disc boxes.

German American Musical Boxes. See Adler Musikwerke.

Gilbert & Co., London. Agent for Monopol disc boxes.

Graf, Heinrich. Patented in 1910 a type of disc musical box using a disc on which the tunes were interchangeable. The projections were in the form of movable pegs, which could be arranged to play the tune required.

Grosz, B. & Co., Leipzig, Germany. Manufacturers (?) of 'Troubadour' disc musical boxes.

Guldman & Co., Manchester, England. Agent for Polyphon.

Hahn, P.H. & Co., Dresden, Germany. Main agent and member of *V.D.M-G*.

Harmonia A.-G. L'Auberson. Founded 1896, makers of the Harmonia, one of the first disc musical boxes to use projectionless discs with sprung star wheels. (See Junod, André).

Hasse, William F., 107 E. 14th Street, New York City. c.1894 agent for Polyphon, Symphonion, and Regina.

Hawsky, Adalbert, Leipzig, Germany. Main agent and member of *V.D.M-G*.

Heilbrunn, K. Söhne, Berlin, Germany. Advertised, and exhibited at Leipzig Easter Fair of 1895, the Polyhymnia disc musical box. Member of *V.D.M-G*.

Helbig, Otto, & Polikeit, Gohlis, Leipzig, Germany. In September, 1895, began production of the Euterpephon disc musical box at the same address as A. W. Neumann, after the firm was bankrupted in December 1894. May also have been makers of the Celesta disc box. Accorded patents appertaining to disc musical boxes.

LIST OF MANUFACTURERS AND AGENTS

Hirsch, Martin, London. Agent for Symphonion, Celesta and Troubadour disc boxes.

Holzweissig, Ernst, Leipzig, Germany and Newman Street, London. Wholesale agent. Member of *V.D.M-G.* Manufacturer of pianos and orchestrions. Original shareholder in the firm of Kalliope Musikwerke A.G.

Hössly, Louis, Ste-Croix, Switzerland. Patentee of 'lever-plucker' mechanism used by Thorens in this version of their Edelweiss and Helvetia boxes.

Hupfeld, Ludwig, Leipzig, Germany. Took controlling interest in *Symphonion Musikwerke* c.1900, Main agent and member of *V.D.M-G.* Large manufacturer of mechanical musical instruments.

Imhof & Mukle, 547 Oxford Street, London, W.1. This company has a history going back to 1845. At the above address they were agents for, among others, Stella, Regina and Polyphon.

Jacot Music Box Co., 31 and also 39 Union Square, New York City. Main agent for 'Mira' disc box by Mermod Frères. Published 'How to Repair (cylinder) Musical Boxes' in 1883. Invented Jacot's Safety Check in 1886.

Jentzsch,-., Germany. In September, 1894, introduced the Sirion 'shifting-disc' musical box. Ceased trading in February, 1896, when production taken over by G. Bortmann & A. Keller. See also Seidel & Maumann and Mermod Frères.

Junghans (Junghanssche Uhrenfabrik) Schramberg, Germany. Clockmakers who had made a series of small disc-playing clocks. Since the discs of Junghans' clocks and Symphonion clocks of the same size are interchangeable, and some of the clocks identical, it would seem that Symphonion made the Junghans discs and movements, while Junghans returned the compliment with clocks. Junghans used their own trademark on the discs, an eight-pointed star in a circle with a 'J' in the centre, and the name 'Junghans'. The firm also marketed a series of small disc boxes under the name 'Silvanigra'.

Junod, André, Switzerland. Credited with the design of the machine to play projectionless discs, of which the Stella was one. Employed by Mermod Frères.

Kalliope Musikwerke, Leipzig, Germany. 1895–1919. Makers of the Kalliope range of disc boxes. The firm consisting of Gustave Max Espenhain, a merchant, Emil Moritz Anton Wacker, and Christian Heinrich Richard Bock, became a limited company, with the same

LIST OF MANUFACTURERS AND AGENTS

three shareholders, in 1898. The last two mentioned, Wacker and Bock, were responsible for at least ten patents for disc boxes. The firm entered the gramophone market in 1904, and in the same year began manufacture of American organs. Disc box manufacture also continued. In 1919 the firm merged with Menzenhauer & Schmidt of Berlin, makers of the Guitarophone, a disc-playing mechanical zither.

Keller, Alfred, Leipzig, Germany. Co-patentee in 1896 of 'shifting-disc' mechanism (see Bortmann, G.)

Klein, Henry & Co., Oxford Street and Wardour Street, London. Until 1903 were agents for Polyphon. When Klein retired, business taken over by New Polyphon Supply Co.

Komet Musikwerke (Pollnitz & Bauer), Leipzig, Germany. Incorporation 1st. July, 1895, of the firm of Franz Louis Bauer, he joining with Hans Bruno Ulrich Pancratius Golzo von Pollnitz, a backer. Bauer had commenced making the Komet, a projectionless metal disc machine, in the summer of 1884. The firm continued until 1902, Bauer having left at the beginning of 1899. The Komet is known in both projectionless and normal disc models.

Kraft Behrens, Leipzig, Germany. Main agent and member of *V.D.M-G*.

Langdorff, John-Baptiste. Geneva, Switzerland. Son of David Langdorff of cylinder musical box fame. Member of firm which made the 'Gloria' and 'Polymnia' disc musical boxes (see Société Anonyme, late Maison Billon).

Leipziger Musikwerke, (Paul Ehrlich), Leipzig, Germany. See Ehrlich, F.E. Paul.

Leipzig Music Works, 57, Basinghall Street, London. Agent in 1898 for Monopol disc boxes made by Fabrik Leipziger Musikwerke (Paul Ehrlich).

Liebermann & Co., Berlin, Germany. Manufacturer of the disc musical box invented by H. Graf.

Lochmann, (Oskar) Paul, Leipzig, Germany. Manufacturer of the first practical disc musical box, patented 1885/6. The machine was called a 'Symphonion' and was made at the Lochmannscher Musikwerke A.G. in Gohlis, Leipzig. See the chapter 'The Principal Manufacturers', under the heading 'Symphonion'. In 1901 he opened a factory in Zeulenrode, where the 'Lochmann Original' disc boxes were made, after the Symphonion company had passed to Ludwig Hupfeld & Co.

LIST OF MANUFACTURERS AND AGENTS

Lochmann Original, Zeulenroda (Thuringen), Germany, c.1901. The factory was set up by Paul Lochmann after leaving the Symphonion works. Here was made the 'Lochmann Original' range of disc machines. These models used a disc which had a beaded edge, and the range included a large double-disc machine, playing bells, with 24½-inch disc. Also manufactured was the 'Original Konzert Piano', a disc orchestrion playing on piano strings, tubular bells, drum and triangle and using a 25½-inch disc.

Ludwig & Wild, Leipzig, Germany. Manufacturers of the 'Orpheus' disc musical box.

Ludwig & Fries, Frankfurt-am-Main, Germany. Main agent and member of *V.D.M-G*.

Lyon & Healy, Chicago, Illinois. Agent for disc musical boxes. Mermod Frères manufactured a line of their Mira disc boxes under the name 'Empress' expressly for this company.

Malke, (F.) Ernst, Gohlis, Leipzig, Germany. Co-founder of Adler Musikwerke with F.H. Oberlander, 1895.

Menzenhauer & Schmidt, Berlin, Germany. Makers of the Guitarophone, a disc-played mechanical zither, using a 14½-inch disc. A coin-operated table model is in the collection of the Fowler family of Raleigh, North Carolina. Took over the firm of Kalliope Musikwerke A.-G in 1919.

Mermod Frères, Ste-Croix, Switzerland. 1815–191-. Having had a long and successful career manufacturing cylinder musical boxes, Mermod entered the disc box field with the famous 'Stella'. They also made the 'Mira' disc box. The firm is also credited with the mechanisms for 'New Century' and 'Sirion' disc boxes, though it is likely that only the 'shifting-disc' mechanisms were made by them. Other more orthodox mechanisms used in 'New Century' machines are thought to have been made by Vidoudez of Ste-Croix, Switzerland. The Stella was exhibited for the first time in 1896 at the Geneva Exposition.

Metall-Industrie Schönebeck A.G., Leipzig, Germany. Makers of the Polyhymnia disc musical box from 1900–1903.

Munkwitz, R. Leipzig, Germany. Co-patentee of disc machine improvements (See Bortmann, G.).

Neumann, A.W., Gohlis, Leipzig, Germany. Introduced the Euterpephon disc musical box in 1893. Was bankrupt by 7th. December, 1894.

LIST OF MANUFACTURERS AND AGENTS

New Polyphon Supply Company Ltd. Established c.1898. Oxford Street, London, W.1. Agent for Polyphon with branches in Glasgow and Paris. In 1906 took over bankrupt Nicole Frères. In 1914 both partners interned and the company became British Polyphon Company.

Nicole Frères, Geneva, Switzerland, and 21, Ely Place, Holborn Circus, London. c.1839–1903. After being leading manufacturers in the cylinder musical box field, Nicole Frères became main agents for Polyphon and others. A common mistake is to think that this company had anything to do with the manufacture of Polyphon. This has arisen from the large transfer bearing the name of Nicole Frères which was fixed to the Polyphons sold by Nicole as agents. It was common practice for the agent to put his name on any machine sold through him.

Oberlander, F.H., Gohlis, Leipzig, Germany. Co-founder of Adler Musikwerke with F. Ernst Malke, 1895.

Otto, Frederick G. & Sons (later Otto Mfg. Co.), Jersey City, New Jersey. Makers of first the 'Capital' music box that used a 'cuff' of metal with projections, and, in 1896 the 'Criterion' disc box. Later the company made the 'Olympia' disc box, and the Euphonia and the Sterling, developments of the Criterion (1902). Their agents, M.J. Paillard of New York City were sued for infringements of patents by Regina in 1896/97. Sons were: Edmund, Gustav and Albert.

Paillard, E. et Cie. Ste-Croix, Switzerland. Member of the large cylinder musical box family. In the Paris Exposition of 1900 the firm showed an interesting disc musical box. According to a report (mentioned in *Histoire de la Boîte à Musique*), it was the latest creation of the firm. It was '. . . with a mechanism that automatically replaces the discs. This mechanism can be adapted to all formats without increasing the size of the box'. None of these are known.

In 1906, Paillard were again exhibiting, this time in Milan (*Histoire* etc.). The firm displayed among other things: A four-comb 'Sublime Harmonie Tremolo Zither' disc box—Paillard introduced the 'Sublime Harmonie' cylinder box, invented by Amedee Paillard, in 1875; a shifting-disc box, and an auto-change disc box.

Paillard, M.J. & Co., 1880–95, 680 Broadway, New York City, and Ste-Croix, Switzerland. Agents for the 'Capital' cuff box and the 'Criterion', both manufactured by F.G. Otto & Sons, New Jersey. The firm was sued by Regina for patent infringements.

LIST OF MANUFACTURERS AND AGENTS

Paoli, John, Rahway, New Jersey. Patented disc machine improvements with Regina.

Parr, Ellis & Co., Long Lane, London. An agent for musical instruments who took out a patent for a disc playing mechanism of which he claimed infringement by Paul Lochmann when he publicized his Symphonion. Some arrangement was entered between the two, and Parr became 'co-patentee', and in England 'sole patentee'. The firm was sole agent for Symphonion for a short while.

The earliest known Symphonion, in the posession of the author, bears the legend on the centre drive wheel 'Lochmanns and Ellis Parrs Patent'.

Perfection Music Box Co. 1897–1901. Jersey City, New Jersey and later Newark, New Jersey. Not a large company, this firm produced the 'Perfection' disc musical box, which used felt pressed between two outside plates of the star wheels to dampen the teeth. The main problem with this method was the wear sustained by the felt. Renewal would have been extremely expensive.

Peters, H. & Co., London and Leipzig, Germany. Established 1887. First main agent for Polyphon.

Phönix Musikwerke (Schmidt & Co), Leipzig, Germany. Makers of the Saxonia range of disc boxes. Makers also of the 'Phönix' (Phoenix) range of organettes, and other instruments.

Pietschmann & Sohn, Berlin, Germany. Maker of the Celesta range of disc boxes. The company was a large one making mechanical instruments, mainly organettes, well before the advent of the disc musical box. In 1888 it was second in importance in the field in Germany, turning out some 13,000 instruments per year and employing 240 workmen, this at a time when the only disc boxes being made were Symphonion.

Plato & Co., Berlin, Germany. Main agent and member of *V.D.M-G*.

Plessing, T. Alwin. (See Caspar & Plessing).

Pollnitz, Hans (see Bauer, Franz Louis).

Polyphon & Regina Music Box Co., Ely Place, London. A company formed by Nicole Frères to handle the sale and repair of disc musical boxes.

Polyphon Musikwerke, Wahren, Leipzig, Germany. Described under 'Polyphon' in the chapter 'The Principal Manufacturers'. See also 'A List of Disc Musical Boxes'.

LIST OF MANUFACTURERS AND AGENTS

Polyphon Supply Co., 3 Bishopsgate Street Without, London, E.C. Main agent for Polyphon in 1898.

Preussner, H., Leipzig, Germany. A director of Leipziger Musikwerke (Paul Ehrlich & Co) who was also a member of the committee of the Association of German Musical Instrument Manufacturers. (*Verein Deutscher Musikwerke-Fabrikanten*).

Regina Music Box Company, Rahway, New Jersey. Described under 'Regina' in the chapter 'The Principal Manufacturers'.

Richter, Friedrich Adolf & Co., 65 Schwartzburgstrasse, Rudolstadt, Germany. Manufacturers of the 'Imperator' disc box which, in the upright models used two sets of opposed combs, one set above the centre dome and one below. This company also made the 'Libellion', which played a steel comb by means of levers and a 'book' of card music. The case of this machine could easily be taken for that of a disc box.

Riessner, Paul, Leipzig, Germany. See chapter 'The Principal Manufacturers' under 'Polyphon' and 'Regina'.

Rückert, Bruno, Leipzig, Germany. In 1891, introduced the Lyraphon disc box, which was made until 1893, when the firm introduced the Orphenion disc box, made from c.1893–1897. See also *V.D.M-G*.

Schaub, Ferdinand, Jersey City, New Jersey. Employed by F.G. Otto & Sons, this man was responsible for several innovations used by the firm.

Schrämli & Tschudin, Geneva, Switzerland. Manufacturers (?) of the 'Sun' disc musical box. None of these machines are known.

Schureman, J.L. Jr., U.S.A. Patented, in March, 1904, a gramophone attachment for music boxes.

Schweichert, N., Leipzig, Germany. A composer who composed and arranged for Polyphon.

Seidel & Maumann, Leipzig, Germany. In September, 1899, introduced a version of the Sirion 'shifting-disc' musical box. Last exhibited at Leipzig Easter Fair for 1901.

Société Anonyme (late Maison Billon). This was a group of three famous Swiss cylinder musical box companies, Rivenc, Langdorff and Billon, who, in 1896, were manufacturers of the 'Gloria' disc musical boxes. Later the group made the 'Polymnia' disc box, which used dimple projections.

Société Anonyme Harmonia. See Harmonia S.A.

LIST OF MANUFACTURERS AND AGENTS

Spiegel L. & Söhn, Ludwigshafen, Germany. Established in 1862 as agent for mechanical musical instruments. Sold Lochmann Original disc boxes under their own name.

Staffelstein, A.C.F. & Kluge, H.F.F., Leipzig, Germany. In March, 1901, introduced the Phänomenal 'disc' musical box, using helicoidal tune-sheets for playing longer tunes. British patent 4469, 8th. March 1900.

Star Silver Depot, London. Sole agents for the 'Britannia' and 'Imperial' disc boxes. These machines, manufactured by B.H. Abrahams of Switzerland, were in fact identical apart from the names. The 'Britannia' was so called for the English market.

Sueur, Alfred. A Swiss national who patented many improvements to musical boxes. He later went to the U.S.A. and worked for M.J. Paillard & Co., in New York. In 1893 he patented a mechanism to operate musical boxes with a coin, which was used almost universally on coin-operated machines.

Symphonion, Leipzig, Germany. See under 'Symphonion' in the chapter 'The Principal Manufacturers'.

Symphonion Music Box Co., Asbury Park, New Jersey. A company set up to produce the 'Imperial Symphonion' in America. See 'The Principal Manufacturers', under 'Symphonion'.

Tannhauser Musikwerke Otto Caspar, Leipzig, Germany. Makers of 'Tannhauser' 'shifting-disc' musical boxes. The firm made several models under a patent granted to T. Alwin Plessing in 1897. The company was short-lived.

Thorens, Hermann, Ste-Croix, Switzerland. Established in 1882, making small and large cylinder boxes—he exhibited a Plerodienique box at the Geneva Exposition of 1896. Responsible for the 'Edelweiss' and 'Helvetia' disc musical boxes.

At the Paris Exposition of 1900 he exhibited three coin-operated disc musical boxes: one with bell accompaniment; one with free reeds and two steel combs, and an autochange ('*Histoire* etc'.).

Thorens musical boxes, disc and cylinder, are still being made by Melodies S.A., L'Auberson. The firm headed by Jean Paul Thorens.

Ullmann, Charles & Jacques, Paris. In 1909, main agent for Symphonion.

Verein Deutscher Musikwerke-Grossisten. (V.D.M-G.). Association of German Wholesale Dealers in Musical Products. Founded in 1896, it

LIST OF MANUFACTURERS AND AGENTS

consisted of eighteen main wholesale agents as follows, some of them large manufacturers in their own right:

Ernst Holzweissig, Leipzig and Berlin.
Wilhelm Dietrich, Leipzig and Berlin.
Ludwig Hupfeld, Leipzig.
J.M. Bon, Leipzig.
Kraft Behrens, Leipzig.
Zuleger & Mayenburg, Leipzig.
Adalbert Hawsky, Leipzig.
P.H. Hahn & Co., Dresden.
K. Heilbrunn Söhne, Berlin.
E. Dienst, Leipzig.
Berger & Wurker, Leipzig.
J.H. Zimmermann, Leipzig.
H.L. Ernst, Leipzig.
C.H. Weigel, Leipzig.
Wilhelm Benzing, Leipzig.
Ludwig & Fries, Frankfurt-am-Main.
Plato & Co., Berlin.
Deurer & Kaufmann, Hamburg.

By 1898 Hahn of Dresden had been replaced by Ph. Brunnbauer & Söhne of Vienna. The association held sole agency rights for Symphonion, Orphenion, and Kalliope instruments from the year of its foundation. By 1898 Orphenion had been dropped, and presumably ceased to do business, since Adler had moved into the Orphenion factory and had taken its place as subject to the sole agency of the association. It is fascinating to see that at least four members of the association eventually held a strong position in the companies mentioned. Hupfeld took over the Lochmann Symphonion firm in c. 1900; Julius H. Zimmermann took over Adler to make it Fortuna in 1900, and earlier both Holzweissig and Wilhelm Dietrich were shareholders from the limitation of the Kalliope firm in 1898.

Verein Deutscher Musikwerke-Fabrikanten. Association of German Musical Instrument Manufacturers, founded in 1897. Of the seven committee members two represented mechanical music: H. Preussner, a director of Leipziger Musikwerke and G. Espenhain, of Kalliope Musikwerke.

Vidoudez, Henri, Ste-Croix, Switzerland. At least agents for the 'New Century' range of disc boxes. There is some evidence to suggest that Mermod Frères, or possibly E. Paillard et Cie., made the movements for at least the 'shifting-disc' models bearing this name.

Voigt, Alban, 14, Edmund Place, London. Agent for and repairer of Symphonion.

LIST OF MANUFACTURERS AND AGENTS

Wacker, Emil M.A., Leipzig, Germany. Partner, then director, of Kalliope Musikwerke.

Weigel, C.H., Leipzig, Germany. Main agent and member of *V.D.M-G*.

Wendland, Max. Brother of Paul, who worked for Polyphon in Leipzig and later repaired Polyphons for the firm in London.

Wendland, Paul, Leipzig, Germany. A worker for Symphonion who patented the first design for a star wheel for use in disc musical boxes.

Zimmermann, Julius H., Leipzig, Germany. A wholesale agent with outlets in Leipzig, St. Petersburg, Moscow and London, who with other member companies of *V.D.M-G* handled the output of Symphonion, Kalliope and Adler until 1899. In 1900, the year in which the reed organ accompaniment disc box 'Fortuna Marvel' was presented, he became head of the Adler firm, changing the name of the range to Fortuna in order to take advantage of the success of the new machine.

Zuleger & Mayenburg, Leipzig, Germany. Main agents and members of *V.D.M-G*.

AN ESSENTIAL BIBLIOGRAPHY

Bowers, Q. David. *Encyclopedia of Automatic Musical Instruments.* 1972, The Vestal Press, Ltd., Vestal, New York. A wealth of information, including many original advertisements, for disc musical boxes and other instruments.

Chapuis, Alfred. *History of the Musical Box and of Mechanical Music.* 1980, The Musical Box Society International, Summit, New Jersey. A translation of *Histoire de la Boîte à Musique et de la Musique Mécanique* (1955) made by Joseph E. Roesch.

Ord-Hume, Arthur W. J. G. *Musical Box,* a history and collector's guide. 1980, Allen and Unwin, Inc., Winchester, Massachusetts.

Ord-Hume, Arthur W. J. G. *Restoring Musical Boxes.* 1980, Allen and Unwin, Inc., Winchester, Massachusetts.

Webb, Graham. *The Disc Musical Box Handbook.* 1971, Faber and Faber, London. Illustrated by Philip Weston, includes (pp. 216-319) "Polyphon Tune Titles."

Webb, Graham. *The Musical Box Handbook,* volume 1—cylinder boxes. 1984, The Vestal Press, Ltd., Vestal, New York.

Young, David R. *How Old is my Music Box?* 1980, David R. Young, Rochester, New York.

INDEX

Bells, 38–41
Boom, Miguel, 4, 6, 19, 302
Brachhausen, Gustave, 14, 27, 28, 33–34, 42, 303

Clocks, 49–53, 306
Combs, 64, 90, 92, 171, 176–177, 212–213

Dampers, 65, 86–87, 91–92, 157, 200–215

Ehrlich, Paul, 5–7, 10–11, 21–22, 304

Gambling machines, 58–59
Geneva stop, 95–96, 102
Gramophones, 60–61

Handles, 142–146
Hennig, Hugo, 14
Hupfeld, Ludwig, 19, 25, 313

Lochmann, Paul, 8, 10, 20, 41, 45, 228–229, 307–308
Locks, 115–116

Mermod Frères, 15, 52, 308
Monopol, 230–232

Paillard et Cie., 16, 18, 45, 309
Parr, Ellis, 8–9, 310
Polyphon, 27–31, 235–237, 310

Regina, 31–36, 237–238
Riessner, Paul, 14, 27, 33, 42, 311

Star wheels, 88, 155–157, 190–192, 194
Symphonion, 20–26, 226, 241–242, 312

Thorens, Hermann, 16, 45
Titles, 131–133
Tuning scales, 245–300

Veneer, 112-113

Wendland, Paul, 10, 314
Woodworm, 111, 113